HTML5 and JavaScript Projects

Jeanine Meyer

Apress®

HTML5 and JavaScript Projects

To my expanding family, including Annika Lyyli and her parents and brothers;
and Esther, Aviva, and Anne, who take care of me now;
and to my father, who takes care of me still.

Contents at a Glance

Contents

About the Author

Jeanine Meyer is a full professor at Purchase College/State University of New York. She teaches courses for students majoring in mathematics/computer science and new media. She developed and teaches a course on understanding quantitative information for humanities students. The web site for her academic activities is http://faculty.purchase.edu/jeanine.meyer. Before coming to academia, she was a research staff member and manager at IBM Research, focusing on robotics and manufacturing research, and she later worked as a research consultant at IBM for educational grant programs.

After having a great time in 2010 developing *The Essential Guide to HTML5: Using Games to Learn HTML5 and JavaScript*, Jeanine looked forward to a similar experience doing this book, and her expectations were met. She also needed to be occupied while awaiting the birth of her granddaughter (see Chapter 2). Family members also are documented in Chapters 3, 5, and 8. She continues to enjoy doing crossword puzzles and ken ken, knitting and crocheting, reading novels and history, gardening, eating Aviva's extraordinary cooking, listening to her mother on piano, and playing the flute. She still and again is an active volunteer and letter-to-the-editor writer for progressive causes and candidates.

About the Technical Reviewer

Andrew Zack is the CEO of ZTMC (`http://ztmc.com`), specializing in search engine optimization (SEO) and Internet marketing strategies. His project background includes almost 20 years of site development and project management experience and over 15 years as an SEO and Internet marketing expert.

Andrew has also been very active in the publishing industry, having coauthored *Flash 5 Studio* (Apress, 2001) and served as a technical reviewer on over ten books and industry publications.

Acknowledgments

Much appreciation to my students and colleagues at Purchase College/State University of New York. In particular, for Chapter 5, which covers the map portal, I want to thank Jennifer Douglas, Jeremy Martinez, and Nik Dedvukaj for the maze video clip produced in my Robotics class in 2008, and my mother for her piano playing recorded as an audio clip. Thanks also to the LA HTML5 MeetUp group, especially Samy Kamkar, Matthew Sacks, and Tiffany Brown for their help and also their requests for help, which gave me ideas. Thanks to Daniel Davis for his HTML5 logo; Mike Taylor for video advice; David Keefe, who always is an inspiration; Aviva Meyer, Anne Kellerman, John McMullen, and Barbara McMullen for their testing help on iPhones and iPads; and Palmer Agnew and Daniel Meyer for general support and helping me better understand geolocation.

Thanks to the crew at Apress/friends of Ed: Ben Renow-Clarke, Adam Heath, Andrew Zack, Damon Larson, Nancy Wright, Michael Spano and others who made this book much better than I could have on my own.

Introduction

This book continues my exploration of HTML5. My approach in developing the projects was to combine features such as canvas and video; attempt more intricate drawing, making use of mathematics; and make use of standard programming techniques such as object-oriented programming and separation of content and logic. I was also interested in building applications combining HTML5 and JavaScript with other technologies, including Google Maps, geolocation, and server-side programming.

Each chapter in the book is focused on an application or set of related applications. This is because my experience as a teacher and a learner has shown that concepts and mechanics are best understood in the context of actual use. The applications start off with drawing the HTML5 official logo. As you will find out in Chapter 1, the way I developed this application prompted a use of coordinate transformations. The project in Chapter 2, involving a family collage, was inspired by my growing family and the desire to teach about object-oriented programming. It is a good application for you to use as a foundation to create your own, with your own photos and objects of your own invention. Chapter 3, which shows how to create a bouncing video, was built on other two-dimensional applications I have created, and features two different ways to combine canvas and video.

Chapters 4, 5, and 6 demonstrate use of the Google Maps API (Application Programming Interface), a powerful facility that allows you to incorporate access to Google Maps as part of your own projects. Chapter 4 presents a user interface combining a map and canvas, and includes a custom-designed cursor and the use of alpha (transparency) in drawing paths. The three applications discussed in Chapter 5 all demonstrate the use of mapping as a portal to media. The sequence of applications shows you how to separate content and logic so you can scale up to various applications (e.g., a tour of a region or a geography quiz with many locations). Chapter 6 features geolocation, technology to determine the location of your end-user. I combine this with server-side programming using PHP that allows you to send an e-mail of where you are to someone the end-user chooses.

In Chapter 7, I use the production of directions for origami to show how to combine line drawings, often using mathematical expressions, and video and photographs. You can use this as a model for your own set of directions using drawings, video, and images, or let the reading refresh your memory for topics in algebra and geometry. Chapter 8 was inspired by a project I produced using Adobe Flash, in which a jigsaw puzzle is transformed into a video. In the project in this chapter, you'll also learn how to make this work on an iPod and iPad, including how to incorporate the handling of finger touch events. Similarly, Chapter 9 was initially inspired by an identify-and-name-the-state game I made using Flash. This chapter includes the challenge of mixing up the states in the form of a jigsaw puzzle, including the feature of saving the puzzle-in-progress using localStorage. The resulting educational game presents a user interface that must handle multiple types of player actions. Chapter 10, the last chapter, demonstrates use of a database. In this chapter, HTML5 and JavaScript are combined with PHP and Structured Query Language (SQL), which is the standard language for most databases. The database featured in the chapter is MySQL. The form validation features of HTML5 along with localStorage address common requirements of many database applications. The database application also demonstrates one-way encryption for user passwords and the combination of client-side and server-side form validation.

Who Is This Book For?

I do believe my explanations are complete, but I am not claiming, as I did for my previous book, *The Essential Guide to HTML5*, that this book is for the total beginner. This book is for the developer who has some knowledge of programming and who wants to build (more) substantial applications by combining basic features and combining JavaScript with other technologies. It also can serve as an idea book for someone working with programmers to get an understanding of what is possible.

How Is This Book Structured?

This book consists of ten chapters, each organized around an application or type of application. You can skip around. However, it probably makes sense to read Chapter 4 before 5 or 6. Also, the PHP server-side language is used in a simple way in Chapter 6 and then more fully in Chapter 10. Other cross-references are indicated in the text. Each chapter starts with an introduction to the application, with screenshots of the applications in use. In several cases, the differences between browsers are shown. The chapters continue with a discussion of the critical requirements, where concepts are introduced before diving into the technical details. The next sections describe how the requirements are satisfied, with specific constructs in HTML5, JavaScript, PHP, and/or SQL, and with standard programming techniques. I then show the application coding line by line with comments. Each chapter ends with instructions and tips for testing and uploading the application to a server, and a summary of what you learned.

The code (with certain exceptions noted for Chapter 10) is all included as downloads available from the publisher. In addition, the figures are available as full-color TIFF files. Of course, you will want to use your own media for the projects shown in Chapters 2, 3, 5, and 8. My media (video, audio, images) is included with the code and this includes images for the 50 states for the states game in Chapter 9. You can use the project as a model for a different part of the world or a puzzle based on an image or diagram. Let's get started.

CHAPTER 1

Building the HTML5 Logo – Drawing on Canvas, with Scaling, and Semantic Tags

In this chapter, we will review

- Drawing paths on a canvas
- Placing text on a canvas
- Coordinate transformations
- Fonts for text drawn on canvas and fonts for text in other elements
- Semantic tags
- The range input element

Introduction

The project for this chapter is a presentation of the official HTML5 logo, with accompanying text. The shield and letters of the logo are drawn on a canvas element and the accompanying text demonstrates the use of semantic tags. The viewer can change the size of the logo using a slider input device. It is an appropriate start to this book, a collection of projects making use of HTML5, JavaScript and other technologies, because of the subject matter and because it serves as a good review of basic event-driven programming and other important features in HTML5. The way I developed the project, building on the work of others, is typical of how most of us work. In particular, the circumstances provide motivation for the use of coordinate transformations. Lastly, at the time of writing, Firefox does not fully implement the slider input element. Unfortunately, this also is a common situation and I will discuss the implications.

The approach of this book is to explain HTML5, Cascading Style Sheets and JavaScript chapters in the context of specific examples. The projects represent a variety of applications and, hopefully, you will find something in each one that you will learn and adapt for your own purposes.

■ **Note** If you need an introduction to programming using HTML5 and JavaScript, you can consult my book the Essential Guide to HTML5 or other books published by Apress or others. There also is considerable material available online.

Figure 1-1 shows the opening screen for the logo project on the Chrome browser. (Skip ahead to Figure 1-3 for the appearance on Firefox.)

Scale percentage: ⎴ Note: slider treated as text field in some browsers.
Built on work by Daniel Davis, et al, but don't blame them for the fonts. Check out the use of *font-family* in the style element and the *fontfamily* variable in the script element for safe ways to do fonts. I did the scaling. Note also use of semantic elements.

HTML5 Logo by W3C.

Figure 1-1. Opening Screen for HTML5 Logo

Notice the slider feature, the accompanying text, which contains what appears to be a hyperlink, and the text in a footer below a yellow line. The footer also includes a hyperlink. As I will explain later, the function and the formatting of the footer and any other semantic element is totally up to me, but providing a reference to the owners of the logo, The World Wide Web Consortium would be deemed an appropriate use.

The viewer can use the slider to change the size of the logo. **Figure 1-2** shows the application after the slider has been adjusted to show the logo reduced to about a third in width and in height.

Scale percentage: Note: slider treated as text field in some browsers.

Built on work by Daniel Davis, et al, but don't blame them for the fonts. Check out the use of *font-family* in the style element and the *fontfamily* variable in the script element for safe ways to do fonts. I did the scaling. Note also use of semantic elements.

HTML5 Logo by W3C.

Figure 1-2. *Logo scaled down*

The implementation of HTML5 is not complete by any browsers and, as it turns out, Firefox treats all slider inputs as simple text fields. This is termed 'graceful degradation' and it certainly is better than producing nothing at all. **Figure 1-3** shows the opening screen in Firefox. Notice the initial value is displayed as 100.

Scale percentage: 100 Note: slider treated as text field in some browsers.

Built on work by Daniel Davis, et al, but don't blame them for the fonts. Check out the use of *font-family* in the style element and the *fontfamily* variable in the script element for safe ways to do fonts. I did the scaling. Note also use of semantic elements.

HTML5 Logo by W3C.

Figure 1-3. *Application using Firefox*

As will be the practice in each chapter, I now explain the critical requirements of the application, more or less independent of the fact that the implementation will be in HTML5, and then describe the features of HTML5, JavaScript, and other technologies as needed that will be used in the implementation. The Building section includes a table with comments for each line of code and also guidance for building similar applications. The Testing section provides details for uploading and testing. This section is more critical for some projects than others. Lastly, there is a Summary that reviews the programming concepts covered and previews what is next in the book.

Project History and Critical Requirements

The critical requirements for this project are somewhat artificial and not easily stated as something separate from HTML. For example, I wanted to draw the logo as opposed to copying an image from the Web. My design objectives always include wanting to practice programming and prepare examples for my students. The shape of the shield part of the logo seemed amenable to drawing on canvas and the HTML letters could be done using the draw text feature. In addition, there are practical advantages to drawing images instead of using image files. Separate files need to be managed, stored, and downloaded. The image shown in Figure 1-4 is 90KB. The file holding the code for the program is only 4KB. Drawing a logo or other graphic means that the scale and other attributes can be changed dynamically using code.

Figure 1-4. Image of logo

I looked online and found an example of just the shield done by Daniel Davis, who works for Opera. This was great because it meant that I did not have to measure a copy of the logo image to get the coordinates. This begs the question of how he determined the coordinates. I don't know the answer, even though we had a pleasant exchange of emails. One possibility is to download the image and use the grid feature of image processing programs such as Adobe Photoshop or Corel Paint Shop Pro. Another possibility is to use (old-fashioned) transparent graph paper.

However, there was a problem with building on Daniel Davis's work. His application did not include the HTML letters. The solution to this was to position the letters on the screen and then move down so to speak to position the drawing of the shield using the coordinates provided in Daniel's example. The technical term for 'moving down the screen' is performing a coordinate transformation. So the ability to perform coordinate transformations became a critical requirement for this project.

I chose to write something about the logo and, in particular, give credit and references in the form of hyperlinks. I made the decision to reference the official source of the logo as brief text at the bottom of the document below a line. The reference to Daniel Davis was part of the writing in the body. We exchanged notes on font choices and I will discuss that more in the next section.

In order to give the viewer something to do with the logo, I decided to present a means of changing the size. A good device for this is a slider with the minimum and maximum values and steps all specified. So the critical requirements for this application include drawing shapes and letters in a specific font, coordinate transformations, formatting a document with a main section and a footer section, and including hyperlinks.

HTML5, CSS, and JavaScript features

I assume that you, the reader, have some experience with HTML and HTML5 documents. One of the most important new features in HTML5 is the canvas element for drawing. I describe briefly the drawing of filled-in paths of the appropriate color and filled-in text. Next, I describe coordinate transformations, used in this project for the two parts of the logo itself and for scaling, changing the size, of the whole logo. Lastly, I describe the range input element. This produces the slider.

Drawing paths on canvas

Canvas is a type of element introduced in HTML5. All canvas elements have a property (aka attribute) called the 2D context. Typically, a variable is set to this property after the document is loaded:

```
ctx = document.getElementById('canvas').getContext('2d');
```

It is important to understand that canvas is a good name: code applies color to the pixels of the canvas, just like paint. Code written later can put a different color on the canvas. The old color does not show through. Even though our code causes rectangles and shapes and letters to appear, these distinct entities do not retain their identity as objects to be re-positioned.

The shield is produced by drawing six filled-in paths in succession with the accumulated results as shown in Figure 1-5. You can refer to this picture when examining the code. Keep in mind that in the coordinates, the first number is the distance from the left edge of the canvas and the second number is the distance from the top edge of the canvas.

Figure 1-5. Sequence of paths for drawing logo

By the way, I chose to show you the sequence with the accumulated results. If I displayed what is drawn, you would not see the white parts making up the left side of the five. You can see it because it is two white filled-in paths on top of the orange.

All drawing is done using methods and properties of the `ctx` variable holding the 2D context property of the canvas element. The color for any subsequent fill operation is set by assigning a color to the `fillStyle` property of the canvas context.

```
ctx.fillStyle = "#E34C26";
```

This particular color, given in the hexadecimal format, where the first two hexadecimal (base 16) digits represent red, the second two hexadecimal digits represent green and the last two represent blue, is provided by the W3C website, along with the other colors, as the particular orange for the background of the shield. It may be counterintuitive, but in this system, white is specified by the value #FFFFFF. Think of this as all colors together make white. The absence of color is black and specified by #000000. The pearly gray used for the right hand side of the 5 in the logo has the value #EBEBEB. This is a high value, close to white. It is not necessary that you memorize any of these values, but it is useful to know black and white, and that a pure red is #FF0000, a pure green is #00FF00 and a pure blue #0000FF. You can use the eyedropper/color picker tool in drawing programs such as Adobe Photoshop, Corel Paint Shop Pro on the on-line tool: http://pixlr.com/ to find out values of colors in images OR you can use the official designation, when available, for official images.

All drawing is done using the 2 dimensional coordinate systems. Shapes are produced using the path methods. These assume a current location, which you can think of as the position of a pen or paint brush over the canvas. The critical methods are moving to a location and setting up a line from the current location to the indicated location. The following set of statements draws the five sided orange shape starting at the lower, left corner. The closePath method closes up the path by drawing a line back to the starting point.

```
ctx.fillStyle = "#E34C26";
ctx.beginPath();
ctx.moveTo(39, 250);
ctx.lineTo(17, 0);
ctx.lineTo(262, 0);
ctx.lineTo(239, 250);
ctx.lineTo(139, 278);
ctx.closePath();
ctx.fill();
```

If you haven't done any drawing on canvas, here is the whole HTML script needed to produce the 5-sided shape. The onLoad attribute in the <body> tag causes the init function to be invoked when the document is loaded. The init function sets the ctx variable, sets the fillStyle property and then draws the path.

```
<!DOCTYPE html>
<html>
<head>
<title>HTML 5 Logo</title>
<meta charset="UTF-8">
<script>
function init() {
 ctx = document.getElementById('canvas').getContext('2d');
 ctx.fillStyle = "#E34C26";
 ctx.beginPath();
 ctx.moveTo(39, 250);
 ctx.lineTo(17, 0);
 ctx.lineTo(262, 0);
 ctx.lineTo(239, 250);
 ctx.lineTo(139, 278);
 ctx.closePath();
 ctx.fill();
}
```

```
</script>
</head>
<body onLoad="init();">
<canvas id="canvas" width="600" height="400">
Your browser does not support the canvas element .
</canvas>
</body>
</html>
```

Do practice and experiment with drawing on the canvas if you haven't done so before, but I will go on. The other shapes are produced in a similar manner. By the way, if you see a line down the middle of the shield, this is an optical illusion.

Placing text on canvas and in the body of a document

Text is drawn on the canvas using methods and attributes of the context. The text can be filled in, using the `fillText` method or drawn as an outline using the `strokeText` method. The color is whatever the current `fillStyle` property or `strokeStyle` property holds. Another property of the context is the `font`. This property can contain the size of the text and one or more fonts. The purpose of including more than one font is to provide options to the browser if the first font is unavailable on the computer running the browser. For this project, I use

```
var fontfamily = "65px 'Gill Sans Ultra Bold', sans-serif";
```

and in the `init` function

```
ctx.font = fontfamily;
```

This directs the browser to use the Gill Sans Ultra Bold font if it is available and if not, use whatever the default sans-serif font on the computer.

I could have put this all in one statement, but chose to make it a variable. You can decide if my choice of font was close enough to the official W3C logo.

■ **Note** There are at least two other approaches to take for this example. One possibility is to NOT use text but to draw the letters as filled-in paths. The other is to locate and acquire a font and place it on the server holding the HTML5 document and reference it directly using @font-face.

With the font and color set, the methods for drawing text require a string and a position: x and y coordinates. The statement in this project to draw the letters is

```
ctx.fillText("HTML", 31,60);
```

Formatting text in the rest of the HTML document, that is, outside a canvas element, requires the same attention to fonts. In this project, I choose to make use of the semantic elements new to HTML5 and follow the practice of putting formatting in the style element. The body of my HTML script contains two article elements and one footer elements. One article holds the input element with a comment and the other article holds the rest of the explanation. The footer element contains the reference to W3C. Formatting and usage of these are up to the developer/programmer. This includes making sure the footer is the last thing in the document. If I placed the footer before one or both articles, it would no longer be displayed at the foot, that is, the bottom of the document. The style directives for this project are the following:

```
footer {display:block; border-top: 1px solid orange; margin: 10px;↵
 font-family: "Trebuchet MS", Arial, Helvetica, sans-serif; font-weight: bold;}
article {display:block; font-family: Georgia, "Times New Roman", Times, serif; margin: 5px;}
```

The styles each set up all instances of these elements to be displayed as blocks. This puts a line break before and after. The footer has a border on the top, which produces the line above the text. Both styles specify a list of four fonts each. So the browser first sees if Trebuchet MS is available, then checks for Arial, then for Helvetica and then, if still unsuccessful, uses the system default sans-serif font for the footer element. Similarly, the browser checks for Georgia, then Times New roman, then Times and then, if unsuccessful, uses the standard serif font. This probably is overkill, but it is the secure way to operate. The footer text is displayed in bold and the articles each have a margin around them of 5 pixels.

Formatting, including fonts, is important. HTML5 provides many features for formatting and for separating formatting from structure and content. You do need to treat the text on the canvas differently than the text in the other elements.

Coordinate transformations

I have given my motivation for using coordinate transformations, specifically to keep using a set of coordinates. To review, a coordinate system is the way to specify positions on the canvas. Positions are specified as distances from an origin point. For the two-dimensional canvas, two coordinates are necessary: the first coordinate, governing the horizontal, often called the x and the second coordinate, governing the vertical, called the y. A pesky fact is that when drawing to screens the y axis is flipped so the vertical is measured from the top of the canvas. The horizontal is measured from the left. This means that the point (100,200) is further down the screen than the point (100,100).

In the logo project, I wrote code to display the letters HTML and then move the origin to draw the rest of the logo. An analogy would be that I know the location of my house from the center of my town and so I can give directions to the center of town and then give directions to my house. The situation in which I draw the letters in the logo and 'move down the screen' requires the translate transformation. The translation is done just in the vertical. The amount of the translation is stored in a variable I named offsety:

```
var offsety = 80;
…
ctx.fillText("HTML", 31, 60);
ctx.translate(0, offsety);
```

Since I decided to provide a way for the viewer to change the size of the logo, I made use of the scale transformation. Continuing the analogy of directions, this is equivalent to changing the units. You may give some directions in miles (or kilometers) and other directions in yards or feet or meters or, maybe, blocks. The scaling can be done separately for each dimension. In this application, there is a variable called factorvalue that is set by the function invoked when the input is changed. The statement

```
ctx.scale(factorvalue, factorvalue);
```

changes the units for both the horizontal and vertical direction.

HTML5 provides a way to save the current state of the coordinate system and restore what you have saved. This is important if you need your code to get back to a previous state. The saving and restoring is done using what is termed a stack: last in first out. Restoring the coordinate state is termed popping the stack and saving the coordinate state is pushing something onto the stack. My logo project does not use this in its full power, but it is something to remember to investigate if you are doing more complex applications. In the logo project, my code saves the original state when the document is first loaded. Then before drawing the logo, it restores what was saved and then saves it again so it is available the next time. The code at the start of the function dologo, which draws the logo, starts off as follows:

```
function dologo() {
var offsety = 80 ;
ctx.restore();
ctx.save();
ctx.clearRect(0,0,600,400);
ctx.scale(factorvalue,factorvalue);
ctx.fillText("HTML", 31,60);
ctx.translate(0,offsety);

// 5 sided orange background
ctx.fillStyle = "#E34C26";
ctx.beginPath();
ctx.moveTo(39, 250);
ctx.lineTo(17, 0);
ctx.lineTo(262, 0);
ctx.lineTo(239, 250);
ctx.lineTo(139, 278);
ctx.closePath();
ctx.fill();

// right hand, lighter orange part of the background
ctx.fillStyle = "#F06529";
ctx.beginPath();
ctx.moveTo(139, 257);
ctx.lineTo(220, 234);
ctx.lineTo(239, 20);
ctx.lineTo(139, 20);
ctx.closePath();
ctx.fill();
...
```

Note that the canvas is cleared (erased) of anything that was previously drawn.

Using the range input element

The input device, which I call a slider, is the new HTML5 input type range, and is placed in the body of the HTML document. Mine is placed inside an article element. The attributes of this type and other input elements provide ways of specifying the initial value, the minimum and maximum values, the smallest increment adjustment and the action to take if the viewer changes the slider. The code is

```
<input id="slide" type="range" min="0" max="100" value="100"↵
  onChange="changescale(this.value)" step="10"/>
```

The min, max, (initial) value, and the step can be set to whatever you like. Since I was using percentage and since I did not want the logo to get bigger than the initial value or deal with negative values, I used 0 and 100.

In the proper implementation of the slider, the viewer does not see the initial value or the maximum or minimum. My code uses the input as a percentage. The expression `this.value` is interpreted as the value attribute of THIS element, emphasis given in capitals to convey the switch to English! The term `this` has special meaning in JavaScript and several other programming languages. The `changescale` function takes the value, specified by the parameter given in the assignment to the `onChange` attribute, and uses it to set a global variable (a variable declared outside of any function so it persists and is available to any function).

```
function changescale(val) {
        factorvalue = val / 100;
        dologo();
}
```

It is part of the specification of HTML5 that the browsers will provide form validation, that is, check that the conditions specified by attributes in the input elements are obeyed. This can be a significant productivity boost in terms of reducing the work programmers need to do and a performance boost since the checking probably would be faster when done by the browser. We will discuss it more in Chapter 10 on databases and php. In the HTML5 logo project, an advantage of the slider is that the viewer does not need to be concerned with values but merely moves the device. There is no way to input an illegal value. I do not want to disparage the Firefox browser, and, as I indicated, producing a text box is better than producing nothing, but, at least at the time of writing, it does not display a slider or do any checking. Figure 1-6 shows the results of entering a value of 200 in the input field.

Scale percentage: 200   Note: slider treated as text field in some browsers.

Built on work by Daniel Davis, et al, but don't blame them for the fonts. Check out the use of *font-family* in the style element and the *fontfamily* variable in the script element for safe ways to do fonts. I did the scaling. Note also use of semantic elements.

HTML5 Logo by W3C.

Figure 1-6. Display in Firefox of scale of 200

The canvas is of fixed width and height and drawing outside the canvas, which is what is done when the scaling is done to accept numbers and stretch them out to twice the original value, is ignored.

Building the application and making it your own

The project does one thing, draw the logo. A function, `dologo`, is defined for this purpose. Informally, the outline of the program is

1. *init: initialization*

2. *dologo: draw the logo starting with the HTML letters and then the shield*

3. *changescale: change the scale*

The function called and calling table shows the relationship of the functions. The `dologo` function is invoked when the document is first loaded and then whenever the scale is changed.

Table 1-1. *Functions in the HTML5 Logo project*

Function	Invoked / Called By	Calls
init	invoked by action of the `onLoad` attribute in the `<body>` tag	dologo
dologo	init and changescale	
changescale	invoked by action of the `onChange` attribute in the `<input type="range"...>` tag	dologo

The coding for the `dologo` function puts together the techniques previously described. In particular, the code brings back the original coordinate system and clears off the canvas.

The global variables in this application are

```
var ctx;
var factorvalue = 1;
var fontfamily = "65px 'Gill Sans Ultra Bold', sans-serif";
```

As indicated earlier, it would be possible to not use the `fontfamily` but use the string directly in the code. It is convenient to make `ctx` and `factorvalue` global.

Table 1-2 shows the code for the basic application, with comments for each line.

Table 1-2. Complete Code for the HTML5 Logo project

Code Line	Description
`<!DOCTYPE html>`	header
`<html>`	opening html tag
`<head>`	opening head tag
`<title>HTML5 Logo </title>`	complete title element
`<meta charset="UTF-8">`	meta tag
`<style>`	opening style tag
`footer {display:block; border-top: 1px solid orange; margin: 10px; font-family: "Trebuchet MS", Arial, Helvetica, sans-serif; font-weight: bold;}`	style for the footer, including the top border and font family
`article {display:block; font-family: Georgia, "Times New Roman", Times, serif; margin: 5px;}`	style for the 2 articles
`</style>`	close the style element
`<script language="JavaScript">`	opening script tag. Note: case doesn't matter for the JavaScript.
`var ctx;`	variable to hold the context. Used in all drawing
`var factorvalue = 1;`	set initial value for scaling
`var fontfamily = "65px 'Gill Sans Ultra Bold', sans-serif";`	set the fonts for the text drawn on the canvas
`function init() {`	start of init function
`    ctx = document.getElementById('canvas').getContext('2d');`	set ctx
`    ctx.font = fontfamily;`	set font for text drawn on canvas
`    ctx.save();`	save the original coordinate state
`    dologo();`	invoke function to draw the logo

Code Line	Description
`}`	close function
`function dologo() {`	start of dologo function
`var offsety = 80 ;`	specify amount to adjust the coordinates to draw the shield part of the logo.
`ctx.restore();`	restore original state of coordinates
`ctx.save();`	save it (push onto stack) so it can be restored again
`ctx.clearRect(0,0,600,400);`	erase the whole canvas
`ctx.scale(factorvalue,factorvalue);`	scale horizontally and vertically using value set by slider
`ctx.fillText("HTML", 31,60);`	draw the letters: HTML
`    ctx.translate(0,offsety);`	move down the screen (canvas)
`// 5 sided orange background`	
`ctx.fillStyle = "#E34C26";`	set to official bright orange
`ctx.beginPath();`	start a path
`ctx.moveTo(39, 250);`	move to indicated position at lower left
`ctx.lineTo(17, 0);`	draw line up and more to the left
`ctx.lineTo(262, 0);`	draw line straight over to the right
`ctx.lineTo(239, 250);`	draw line down and slightly to the left
`ctx.lineTo(139, 278);`	draw line to the middle, low point of the shield
`ctx.closePath();`	close the path

Code Line	Description
`ctx.fill();`	fill in with the indicated color
`// right hand, lighter orange part of the // background`	
`ctx.fillStyle = "#F06529";`	set color to the official darker orange
`ctx.beginPath();`	start the path
`ctx.moveTo(139, 257);`	move to middle point, close to the top
`ctx.lineTo(220, 234);`	draw line to the right and slightly up
`ctx.lineTo(239, 20);`	draw line to the right and up
`ctx.lineTo(139, 20);`	draw line to the left (point at the middle)
`ctx.closePath();`	close path
`ctx.fill();`	fill in with the indicated color
`//light gray, left hand side part of the //five`	
`ctx.fillStyle = "#EBEBEB";`	set color to gray
`ctx.beginPath();`	start path
`ctx.moveTo(139, 113);`	move to middle horizontally, midway vertically
`ctx.lineTo(98, 113);`	draw line to the left
`ctx.lineTo(96, 82);`	draw line up and slightly further left
`ctx.lineTo(139, 82);`	draw line to right
`ctx.lineTo(139, 51);`	draw line up
`ctx.lineTo(62, 51);`	draw line to the left

Code Line	Description
`ctx.lineTo(70, 144);`	draw line to the left and down
`ctx.lineTo(139, 144);`	draw line to the right
`ctx.closePath();`	close path
`ctx.fill();`	fill in with indicated color
`ctx.beginPath();`	start a new path
`ctx.moveTo(139, 193);`	move to middle point
`ctx.lineTo(105, 184);`	draw line to the left and up
`ctx.lineTo(103, 159);`	draw line slightly to the left and up
`ctx.lineTo(72, 159);`	draw line more to the left
`ctx.lineTo(76, 207);`	draw line slightly to the right and down
`ctx.lineTo(139, 225);`	draw line to the left and down
`ctx.closePath();`	close path
`ctx.fill();`	fill in the shape in the indicated color
`// white, right hand side of the 5`	
`ctx.fillStyle = "#FFFFFF";`	set color to white
`ctx.beginPath();`	start path
`ctx.moveTo(139, 113);`	start at middle pint
`ctx.lineTo(139, 144);`	draw line down
`ctx.lineTo(177, 144);`	draw line to the right
`ctx.lineTo(173, 184);`	draw line slightly left and down

Code Line	Description
`ctx.lineTo(139, 193);`	draw line more left and down
`ctx.lineTo(139, 225);`	draw line down
`ctx.lineTo(202, 207);`	draw line to the right and up
`ctx.lineTo(210, 113);`	draw line slightly right and up
`ctx.closePath();`	close path
`ctx.fill();`	fill in white
`ctx.beginPath();`	start a new path
`ctx.moveTo(139, 51);`	move to middle point
`ctx.lineTo(139, 82);`	move down
`ctx.lineTo(213, 82);`	move to the right
`ctx.lineTo(216, 51);`	move slightly to the right and up
`ctx.closePath();`	close path
`ctx.fill();`	fill in white
`}`	close dologo function
`function changescale(val) {`	open function changevalue with parameter
`    factorvalue = val / 100;`	set factorvalue to the input divided by 100
`    dologo();`	invoke function to draw logo
`}`	close changevalue function
`</script>`	close script element
`</head>`	close head element

Code Line	Description
`<body onLoad="init();">`	body tag with attribute set to invoke init
`<canvas id="canvas" width="600" height="400">`	canvas tag setting dimensions and with id to be used in code
`Your browser does not support the canvas element.`	message to appear if canvas not supported
`</canvas>`	close canvas tag
`<article>`	article tag
`Scale percentage:  <input id="slide" type="range" min="0" max="100" value="100" onChange="changescale(this.value)" step="10"/>`	the slider (range) input with settings
`Note: slider treated as text field in some browsers.`	Comment to note that slider may be text field. It is still usable.
`</article>`	article close tag
`<article>Built on <a href="http://people.opera.com/danield/html5/html5logo/">work by Daniel Davis, et al</a>, but don't blame them for the fonts. Check out the use of <em>font-family</em> in the style element and the <em>fontfamily</em> variable in the script element for safe ways to do fonts. I did the scaling. Note also use of semantic elements.</article>`	article tag with some text, including hyperlink
`<footer>HTML5 Logo by <a href="http://www.w3.org/"><abbr title="World Wide Web Consortium">W3C</abbr></a>.`	footer tag and footer content, including abbr element
`</footer>`	footer close tag
`</body>`	body close
`</html>`	html close

You can make this application your own by using all or parts of it with your own work. You probably want to omit the comments about fonts.

Testing and uploading the application

This is a simple application to test and upload (and test) because it is a single file. I am told that the logo does display on iPhone4 and iPad2, but the slider is a text box in each case. I also tested it on Safari and Opera on a PC. You can skip ahead to Chapter 8 for a project displaying a jigsaw puzzle turning into a video that does work with finger touches on the iPhone and iPad as well as mouse moves on computers.

Summary

In this chapter, you learned how make a specific drawing and also steps to take in producing other, similar, applications. The features used include

- paths
- text on the canvas and text in semantic elements in the body
- the range input element and its associated change event
- coordinate transformations, namely translate and scale
- specification of sets of fonts
- styles for semantic elements, including the border top to make a line to go before the footer

The next chapter describes how to build a utility application for making compositions or collages of photographs and shapes. It combines techniques of drawing on canvas and creating HTML elements with a standard technique in computing, objects. It also makes use of coordinate transformations.

CHAPTER 2

Family Collage: Manipulating Programmer-defined Objects on a Canvas

In this chapter, you will learn about

- Creating and manipulating object-oriented programming for drawing on canvas

- Handling mouse events, including double-click

- Saving the canvas to an image

- Using try and catch to trap errors

- Browser differences involving the location of the code

- Using algebra and geometry to construct shapes and determine when the cursor is over a specific object

- Controlling the icon used for the cursor

Introduction

The project for this chapter is a utility for manipulating objects on a canvas to produce a picture. I call it a utility because one person does the programming and gathers photographs and designs and then can offer the program to friends, family members, colleagues and others to produce the compositions / collages. The result can be anything from an abstract design to a collage of photographs. The objects in my example include two rectangles, an oval, a circle, a heart, and five family photographs. It is possible for you, or, perhaps, your end-user/customer/client/player, to make duplicate copies of any of the objects or to remove any of the objects. The end-user positions the object using drag and drop with the mouse. When the picture is judged to be complete, it is possible to create an image that can be downloaded into a file.

Figure 2-1 shows the opening screen for my program. Notice that you start off with ten objects to arrange.

Mouse down, move and mouse up to move objects. Double click for new object. Click re-load if images fail to appear.

Open window with image (which you can save into image file)

Remove last object moved

Figure 2-1. Opening screen for Family Pictures

Figure 2-2 shows what I, as an end-user, produced as a final product. I have arranged the photographs to represent my son's family, including my new granddaughter. I deleted the two rectangles and the oval and made duplicates of the circle to position as decoration in the corners of the picture.

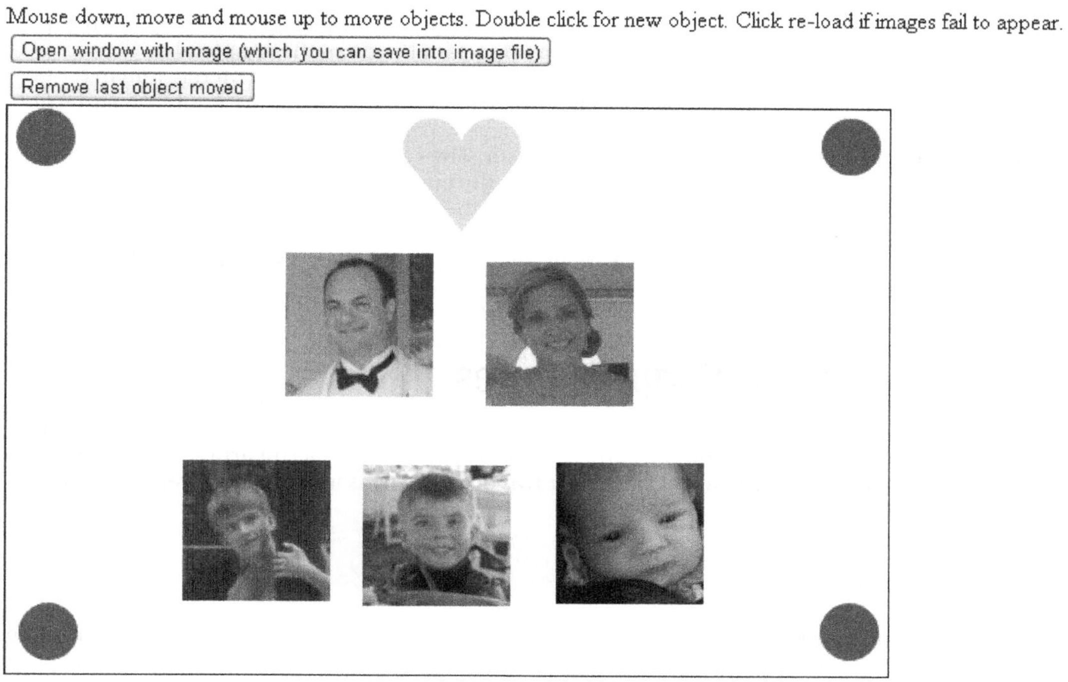

Mouse down, move and mouse up to move objects. Double click for new object. Click re-load if images fail to appear.

[Open window with image (which you can save into image file)]
[Remove last object moved]

Figure 2-2. *Sample final product: rearranged objects*

I decided on including a heart, not just for sentimental reasons, but because it required me to use algebra and geometry. Don't be afraid of mathematics. It is very useful. I invented, so to speak, a canonical heart. For other shapes, you may be able to find a standard definition in terms of mathematical expressions.

In this situation, I created the set of objects and then I used the program to make a composition. You can plan your application to take family photographs or photographs categorized by another theme and some set of circles, ovals, rectangles, and hearts. When you are finished, you can offer this program to others for them to use. This is analogous to building a game program for players. The end-users for this application may be family members, friends, or colleagues.

Of course, it certainly is possible to use a drawing program such as Adobe Photoshop or Corel Paint Shop Pro to create compositions such as these, but this application provides considerable ease-of-use for its specific purpose. The project also serves as a vehicle to learn important programming techniques as well as features of HTML5 and JavaScript. And, as will be a continual refrain, there are differences among the browsers to discuss.

Critical Requirements

The critical requirements for this project include constructing a framework for manipulating objects on the screen, including detecting mouse events on the objects, deleting objects and creating copies of objects. The current framework provides a way to specify rectangles, ovals, hearts and images, but the approach can accommodate other shapes and this is an important lesson of the chapter.

The objective is for the drag and drop operations to be reasonably precise: not merely moving something from one region of the window to another. I will re-visit this topic in the Chapters 8 and 9 on making jigsaw puzzles.

I also made the decision to control the look of the cursor. The cursor when the mouse is not on the canvas is the standard arrow. When on the canvas element, the cursor will be the cross-hairs. When the user presses down on the mouse button and drags an object, the cursor changes to a hand with pointer finger.

When the work is complete, it is a natural desire to save it, perhaps as an image file, so this also is a requirement for the project.

HTML5, CSS, and JavaScript features

We now explore the features of HTML5 and JavaScript that are used for the Family Collage project. The idea is to maintain a list of the material on the canvas. This list will be a JavaScript array. The information will include the position of each item, how it is to be drawn on the canvas and how to determine if the mouse cursor is on the item.

JavaScript objects

Object oriented programming is a standard of computer science and a critical part of most programming languages. Objects have *attributes*, also called *properties*, and *methods*. A method is a function. Put another way, an object has data and code that may make use of the data. HTML and JavaScript have many built-in objects, such as `document` and `window` and also arrays and strings. For the Family Picture project, I make use of a basic facility in JavaScript (established before HTML5) for defining my own objects. These sometimes are called user-defined objects, but the term I and others prefer is programmer-defined objects. This is an important distinction for the Family Collage project in which you, the programmer, may create an application, with pictures and other shapes you identify and design, and then offer it to a family member to use.

The objective of this project is to set up a framework for creating and manipulating different shapes on the canvas, keeping in mind that once something is drawn to the canvas, its identity as a rectangle or image is lost. The first step for each shape is to define what is called a *constructor* function that stores the information that specifies the shape. The next step is to define the methods, code for using the information to do what needs to be done.

My approach gives the appearance of moving things on the canvas. In fact, information kept in internal variables is changed and the canvas is cleared and new drawings made each time something happens to change the look of the canvas.

My strategy is to define new types of objects, each of which will have two methods defined

- `draw` for drawing the object on the canvas

- `overcheck` for determining if a given position, specifically the mouse position, is on the object

These methods reference the attributes of the object and use these values in mathematical expressions to produce the results. Once the constructor functions are defined, values can be created as new instances of these objects. An array called `stuff` holds all the object instances.

■ **Note** Object oriented programming in all its glory has a rich and often daunting vocabulary. Classes are what define objects. I have hinted here at what is called an interface. Classes can be subclasses of other classes and this may have been useful for pictures and rectangles. I'm aiming for a more casual tone here. For example, I will speak of objects and object instances.

Let's move away from generalities and show how this works. I created functions I named Rect, Oval, Picture and Heart. These will be what are called the constructor functions for the Rect, Oval, Picture and Heart object instances. It is a convention to give such functions names starting with capital letters.

Rect

The definition of the Rect constructor function is

```
function Rect(x,y,w,h,c) {
        this.x = x;
        this.y = y;
        this.w = w;
        this.h = h;
        this.draw = drawrect;
        this.color = c;
        this.overcheck = overrect;
}
```

The function is used as follows in the init function invoked when the document is loaded:

```
var r1 = new Rect(2,10,50,50,"red");
```

The variable r1 is declared and set to a new object constructed using the function Rect. The built-in term new does the task of creating a new object. The newly constructed object holds the values 2 and 10 for the initial x and y position, accessed using the attribute names x and y and the values 50 and 50 for width and height accessed using the attribute names w and h. The term this refers to the object being constructed. The English meaning and the computer jargon meaning of *new* and *this* match. The Rect function also stores away values for the attributes draw and overcheck. It is not obvious from what you have seen so far, but these values will be used to invoke functions named drawrect and overrect. This is the way to specify methods for the programmer-defined objects. Lastly, the color attribute is set to "red".

Oval

Moving on, the constructor function for Oval is similar.

```
function Oval(x,y,r,hor,ver,c) {
        this.x = x;
        this.y = y;
        this.r = r;
        this.radsq = r*r;
        this.hor = hor;
```

```
        this.ver = ver;
        this.draw = drawoval;
        this.color = c;
        this.overcheck = overoval;
}
```

The x and y values refer to the center of the Oval. The hor and ver attributes will be used to scale the horizontal and vertical axis respectively and, depending on the values, produce an oval that is not a circle. The radsq attribute is calculated and stored to save time in the overoval function.

■ **Note**   Computers are very fast and I am showing my age by storing away and then using the square of the radius. Still, making this trade-off of extra storage for savings in computation time may be justified.

In my example,

```
var oval1 = new Oval(200,30,20,2.0,1.0, "teal");
```

produces the teal colored oval in Figure 2-1. Notice that it is stretched out in the horizontal dimension. In contrast, the purple oval is declared in the following declaration:

```
var cir1 = new Oval(300,30,20,1.0,1.0,"purple");
```

The purple circle has the hor and ver values the same and so is a circle. You have every right to ask how or where this information is used to produce an oval or circle. The answer is in the drawoval function that will be shown later on. Similarly, the checking if a given x,y position is on the oval is performed by the overoval function.

Picture

The constructor for Picture objects stores away position, width and height, and the name of an Image object.

```
function Picture(x,y,w,h,imagename) {
        this.x = x;
        this.y = y;
        this.w = w;
        this.h = h;
        this.imagename = imagename;
        this.draw = drawpic;
        this.overcheck = overrect;
}
```

My example has four Picture objects. Here is code for setting up one of them:

```
var dad = new Image();
dad.src = "daniel1.jpg";
var pic1 = new Picture(10,100,100,100,dad);
```

Setting up one of the Picture objects takes more work than Rect objects. I need to write the code to create an Image object. This is a built-in object type in JavaScript. I need to acquire an image file and move it into the same folder as the HTML file and write code to assign the correct file name to the src attribute of the Image variable. (Alternatively, you can put all images into a subfolder or several subfolders. For example, the string for the src would be "images/daniel1.jpg".) Then I write the line of code that constructs the pic1 variable.

Heart

We have one more of the programmer defined objects to cover. The challenge I set myself was to define values that specify a heart shape. I came up with the following: a heart shape is defined by the position, an x, y pair of values that will be the location of the cleft of the heart; the distance from the cleft to the bottom point, and the radius for the two partial circles representing the curved parts of the heart. You can think of this as a canonical heart. The critical pieces of information are shown in Figure 2-3. If and when you add new types of shapes to your application, you will need to invent or discover the data that defines the shape.

Figure 2-3. *Data defining a heart*

The constructor function saves the indicated values, along with the color, into any newly constructed object. You might be suspecting that the drawing and the overcheck will be somewhat more complicated than the functions for rectangles and you would be correct. The constructor function resembles the other constructor function.

```
function Heart(x,y,h,drx,color) {
        this.x = x;
        this.y = y;
        this.h = h;
        this.drx = drx;
        this.radsq = drx*drx;
        this.color = color;
        this.draw = drawheart;
        this.overcheck = overheart;
        this.ang = .25*Math.PI;

}
```

The ang attribute is a case of my hedging my bets. You notice that it is a constant and I could avoid making it an attribute. You will see later when I explain drawheart how my coding uses it to make the heart rounded. I made it an attribute just in case I want to change to allow hearts to have more variability.

Drawing

I have the different method functions to explain, but let's go to where the drawing is done in order to demonstrate how all of this works together. I define an array, initially empty,

```
var stuff = [];
```

Then my code adds to this array with statements such as

```
stuff.push(pic1);
stuff.push(pic2);
stuff.push(pic3);
stuff.push(pic4);
stuff.push(r1);
stuff.push(s1);
stuff.push(oval1);
stuff.push(cir1);
```

At appropriate times, namely after any changes, the function `drawstuff` is invoked. It works by erasing the canvas, drawing a rectangle to make a frame, and then iterating over each element in the `stuff` array and invoking the `draw` methods. The function is

```
function drawstuff() {
        ctx.clearRect(0,0,600,400);
        ctx.strokeStyle = "black";
        ctx.lineWidth = 2;
        ctx.strokeRect(0,0,600,400);
        for (var i=0;i<stuff.length;i++) {
                stuff[i].draw();
        }
}
```

Notice that there is no coding that asks, is this an oval, if so do this, or is it a picture, if so do that…. Instead, the `draw` method that has been established for each member of the array does its work! The same magic happens when checking if a position (the mouse) is on an object. The benefit of this approach increases as more object types are added.

I did realize that since my code never changes the `strokeStyle` or the `lineWidth`, I could move those statements to the `init` function and just do them one time. However, it occurred to me that I might have a shape that does change these values and so to prepare for that possible change in the application at a later time, I would set `strokeStyle` and `lineWidth` in `drawstuff`.

Now I will explain the methods for drawing and the methods for checking if a position is on the object. The `drawrect` function is pretty straight-forward:

```
function drawrect() {
        ctx.fillStyle = this.color;
        ctx.fillRect(this.x, this.y, this.w, this.h);
}
```

Remember the term `this` refers to the object for which `drawrect` serves as a method. The `drawrect` function is the method for rectangles and for pictures.

The `drawoval` function is slightly, but only slightly, more complex. You need to recall how coordinate transformations work. HTML5 JavaScript only allows circular arcs but does allow scaling the coordinates to produce ovals (ellipses) that are not circles. What the coding in the `drawoval` function does is to save the current state of the coordinate system and then perform a translation to the center of the object.

Then a scaling transformation is applied, using the hor and ver properties. Now, after setting the fillStyle to be the color specified in the color attribute, I use the coding for drawing a path made up of a circular arc and filling the path. The last step is to restore the original state of the coordinate system.

```
function drawoval() {
        ctx.save();
        ctx.translate(this.x,this.y);
        ctx.scale(this.hor,this.ver);
        ctx.fillStyle = this.color;
        ctx.beginPath();
        ctx.arc(0,0,this.r,0,2*Math.PI,true);
        ctx.closePath();
        ctx.fill();
        ctx.restore();
}
```

This is the way ovals that may or may not be circles are drawn on the canvas. Since my code restored the original state of the coordinate system, this has the effect of undoing the scaling and translation transformations.

The drawpic function is the easiest one, just one line:

```
function drawpic() {
        ctx.drawImage(this.imagename,this.x,this.y,this.w,this.h);
}
```

Again, the terms starting with this followed by a dot and then the attribute names reference the stored attributes.

■ **Note** Please keep in mind that I didn't plan and program this whole application all at once. I did the rectangles and ovals and later added the pictures and much later the heart. I also added the duplication operation and the deletion operation much later. Working in stages is the way to go. Planning is important and useful, but you do not have to have all the details complete at the start.

The drawheart function starts by defining variables to be used later. The leftctrx is the x coordinate of the center of the left arc and the rightctrx is the x coordinate of the center of the right arc. The arcs are each more than a half circle. How much more? I decided to make this be .25* Math.PI and to store this value in the ang attribute.

The tricky thing was to determine where the arc stops on the right side. My code uses trig expressions to set the cx and cy values. The cx, cy position is where the arc meets the straight line. Figure 2-4 indicates the meaning of the variables.

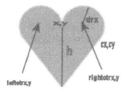

Figure 2-4. *Added pieces of data used in functions*

The path will start at what we are calling the cleft or the cleavage (giggle) and draw the arc on the left, then draw a line to the bottom point, then up to the **cx,cy** point and then finish with the arc on the right. The function is the following:

```
function drawheart() {
        var leftctrx = this.x-this.drx;
        var rightctrx = this.x+this.drx;
        var cx = rightctrx+this.drx*Math.cos(this.ang);
        var cy = this.y + this.drx*Math.sin(this.ang);
        ctx.fillStyle = this.color;
        ctx.beginPath();
        ctx.moveTo(this.x,this.y);
        ctx.arc(leftctrx,this.y,this.drx,0,Math.PI-this.ang,true);
        ctx.lineTo(this.x,this.y+this.h);
        ctx.lineTo(cx,cy);
        ctx.arc(rightctrx,this.y,this.drx,this.ang,Math.PI,true);
        ctx.closePath();
        ctx.fill();
}
```

Checking for mouse over object

Before describing the functions for the overcheck method, I will preview why it is needed. HTML5 and JavaScript provide ways to handle (listen for and respond to) mouse events on the canvas and supply the coordinates of where the event took place. However, our code must do the work of determining what object was involved. Remember: there are no objects actually on the canvas, just the remains, think of it as paint, of whatever drawing was done. My code accomplishes this task by looping through the **stuff** array and invoking the **overcheck** method for each object. As soon as there is a hit (and I will explain the order in which this is done later), my code proceeds with that object as the one selected. The functions in which this checking occurs are **startdragging** and **makenewitem** and will be explained in the next section.

There are three functions to explain for the **overcheck** method since Picture and Rect refer to the same function. Each function takes two parameters. Think of the **mx, my** as the location of the mouse. The **overrect** function checks for four conditions each being true. In English, the question is: Is **mx** greater than or equal to this.x AND is **mx** less than or equal to this.x + this.w AND is **my** greater than or equal to this.y AND is **my** less than or equal to this.y + this.h? The function says this more compactly:

```
function overrect (mx,my) {
        if ( (mx>=this.x)&&(mx<=(this.x+this.w))&&(my>=this.y)&&(my<=(this.y+this.h)))
                {return true;}
        else {return false;}
}
```

The function defining the **overcheck** method for ovals is **overoval**. The overoval function performs the operation of checking if something is within a circle, but in a translated and scaled coordinate system. The check for a point being within a circle could be done by setting the center of the circle to x1,y1 and the point to x2,y2 and see if the distance between the two is less than the radius. I use a variation of this to save time and compare the square of the distance to the radius squared. I define a function **distsq** that returns the square of the distance. But now I need to figure out how to do this in a translated and scaled coordinate system. The answer is to set x1,y1 to 0,0. This is the location of the center of the oval in the translated coordinate system. Then my code sets x2 and y2 as indicated in the code to what would be the scaled values.

```
function overoval(mx,my) {
        var x1 = 0;
        var y1 = 0;
        var x2 = (mx-this.x)/this.hor;
        var y2 = (my-this.y)/this.ver;
        if (distsq(x1,y1,x2,y2)<=(this.radsq) ){
                return true
        }
        else {return false}
}
```

This did not come to me instantly. I worked it out trying values for mx and my located in different positions relative to the oval center. The code does represent what the transformations do in terms of the translation and then the scaling.

The **overheart** function consists of several distinct if statements. This is a case of not trying for a simple expression but thinking about various situations. The function starts off by setting variables to be used later. The first check made by the function is to determine if the mx,my point is outside the rectangle that is the bounding rectangle for the heart. I wrote the outside function to return true if the position specified by the last two parameters was outside the rectangle indicated by the first four parameters. The qx,qy point is the upper left corner. qwidth is the width at the widest point and qheight is the total height. I thought of this as a quick check that would return false most of the time. The next two if statements determine if the mx,my point is contained in either circle. That is, I again use the comparison of the square of the distance from mx,my to the center of each arc to the stored radsq attribute. At this point in the function, that is, if the mx,my position was not close enough to the center of either circle and if my is above (less than) this.y, then the code returns false. Lastly, the code puts the mx value in the equation for each of the sloping lines and compares the result to my. The equation for a line can be written using the slope m and a point on the line x2,y2:

```
y = m * (x - x2) + y2
```

The code sets m and x2, y2 for the line on the left and then modifies it to work for the line on the right by changing the sign of m. One possible concern here is whether or not the fact that the screen coordinate system has upside down vertical values (vertical values increase going down the screen) causes a problem. I checked out cases and the code works.

```
function overheart(mx,my) {
        var leftctrx = this.x-this.drx;
        var rightctrx = this.x+this.drx;
        var qx = this.x-2*this.drx;
        var qy = this.y-this.drx;
        var qwidth = 4*this.drx;
        var qheight = this.drx+this.h;

//quick test if it is in bounding rectangle
        if (outside(qx,qy,qwidth,qheight,mx,my)) {

                return false;}
//compare to two centers

  if (distsq(mx,my,leftctrx,this.y)<this.radsq) return true;
  if (distsq(mx,my,rightctrx,this.y)<this.radsq) return true;
// if outside of circles AND below (higher in the screen) than this.y, return false
  if (my<this.y) return false;

// compare to each slope
 var x2 = this.x
 var y2 = this.y + this.h;
 var m = (this.h)/(2*this.drx);
// left side
 if (mx<=this.x) {
        if (my < (m*(mx-x2)+y2)) {return true;}
        else { return false;}
 }
 else {
 m = -m;

 if (my < (m*(mx-x2)+y2)) { return true}
 else return false;
 }
}
```

The reasoning underlying the outside function is similar to the overrect function. You need to write code comparing the mx,my value to the sides of the rectangle. However, for outside I chose to use the OR operator, ||, and to return its value. This will be true if any of the factors are true and false otherwise.

```
function outside(x,y,w,h,mx,my) {
        return ((mx<x) || (mx > (x+w)) || (my < y) || (my > (y+h)));
}
```

Actually, what I said was true, but misses what could be an important consideration if performance is an issue. The || evaluates each of the conditions starting from the first (leftmost) one. As soon as one of them is true, it stops evaluating and returns true. The && operator does a similar thing. As soon as one of the conditions is false, it returns false.

This is the basis for the four types of objects I designed for manipulation on the canvas. You can look ahead to examine all the code or continue to see how these objects are put in use in the responses to mouse events.

▤ **Note**   This example does not demonstrate the full power of object-oriented programming. In a language such as Java (or the variant Processing designed for artists), I could have programmed this in such a way to check that each additional object was defined properly, that is with the x and y attributes for location and methods for drawing and checking.

User interface

The application requirements for the user interface include dragging, that is, mouse down, mouse move and mouse up, for re-positioning items and double clicking for producing a duplicate copy of an item. I decided to use buttons for the other end-user actions: removing an item from the canvas and creating an image to be saved. The button action is straight-forward. I write two instances of the HTML5 button element with the onClick attributes set to the appropriate function.

```
<button onClick="saveasimage();">Open window with image (which you can save into image file)↵
</button></br>
<button onClick="removeobj();">Remove last object moved </button>
```

The saveasimage function will be explained in the next section. The removeobj function deletes the last moved object from the stuff array. The last moved object is the last one in the array. This makes the coding extremely simple:

```
function removeobj() {
        stuff.pop();
        drawstuff();
}
```

A pop for any array deletes the last element. The function then invokes the drawstuff function to display all but the last element. By the way, if the button is clicked at the start of the application, the last element pushed on the stuff array will be deleted. If this is unacceptable, you can add a check to prevent this from happening. The cost is that it needs to be done every time the user clicks on the button.

Fortunately, HTML5 provides the mouse events that we need for this application. In the init function, I include the following lines:

```
canvas1 = document.getElementById('canvas');
canvas1.onmousedown = function () { return false; };
canvas1.addEventListener('dblclick',makenewitem,false);
canvas1.addEventListener('mousedown',startdragging,false);
```

The first statement sets the canvas1 variable to reference the canvas element. The second statement is necessary to turn off the default action for the cursor. I also included a style directive for the canvas, which made the positioning absolute and then positioned the canvas 80 pixels from the top. This is ample space for the directions and the buttons.

```
canvas {position:absolute; top:80px;
  cursor:crosshair;
}
```

The third and fourth statements set up event handling for double click and mouse button down events. We should appreciate the fact that we as programmers do not have to write code to distinguish mouse down, click and double click.

31

The makenewitem and the startdragging functions start off the same. The code first determines the mouse cursor coordinates and then loops through the stuff array to determine which, if any, object was clicked on. You probably have seen the mouse cursor coordinate code before, in the Essential Guide to HTML5, for example. The looping through the array is done in reverse order. Calls are made to the overcheck method, defined appropriately for the different types of objects. If there is a hit, then the makenewitem function calls the clone function to make a copy of that item. The code modifies the x and y slightly so the new item is not directly on top of the original. The new item is added to the array and there is a break to leave the for loop.

```
function makenewitem(ev) {
        var mx;
        var my;
        if ( ev.layerX ||  ev.layerX == 0) {
                mx= ev.layerX;
                my = ev.layerY;
                } else if (ev.offsetX || ev.offsetX == 0) {
                            mx = ev.offsetX;
                            my = ev.offsetY;
                }
        var endpt = stuff.length-1;
        var item;
        for (var i=endpt;i>=0;i--) {   //reverse order
                if (stuff[i].overcheck(mx,my)) {
                        item = clone(stuff[i]);
                        item.x +=20;
                        item.y += 20;
                        stuff.push(item);
                        break;
                }
        }
        drawstuff();
}
```

As I indicated earlier, the clone function makes a copy of an element in the stuff array. You may ask, why not just write

```
        item = stuff[i];
```

The answer is that this assignment does not create a new, distinct value. JavaScript merely sets the item variable to point to the same thing as the ith member of stuff. This is called 'copy by reference'. We don't want that. We want a brand new, separate thing that we can change. The way to copy is demonstrated in the clone function. A new object is created and then a for-loop is invoked. The for(var info in obj) says: for every attribute of obj, set an equivalently named attribute in item to the value of the attribute.

```
function clone(obj) {
        var item = new Object();
        for (var info in obj) {
                item[info] = obj[info];
        }
        return item;

}
```

So the effect of the two functions is to duplicate whatever element is under the mouse cursor. You or your end-user can then mouse down on the original or the cloned object and move it around.

The startdragged function proceeds as indicated to determine what object was under the mouse. The code then determines what I (and others) call the offsets in x and y of the mouse coordinates versus the x, y position of the object. This is because we want the object to move around maintaining the same relationship between object and mouse. Some folks call this the flypaper effect. It is as if the mouse cursor came down on the object and stuck like flypaper. The offsetx and offsety are global variables. Note that the coding works for objects for which the x, y values refer to the upper left corner (pictures and rectangles), to the center (ovals) and to a specific internal point (hearts).

The coding then performs a series of operations that has the effect of moving this object to the end of the array. The first statement is a copy by reference operation to set the variable item. The next step saves the index for the last element of the stuff array to the global variable thingInMotion. This variable will be used by the function moveit. The splice statement removes the original element and the push statement adds it to the array at the end. The statement referencing cursor is the way to specify a cursor. The "pointer" refers to one of the built-in options. The last two statements in the function set up the event handling for moving the mouse and releasing the button on the mouse. This event handling will be removed in the dropit function.

```
function startdragging(ev) {
        var mx;
        var my;
        if ( ev.layerX ||  ev.layerX == 0) {
                        mx= ev.layerX;
                my = ev.layerY;
                } else if (ev.offsetX || ev.offsetX == 0) {
                mx = ev.offsetX;
                my = ev.offsetY;
                }
        var endpt = stuff.length-1;
        for (var i=endpt;i>=0;i--) {   //reverse order
                if (stuff[i].overcheck(mx,my)) {
                offsetx = mx-stuff[i].x;
                 offsety = my-stuff[i].y;
                 var item = stuff[i];
                 var last = stuff.length-1;
                 stuff.splice(i,1);
                 stuff.push(item);
                 thingInMotion = last;
                 canvas1.style.cursor = "pointer";    // change to finger
                 canvas1.addEventListener('mousemove',moveit,false);
                 canvas1.addEventListener('mouseup',dropit,false);
                 break;
                }
        }
}
```

The moveit function moves the object referenced by thingInMotion and uses the offsetx and offsety variables to move the object. The drawstuff function is invoked to show the modified canvas.

```
function moveit(ev) {
        var mx;
        var my;
        if ( ev.layerX ||  ev.layerX == 0) {
                mx= ev.layerX;
                my = ev.layerY;
                } else if (ev.offsetX || ev.offsetX == 0) {
                mx = ev.offsetX;
                my = ev.offsetY;
                }
        stuff[thingInMotion].x = mx-offsetx; //adjust for flypaper dragging
        stuff[thingInMotion].y = my-offsety;
        drawstuff();
}
```

A mousemove event is triggered if the mouse moves a single pixel in any direction. If this seems too much, remember that the computer does it, not you or I. The user gets a smooth response to moving the mouse.

The dropit function is invoked at a mouseup event. The response is to remove, stop the listening for moving and releasing the mouse and then changing the cursor back to the crosshairs.

```
function dropit(ev) {
        canvas1.removeEventListener('mousemove',moveit,false);
        canvas1.removeEventListener('mouseup',dropit,false);
        canvas1.style.cursor = "crosshair";  //change back to crosshair
}
```

To summarize, the user interface for this application involves two buttons and two types of mouse actions. The drag and drop operation is implemented using a set of functions.

Saving the canvas to an image

After creating a composition, the user may want to save it to an image file. The Firefox browser makes this easy. You can right-click on the canvas when using a PC or do the equivalent operation on a MAC and a pop-up menu will appear with the option to Save Image As... However, Chrome, Safari and Opera do not provide that facility. If you right-click, the options concern the HTML document. There is, however, an alternative provided in HTML5.

A canvas element has a method called toDataURL that will produce an image from the canvas. The method provides a choice of image file types from among png, jpg, or bmp. What I choose to do with the result of this operation is write code to open a new window with the image as the content. The user then can save this image as a file either by the save file option or the right-click for the image. However, there is one more consideration. Chrome and Firefox require that this code run from a server, not on the client computer. The client computer is the one running the browser program. The server computer would be the website to which you will upload your finished work. You may or may not have one. Opera and Safari allow the code to run from the client computer. This has an impact on testing, since, generally speaking, we test programs locally and then upload to a server. Because of this situation, this is an appropriate place to use the try/catch facility of JavaScript for catching errors (so to speak) for the programmer to take action. Here is the code for the saveasimage function. The variable canvas1 has been set to the canvas element in the init function invoked when the document is loaded.

```
function saveasimage() {
 try {
  window.open(canvas1.toDataURL("image/png"));}
  catch(err) {
        alert("You need to change browsers OR upload the file to a server.");
  }
}
```

Building the application and making it your own

You can make this application your own by identifying your own image files, specifying what rectangles, ovals and hearts you want to include in the collection of objects to be manipulated and, after you have something working, adding new object types. The application has many functions but they each are small and many share attributes with others. An informal summary / outline of the application is

1. *init for initialization, including setting up event handling for double click, mouse down, mouse move and mouse up*

2. *object definition methods: constructor functions, draw functions and overcheck functions*

3. *event handling functions: mouse events and button onClick*

More formally, Table 2-1 lists all the functions and indicates how they are invoked and what functions they invoke. Notice that several functions are invoked as a result of the function being specified as a method of an object type.

Table 2-1. *Functions in the HTML5 Family Card project*

Function	Invoked / Called By	Calls
init	invoked by action of the onLoad attribute in the <body> tag	Picture, Rect, Oval, Heart, drawstuff
saveasimage	invoked by action of the onClick attribute in a button tag	
removeobj	invoked by action of the onClick attribute in a button tag	drawstuff
Picture	invoked in init function	
Rect	invoked in init function	
Oval	invoked in init function	
Heart	invoked in init function	
drawheart	invoked in drawstuff	

Continued

Function	Invoked / Called By	Calls
drawrect	invoked in drawstuff	
drawoval	invoked in drawstuff	
drawpic	invoked in drawstuff	
overheart	invoked in startdragging and makenewitem	distsq, outside
overrect	invoked in startdragging and makenewitem	
overoval	invoked in startdragging and makenewitem	distsq
distsq	invoked by overheart and overoval	
drawstuff	invoked by makenewitem, moveit, removeobj, init	draw method of each item in the stuff array
moveit	invoked by action set by addEventListener for mousemove set in startdragging	
dropit	invoked by action set by addEventListener for mouseup set in startdragging	
outside	invoked by overheart	
makenewitem	invoked by action set by addEventListener for dblclick set in init	clone
clone	invoked by makenewitem	
startdragging	invoked by action set by addEventListener for mousedown set in init	

Table 2-2 shows the code for the basic application, with comments for each line.

Table 2-2. *Complete Code for the HTML5 Logo project*

Code Line	Description
`<!DOCTYPE html >`	standard heading for HTML5 documents
`<html>`	html tag
`<head>`	head tag
`<title>Build family picture</title>`	complete title
`<meta charset="UTF-8">`	meta tag
`<style>`	start of style
`canvas {position:absolute; top:80px;`	directive for canvas, setting its position as absolute and its location 80 pixels from the top of the document.
`cursor:crosshair;`	specifying the cursor icon for when the mouse is over the canvas
`}`	close directive
`</style>`	close style
`<script language="Javascript">`	script tag
`var ctx;`	variable to hold the canvas context
`var canvas1;`	variable to hold the canvas element
`var stuff = [];`	array for all the objects on the canvas
`var thingInMotion;`	reference to object being dragged
`var offsetx;`	horizontal offset for object being dragged
`var offsety;`	vertical offset for object being dragged
`function init() {`	function header for init

Code Line	Description
`canvas1 = document.getElementById('canvas');`	sets variable to reference the canvas element
`canvas1.onmousedown = function () { return false; };`	prevents change of cursor to default
`canvas1.addEventListener('dblclick',makenewitem,false);`	sets up the event handling for double clicks on the canvas
`canvas1.addEventListener('mousedown',startdragging,false);`	sets up the event handling for mouse down on the canvas
`ctx = canvas1.getContext("2d");`	sets ctx to reference the context of the canvas. Used for all drawing.
`var r1 = new Rect(2,10,50,50,"red");`	constructs a rectangle
`var s1 = new Rect(60,10, 50,50,"blue");`	constructs a rectangle
`var oval1 = new Oval(200,30,20,2.0,1.0, "teal");`	constructs an oval
`var cir1 = new Oval(300,30,20,1.0,1.0,"purple");`	constructs an oval (which will be a circle)
`var dad = new Image();`	creates an Image element
`dad.src = "daniel1.jpg";`	sets the src to the indicated file
`var mom = new Image();`	creates an Image element
`mom.src = "allison1.jpg";`	sets the src to the indicated file
`var son1= new Image();`	creates an Image element
`son1.src = "liam2.jpg";`	sets the src to the indicated file
`var son2 = new Image();`	creates an Image element
`son2.src = "grant1.jpg";`	sets the src to the indicated file
`var pic1 = new Picture(10,100,100,100,dad);`	constructs a Picture object

Code Line	Description
`var pic2 = new Picture(120,100,100,100,mom);`	constructs a Picture object
`var pic3 = new Picture(230,100,100,100,son1);`	constructs a Picture object
`var pic4 = new Picture(340,100,100,100,son2);`	constructs a Picture object
`var heart1 = new Heart(400,30,60,20,"pink");`	constructs a Heart object
`stuff.push(pic1);`	adds (pushes) pic1 to stuff array
`stuff.push(pic2);`	adds pic2
`stuff.push(pic3);`	adds pic3
`stuff.push(pic4);`	adds pic4
`stuff.push(r1);`	adds r1
`stuff.push(s1);`	adds s1
`stuff.push(oval1);`	adds oval1
`stuff.push(cir1);`	adds cir1
`stuff.push(heart1);`	adds heart1
`drawstuff();`	draws all the objects on the canvas
`}`	end init function
`function distsq (x1,y1,x2,y2) {`	function header for distsq. Takes 2 points (2 x 2 values) as parameters
`var xd = x1 - x2;`	set difference in x
`var yd = y1 - y2;`	set difference in y
`return ((xd*xd) + (yd*yd) );`	returns sum of squares. This is the square of the distance between the two points.
`}`	end distsq function

Code Line	Description
`function Picture(x,y,w,h,imagename) {`	function header for Picture constructor, positioned at x, y, with width w and height h, and the imagename Image object.
`    this.x = x;`	set attribute
`    this.y = y;`	set attribute
`    this.w = w;`	set attribute
`    this.h = h;`	set attribute
`    this.imagename = imagename;`	set attribute
`    this.draw = drawpic;`	set drawpic function to be the draw method
`    this.overcheck = overrect;`	set overrect function to be the overcheck method
`}`	close function
`function Heart(x,y,h,drx,color) {`	function header for Heart constructor, located with the cleavage at x, y, distance from x, y to lower tip h, radius drx and color.
`    this.x = x;`	set attribute
`    this.y = y;`	set attribute
`    this.h = h;`	set attribute
`    this.drx = drx;`	set attribute
`    this.radsq = drx*drx;`	set attribute to avoid doing this operation repeated times later
`    this.color = color;`	set attribute
`    this.draw = drawheart;`	set drawheart function to be the draw method

Code Line	Description
`this.overcheck = overheart;`	set overheart function to be the overcheck method
`this.ang = .25*Math.PI;`	set attribute to be this constant value. May make more general at a later time
`}`	close function
`function drawheart() {`	function header for drawheart
`var leftctrx = this.x-this.drx;`	calculate and set variable to be x coordinate of center of left curve
`var rightctrx = this.x+this.drx;`	calculate and set variable to be x coordinate of center of right curve
`var cx = rightctrx+this.drx*Math.cos(this.ang);`	calculate and set variable to be x coordinate of point where curve on the right changes to straight line
`var cy = this.y + this.drx*Math.sin(this.ang);`	calculate and set variable to be y coordinate of point where curve on the right changes to straight line
`ctx.fillStyle = this.color;`	set fillStyle
`ctx.beginPath();`	begin path
`ctx.moveTo(this.x,this.y);`	move to cleft of heart
`ctx.arc(leftctrx,this.y,this.drx,0,Math.PI-this.ang,true);`	draw left curve
`ctx.lineTo(this.x,this.y+this.h);`	move to bottom point
`ctx.lineTo(cx,cy);`	move to point where straight line meets curve
`ctx.arc(rightctrx,this.y,this.drx,this.ang,Math.PI,true);`	draw right curve
`ctx.closePath();`	close path

Code Line	Description
`ctx.fill();`	fill in path
`}`	close function
`function overheart(mx,my) {`	header for overheart function
`var leftctrx = this.x-this.drx;`	set variable to be x coordinate of center of left curve
`var rightctrx = this.x+this.drx;`	set variable to be x coordinate of center of right curve
`var qx = this.x-2*this.drx;`	calculate and set variable to be x coordinate of left of bounding rectangle
`var qy = this.y-this.drx;`	calculate and set variable to be y coordinate of top of bounding rectangle
`var qwidth = 4*this.drx;`	calculate and set variable to be width of bounding rectangle
`var qheight = this.drx+this.h;`	calculate and set variable to be height of bounding rectangle
`if (outside(qx,qy,qwidth,qheight,mx,my)) {`	quick test if it is in bounding rectangle
`return false;}`	
`if (distsq(mx,my,leftctrx,this.y)<this.radsq) return true;`	check if inside left curve
`if (distsq(mx,my,rightctrx,this.y)<this.radsq) return true;`	or right curve
`if (my<=this.y) return false;`	return false if above y on screen (and not previously determined to be within curves
`var x2 = this.x`	start calculations to compare my to slopes. Set x2 and
`var y2 = this.y + this.h;`	set y2 to have x2,y2 point on each sloping line

Code Line	Description
`var m = (this.h)/(2*this.drx);`	calculate slope of left line
`if (mx<=this.x) {`	If mx is on the left side…
`    if (my < (m*(mx-x2)+y2)) {return true;}`	compare my to the y value corresponding to mx. If my is above (on the screen), then return true
`    else { return false;}`	otherwise return false
`}`	close if if (mx<=this.x) clause
`else {`	else
`m = -m;`	change sign of slope to be slope of the right line
`if (my < (m*(mx-x2)+y2)) { return true}`	Compare my to the value corresponding to mx on the right line and if less than (further up on the screen) return true
`else return false;`	else return false
`}`	close clause
`}`	close function
`function outside(x,y,w,h,mx,my) {`	function header outside
`return ((mx<x) || (mx > (x+w)) || (my < y) || (my > (y+h)));`	returns true if any of factors is true, indicating the mx, my point is outside the rectangle
`}`	close function
`function drawpic() {`	function header drawpic
`ctx.drawImage(this.imagename,this.x,this.y,this.w,this.h);`	draw indicated image
`}`	close function

Code Line	Description
`function Oval(x,y,r,hor,ver,c) {`	function header for Oval constructor, position x, y, horizontal scaling hor, vertical scaling ver, color c.
`this.x = x;`	set attribute
`this.y = y;`	set attribute
`this.r = r;`	set attribute
`this.radsq = r*r;`	store as attribute to avoid repeated calculations later
`this.hor = hor;`	set attribute
`this.ver = ver;`	set attribute
`this.draw = drawoval;`	set drawoval as the draw method
`this.color = c;`	set attribute
`this.overcheck = overoval;`	set overoval as the overcheck method
`}`	close function
`function drawoval() {`	function header for drawoval
`ctx.save();`	save current coordinate state
`ctx.translate(this.x,this.y);`	move to center
`ctx.scale(this.hor,this.ver);`	scale as indicated by attributes
`ctx.fillStyle = this.color;`	set color
`ctx.beginPath();`	start path
`ctx.arc(0,0,this.r,0,2*Math.PI,true);`	draw arc (complete circle)
`ctx.closePath();`	close path
`ctx.fill();`	fill in

Code Line	Description
`ctx.restore();`	restore original coordinate state
`}`	close function
`function Rect(x,y,w,h,c) {`	function header Rect constructor: position x,y, width w and height h, color c.
`this.x = x;`	set attribute
`this.y = y;`	set attribute
`this.w = w;`	set attribute
`this.h = h;`	set attribute
`this.draw = drawrect;`	set drawrect as the draw method
`this.color = c;`	set attribute
`this.overcheck = overrect;`	set overrect as the overcheck method
`}`	close function
`function overoval(mx,my) {`	function header for overovval
`var x1 = 0;`	set variable to be used in call to distsq. This represents x coordinate of point at center of oval
`var y1 = 0;`	set variable to be used in call to distsq. This represents y coordinate of point at center of oval
`var x2 = (mx-this.x)/this.hor;`	calculate the x2 using input and scaling factor
`var y2 = (my-this.y)/this.ver;`	calculate the y2 using input and scaling factor
`if (distsq(x1,y1,x2,y2)<=(this.radsq) ){`	if distance squares is less than stored radius squared….
`return true`	return true

Code Line	Description
`}`	end clause
`else {return false}`	else return false
`}`	close function
`function overrect (mx,my) {`	function header for overrect

`if (`
`(mx>=this.x)&&(mx<=(this.x+this.w))&&(my>=this.y)`
`&&(my<=(this.y+this.h)))`
	If mx, my within bounds (the 4 sides)

`{return true;}`	return true
`else {return false;}`	else return false
`}`	close function
`function makenewitem(ev) {`	function header for makenewitem. Has as a parameter an event ev set by JavaScript
`var mx;`	variable will hold x coordinate of mouse
`var my;`	variable will hold y coordinate of mouse
`if ( ev.layerX ||  ev.layerX == 0) {`	does this browser use layer...
`mx= ev.layerX;`	... set mx
`my = ev.layerY;`	... my
`} else if (ev.offsetX || ev.offsetX ==` `0) {`	does browser use offset...
`mx = ev.offsetX;`	...set mx
`my = ev.offsetY;`	... set my
`}`	end clause
`var endpt = stuff.length-1;`	store index of last item in stuff array

Code Line	Description
`var item;`	will hold the new item
`for (var i=endpt;i>=0;i--) {`	start search from the end
`if (stuff[i].overcheck(mx,my)) {`	is the mouse over this member of stuff
`item = clone(stuff[i]);`	clone (make copy of)
`item.x += 20;`	move over slightly horizontally
`item.y += 20;`	and vertically
`stuff.push(item);`	add newly created item to stuff array
`break;`	leave for loop
`}`	end if clause
`}`	end for loop
`drawstuff();`	draw everything
`}`	close function
`function clone(obj) {`	function header for clone
`var item = new Object();`	create an Object
`for (var info in obj) {`	loop over all attributes of the obj passed as parameter
`item[info] = obj[info];`	set an attribute by that name to the attribute value
`}`	close for loop
`return item;`	return the newly created object
`}`	close function
`function startdragging(ev) {`	function header for startdragging. Has as a parameter an event ev set by JavaScript

Code Line	Description
`var mx;`	variable will hold x coordinate of mouse
`var my;`	variable will hold y coordinate of mouse
`if ( ev.layerX ||  ev.layerX == 0) { //` `Firefox, ???`	does this browser use layer…
`mx= ev.layerX;`	… set mx
`my = ev.layerY;`	… my
`} else if (ev.offsetX || ev.offsetX == 0) {`	does browser use offset…
`mx = ev.offsetX;`	…set mx
`my = ev.offsetY;`	… set my
`}`	end clause
`var endpt = stuff.length-1;`	store index of last item in stuff array
`for (var i=endpt;i>=0;i--) {`	start search from the end
`if (stuff[i].overcheck(mx,my)) {`	is the mouse over this member of stuff
`offsetx = mx-stuff[i].x;`	calculate how far the mx was from the x of this object
`offsety = my-stuff[i].y;`	calculate how far the my was from the y of this object
`var item = stuff[i];`	will now move this item to the end of the array. Set item
`thingInMotion = stuff.length-1;`	set global variable to be used in the dragging
`stuff.splice(i,1);`	remove this item from its original location
`stuff.push(item);`	add item to the end
`canvas1.style.cursor = "pointer";`	change cursor to finger when dragging

Code Line	Description
`canvas1.addEventListener('mousemove', moveit,false);`	set up event handling for moving the mouse
`canvas1.addEventListener('mouseup',dropit, false);`	set up event handling for releasing mouse button
`break;`	leave the for loop
`}`	close if clause
`}`	close for loop
`}`	close function
`function dropit(ev) {`	function header for dropit. Has as a parameter an event ev set by JavaScript
`canvas1.removeEventListener('mousemove',moveit,false);`	Remove (stop) event handling for moving the mouse
`canvas1.removeEventListener('mouseup',dropit,false);`	Remove (stop) event handling for releasing the mouse button
`canvas1.style.cursor = "crosshair";`	change cursor back to crosshair
`}`	close function
`function moveit(ev) {`	function header for moveit. Has as a parameter an event ev set by JavaScript
`var mx;`	variable will hold x coordinate of mouse
`var my;`	variable will hold y coordinate of mouse
`if ( ev.layerX ||  ev.layerX == 0) {`	does this browser use layer…
`mx= ev.layerX;`	… set mx
`my = ev.layerY;`	… my
`} else if (ev.offsetX || ev.offsetX == 0) {`	does browser use offset…

Code Line	Description
mx = ev.offsetX;	...set mx
my = ev.offsetY;	... set my
}	end clause
stuff[thingInMotion].x = mx-offsetx;	set x for the thingInMotion, adjust for flypaper dragging
stuff[thingInMotion].y = my-offsety;	set y for the thingInMotion, adjust for flypaper dragging
drawstuff();	draw everything
}	close function
function drawstuff() {	function header for drawstuff
ctx.clearRect(0,0,600,400);	clear (erase) canvas
ctx.strokeStyle = "black";	set color for frame
ctx.lineWidth = 2;	set lineWidth
ctx.strokeRect(0,0,600,400);	draw frame
for (var i=0;i<stuff.length;i++) {	iterate through the stuff array
stuff[i].draw();	invoke the draw method for each member of the array
}	close for
}	close function
function drawrect() {	function header drawrect
ctx.fillStyle = this.color;	set the color
ctx.fillRect(this.x, this.y, this.w, this.h);	draw a filled rectangle
}	close function

Code Line	Description
`function saveasimage() {`	function header for saveasimage
`try {`	start try clause
`window.open(canvas1.toDataURL("image/png"));}`	create the image data and use it as contents of new window
`catch(err) {`	if that didn't work, that is, threw an error
`alert("You need to change browsers OR upload the file to a server.");`	display alert message
`}`	close catch clause
`}`	close function
`function removeobj() {`	function header for removeobj
`stuff.pop();`	remove the last member of the stuff array
`drawstuff();`	draw everything
`}`	close function
`</script>`	close script element
`</head>`	close head element
`<body onLoad="init();">`	body tag, with onLoad set
`Mouse down, move and mouse up to move objects. Double click for new object. `	Text giving directions
`<canvas id="canvas" width="600" height=400>`	canvas tag
`Your browser doesn't recognize the canvas element`	message for older browsers
`</canvas>`	ending canvas tag

Code Line	Description
`<button onClick="saveasimage();">Open window with image (which you can save into image file) </button></br>`	button for saving image
`<button onClick="removeobj();">Remove last object moved </button>`	button for removing object
`</body>`	close body tag
`</html>`	close html tag

It is obvious how to make this application your own using only the techniques demonstrated in my example: gather photos of your own family or acquire other photographs and use the Rect, Oval, and Heart to create your own set of shapes.

You can define your own objects, using the coding here as a model. For example, the *Essential Guide to HTML5* book included coding for displaying polygons. You can make the over check function for the polygon treat the polygon as a circle, perhaps a circle with smaller radius, and your customers will not object.

The next step could be to build an application that allows the end-user to specify the addresses of image files. You would need to set up a form for doing this. Another enhancement is to allow the end-user to enter text, perhaps a greeting, and position it on the canvas. You would create a new object type and write the **draw** and **overcheck** methods. The **overcheck** method could be **overrect**, that is, the program accepts as being on the text anything in the bounding rectangle.

Testing and uploading the application

You need to gather all the image files you want to include in your application. The testing procedure depends on what browser you are using. Actually, it is a good practice to test with several browsers. If you are using Firefox or Chrome, you need to upload the application: the html file and all image files, to a server to test the feature for creating an image. However, the other aspects of the application can be tested on your own [client] computer.

Summary

In this chapter, you learned how to build an application involving creating and positioning specific shapes, namely rectangles, ovals and hearts, along with pictures such as photographs on the canvas. The programming techniques and HTML5 features included

- programming-defined objects
- mouse events on canvas
- try and catch for trapping errors
- algebra and geometry for several functions.

The next chapter describes creating an application showing a video clip bouncing around like a ball in a box.

Bouncing Video: Animating and Masking HTML5 Video

In this chapter, you will learn how to do the following:

- Produce a moving video clip by drawing the current frame of the video at different locations on a canvas

- Produce a moving video clip by repositioning the video element in the document

- Mask the video so it looks like a circle for both situations

- Build an application that will adapt to different window sizes

Introduction

The project for this chapter is a display of a video clip in the shape of a ball bouncing in a box. An important new feature in HTML5 is the native support of video (and audio). The book *The Definitive Guide to HTML5 Video*, by Silvia Pfeiffer (Apress, 2010), is an excellent reference. The challenge in this project is making the video clip move on the screen. I will describe two different ways to implement the application. The screenshots do not reveal the differences.

Figure 3-1 shows what the application looks like in the full-window view in Opera. The video is a standard rectangular video clip. It appears ball-like because of my coding. You can skip ahead to Figure 3-8 to get an idea of the mask created to ride along with the video. All the figures are static screen captures of animations. You need to take my word for it that the video does move and bounce within the box.

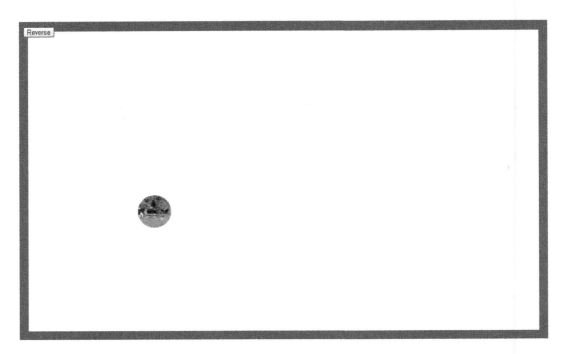

Figure 3-1. *Screen capture, full window*

In all cases, when the virtual ball hits a wall, it appears to bounce off the wall. If, for example, the virtual ball is moving down the screen and to the right, when it hits the right side of the box, it will head off to the left but still moving down the screen. When the virtual ball then hits the bottom wall of the box, it will bounce to the left, heading up the screen. The trajectory is shown in Figure 3-2. To produce this image, I changed the virtual ball to be a simple circle and did not write code to erase the canvas at each interval of time. You can think of it as stop-motion photography. Changing the virtual ball was necessary because of its complexity: an image from a video clip and an all-white mask. I include the code for the trajectory program in the "Building the Application and Making It Your Own" section.

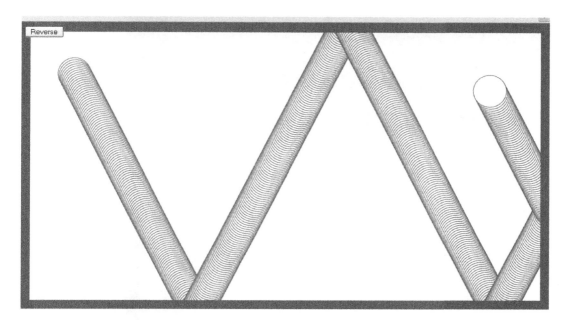

Figure 3-2. *Trajectory of virtual ball*

If I resize the browser window to be a little bit smaller and reload the application, the code will resize the canvas to produce what is shown in Figure 3-3: a smaller box.

Figure 3-3. *Application in smaller window*

If the window is made very small, this forces a change in the size of the video clip itself, as well as the canvas and the box, as shown in Figure 3-4.

Figure 3-4. *Window resized to very small*

The application adapts the box size, and possibly the virtual video ball size, to the window dimensions at the time that the HTML document is first loaded. If the window is resized by the viewer later, during the running of the application, the canvas and video clip are not resized. In this case, you would see something like Figure 3-5, a small box in a big window.

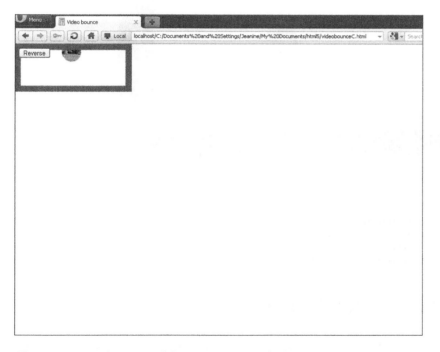

Figure 3-5. *Window resized during running to be larger*

Similarly, if you start the application using a full-size window, or any large window, and resize it to something smaller during the running of the program, you would see something like Figure 3-6, where the scroll bars are displayed by the browser to indicate that the content of the document is wider and longer than the window. If you, the viewer, choose not to use the scroll bars, then the video clip will disappear out of sight periodically for a short period of time before reappearing.

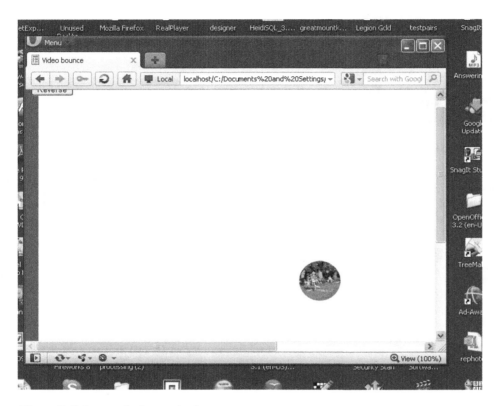

Figure 3-6. *Large window resized*

The two applications (I named them videobounceC for "video drawn on canvas" and videobounceE for "video element") have been tested successfully in Firefox, Chrome, and Opera. The project demonstrates coding techniques using HTML5, JavaScript, and CSS for manipulating video and using video together with the canvas for special effects. The project also explains calculations that are helpful in customizing applications to the dimensions of the browser window.

Project History and Critical Requirements

I have always liked the application of simulating a ball bouncing in a box. Chapter 3 in *The Essential Guide to HTML5* features projects showing a ball produced by a path drawing and a ball produced by an image, each bouncing in a two-dimensional enclosure. I decided I wanted to make a video clip do the same thing. My explanation of the coding is complete in this chapter. However, if the first book is available to you (shameless plug), you may benefit from seeing what is the same and what is different among the various versions. In the ball and image applications, the canvas was set to fixed dimensions and was located with other material in the document. Because I did not want my video clip to be too small, I decided to use the whole window in this case. This objective produced the challenge of determining the dimensions of the document window. In the old ball and image applications, I wanted to demonstrate form validation, so the program provided form elements to change the vertical and horizontal speed. For the bouncing ball video clip, the application just provides one action for the user: a button to reverse direction. After studying this chapter, you should be able to add the other interface operations to the video application.

Since the ability to draw video on canvas is a feature of HTML5, this was the first approach I took for doing the project. However, my reading indicated that this is considered too much of a computation hog and is something to be avoided, so I also developed another approach: moving a video element and moving an element on a canvas on top of it.

Putting off the implementation details, the critical requirements, in addition to determining the dimensions of the window, are to move—reposition—and animate a video clip simultaneously with a graphical element that acts as a mask. The effect of the mask is to make the video clip appear as a circle instead of the standard rectangular shape. The video clip is playing while it is moving. The application is to simulate a ball-like object bouncing within a box. Therefore, the application must display the walls of the box and perform calculations so that when the video clip appears to collide with any of the walls, the direction of motion changes in the appropriate way. A fancy way to describe the change is that the angle of reflection must equal the angle of incidence. In practical terms, what it means is that when the video clip virtually hits the bottom or top walls, it keeps going in the same direction horizontally (to the left if it was traveling to the left and to the right if it was traveling to the right), but switches direction vertically. When the video clip virtually hits either the left or the right wall, it keeps going in the same direction vertically (traveling up if it was traveling up and traveling down if it was traveling down), but switches direction horizontally. If you are interested in simulating real-life physics, you can slow down the motion at each virtual hit of a wall.

HTML5, CSS, and JavaScript Features

Any order of explanation means something is often discussed before the reason for doing it is clear. In this section, I will show how certain variables are set that will be shown in use later on. The general plan is to extract the window dimensions to set variables for the canvas and the video clip that will be referenced in the coding for drawing the video and the mask.

Definition of the Body and the Window Dimensions

The Document Object Model (DOM) provides information about the window in which the HTML document is displayed by the browser. In particular, the attributes `window.innerWidth` and `window.innerHeight` indicate the usable dimensions of the window. My code will use these values when it sets up the application.

Recall that the HTML5 video element can contain as child elements any number of source elements referencing different video files. At this time, this is necessary because the browsers that recognize the video element do not accept the same video formats (codecs). The situation may change in the future. If you know the browser used by *all* your potential customers, you can determine a single video format. If that is not the case, you need to make three versions of the same video clip. The Open Source Miro

Video Converter, downloadable from www.mirovideoconverter.com/, is a good product to convert a video clip into other formats.

With that reminder, I can present the body element for this application. It contains a video element, a button, and a canvas element:

```
<body onLoad="init();">
<video id="vid" loop="loop" preload="auto">
<source src="joshuahomerun.mp4" type='video/mp4; codecs="avc1.42E01E, mp4a.40.2"'>
<source src="joshuahomerun.webmvp8.webm" type='video/webm; codec="vp8, vorbis"'>
<source src="joshuahomerun.theora.ogv" type='video/ogg; codecs="theora, vorbis"'>

Your browser does not accept the video tag.
 </video>
<button id="revbtn" onClick="reverse();">Reverse </button><br/>
<canvas id="canvas" >
This browser doesn't support the HTML5 canvas element.
</canvas>
</body>
```

Style directives will change the location of the three elements: video, canvas, and button.

In the init function invoked when the document is loaded, the following statements set the dimensions of the canvas to match the dimensions of the window:

```
canvas1 = document.getElementById('canvas');
ctx = canvas1.getContext('2d');
canvas1.width = window.innerWidth;
cwidth = canvas1.width;
canvas1.height = window.innerHeight;
cheight = canvas1.height;
```

These statements also set variables that will be used later. So the task of adapting the canvas to the window is accomplished.

Now the next task takes more thought. How much do I want to adapt the video to the window dimensions? I decided that I would reduce the video width and height to one-third of the original width and height in all situations. However, I would reduce it further if the window were very small. The Math.min method returns the smallest of its operands, so the statements

```
v = document.getElementById("vid");
v.width = Math.min(v.videoWidth/3,.5*cwidth);
v.height = Math.min(v.videoHeight/3,.5*cheight);
```

start by setting the variable v to point to the video element, which you can see I have coded in the body to have the id "vid". It then sets the width of the video to either one-third of the original, intrinsic width of the video clip or to half the width of the canvas, whichever is less. The next statement does the same for the height of the video. This approach does not make the video clip proportional to the canvas. When you are working on this or another application, you will need to decide the approach you want to take.

Certain other variables are set in the init function and used for the drawing of the box and for the mask. The code is

```
videow = v.width;
videoh = v.height;
ballrad = Math.min(50,.5*videow,.5*videoh);
maskrad = .4*Math.min(videow,videoh);
ctx.lineWidth = ballrad;
```

The `ballrad` variable is inherited from the previous applications. It is the radius of the ball, assuming the video height and width are equal and less than 50 pixels. Its use in the videobounce applications is to set the width of the line used to draw the box. The radius of the hole in the mask is set to .4 of the minimum of the width and height of the video. You certainly can experiment with these values and also experiment with the shape of the mask.

Animation

Animation is the trick by which still images are presented in succession fast enough so that our eye and brain interprets what we see as motion. The exact mechanics of how things are drawn will be explained in the next two sections. Keep in mind that there are two animations going on: the presentation of the video and the location of the video in the box. In this section, I talk about the location of the video in the box.

The way to get animation in HTML and JavaScript is to use the `setInterval` function. This function is called with two parameters. The first is the name of a function that we want to call and the second indicates the length of the time interval between each call to the function. The unit of time is milliseconds.

The following statement, which is in the `init` function, sets up the animation:

```
setInterval(drawscene,50);
```

`drawscene` refers to a function that will do all the work. The 50 stands for 50 milliseconds. This means that every 50 milliseconds (or 20 times per second), the `drawscene` function will be invoked. Presumably, `drawscene` will do what needs to be done to display something showing the video clip at a new location. You can experiment with interval duration.

If you want to enhance this application or build another one in which it makes sense to stop the animation, you would declare a local variable for the `setInterval` call (let's call it `tid`) and use the statement

```
tid = setInterval(drawscene,50);
```

At the point when you need to stop the animation, or more formally, stop the interval-timing event, you code

```
clearInterval(tid);
```

If you have more than one timing event, you would assign the output for each of them to a new variable. Be careful not to call `setInterval` multiple times with the same function. Doing so has the effect of adding new timing events and invoking the function multiple times.

Much of the details of the `drawscene` function will be described in the next sections. However, two critical tasks are erasing the canvas and then determining the next position of the video clip. The statement for erasing the whole canvas is

```
ctx.clearRect(0,0,cwidth,cheight);
```

Notice that it makes use of the `cwidth` and `cheight` values calculated based on the window dimensions.

The simulation of bouncing is performed by a function called `moveandcheck`. The position of the virtual ball is defined by the variables `ballx` and `bally`. The (ballx,bally) position is the upper-left corner of the video. The motion, also termed the *displacement*, is defined by the variables `ballvx` and `ballvy`. These two variables are termed the horizontal and vertical displacements, respectively.

The objective of the `moveandcheck` function is to reposition the virtual ball by setting `ballx` and `bally`, and when appropriate, change the signs of `ballvx` and `ballvy`. The way the code works is to try out new values (see `nballx` and `nbally` in the function) and then set `ballx` and `bally`. Changing the sign of the displacement values has the effect of making the balls bounce by changing the appropriate horizontal or vertical adjustment on the next interval.

The task now is to determine when to do the bounce. You need to accept that as far as the computer's concerned, there are no balls, bouncing or otherwise, and no walls. There are just calculations. Moreover, the calculations are done at discrete intervals of time. There is no continuous motion. The virtual ball jumps from position to position. The trajectory appears smooth because the jumps are small enough and our eye-brain interprets the pictures as continuous motion. Since the walls are drawn after the video (that will be explained later), the effect is that the virtual ball touches and goes slightly behind the wall before changing direction.

My approach is to set up trial or stand-in values for `ballx` and `bally` and do calculations based on these values. You can think of it logically as asking, If the video ball were moved, would it be beyond any of the walls? If so, readjust to just hit that wall and change the appropriate displacement value. The new displacement value is not used immediately, but will be part of the calculation made at the next iteration of time. If the trial value is not at or beyond the wall, keep the trial value as it is and keep the corresponding displacement value as it is. Then change `ballx` and `bally` to the possibly adjusted stand-in values.

The function definition for the videobounceC program is

```
function moveandcheck() {
        var nballx = ballx + ballvx +.5*videow;
        var nbally = bally + ballvy +.5*videoh;
  if (nballx > cwidth) {
        ballvx =-ballvx;
        nballx = cwidth;
  }
  if (nballx < 0) {

     nballx = 0;
        ballvx = -ballvx;
  }
  if (nbally > cheight) {
        nbally = cheight;
        ballvy =-ballvy;
  }
  if (nbally < 0) {
     nbally = 0;
        ballvy = -ballvy;
  }
  ballx = nballx-.5*videow;
  bally = nbally-.5*videoh;
}
```

The `moveandcheck` function is slightly different for moving a video element because of an issue involving scrolling, which I will discuss later. The basic concepts are the same. The `moveandcheck` function in videobounceE is

```
function moveandcheck() {
var nballx = ballx + ballvx;
        var nbally = bally + ballvy;
  if ((nballx+videow) > cwidth) {
        ballvx =-ballvx;
        nballx = cwidth-videow;
  }
  if (nballx < 0) {
    nballx = 0;
        ballvx = -ballvx;
  }
  if ((nbally+videoh) > cheight) {
        nbally = cheight-videoh;
        ballvy =-ballvy;
  }
  if (nbally < 0) {
    nbally = 0;
        ballvy = -ballvy;
  }
  ballx = nballx;
  bally = nbally;
}
```

Notice that the videobounceC version compares `ballx + ballvx + .5*videow` to `cwidth`, whereas videobounceE compares `ballx + ballvx + videow` to `cwidth`. This means the videobounceE program will force bouncing sooner—that is, turn around sooner—when compared with the right wall. The same holds true for the checking against the bottom wall. I did this to avoid a problem involving automatic scrolling. The video element is not restricted to the canvas, so if it moves out from under the canvas, it is part of the document and is displayed. Because the new display is bigger than the window, this causes scrolling. The scroll bars would appear, and though you would not see anything, I did not like the effect. If you started with a smaller window and made it larger during the program execution, you could see something like what is shown in Figure 3-7.

Figure 3-7. *Video element bouncing with less restrictive checking*

To avoid this, you will see that I changed the checking for the video element application. The downside to doing this is that the video ball barely touches the right and bottom walls.

The reason why these effects do not happen in the video-drawn-on-canvas application, videobounceC, is that drawing on canvas with coordinates outside of the canvas has no visible effect. You can look back to Chapter 1, Figure 1-6, to see an example of drawing "outside the lines" producing nothing outside the canvas.

■ **Note**   There may be other ways to avoid the scrolling problem. This would not prevent the unsightliness shown in Figure 3-7.It may be possible to prevent scrolling in the browser. It is possible to stop the user from scrolling, but automatic scrolling appears to be more of a challenge.

Video Drawn on Canvas and As a Movable Element

I now describe two different implementations: one with material from the video drawn on the canvas and the other with the video element moved around the document.

Video Drawn on Canvas

As I mentioned previously, HTML5 does provide the facility to draw video on the canvas as one would draw an image. This actually is a misnomer. Video clips are made up of sequences of still images called *frames*. Frame rates vary but typically are 15 to 32 frames per second, so you can understand that video files tend to be large. Video is stored using different types of encodings, each of which may make different technical trade-offs in terms of quality and storage size. We do not need to be concerned with these technicalities, but can think of the video as a sequence of frames. Playing a video involves presenting the frames in sequence. What happens in the drawImage command is that the current frame of the video clip is the image drawn on the canvas. If this operation is performed through a timed interval event, then the viewer will see a frame at each interval of time. There is no guarantee that the images shown are successive frames from the video clip, but if done fast enough, the frames drawn will be close enough to the actual sequence that our eye and brain experience it as the live action of the video clip.

The command in pseudocode is

```
ctx.drawImage(video element, x position, y position, width, height);
```

This command, formally a method of the ctx canvas context, extracts the image corresponding to the current frame of the video and draws it at the x and y values, with the indicated width and height. If the image does not have the specified width and height, the image is scaled. This will not occur for this situation.

The goal is to make the traveling video clip resemble a ball. For this application, this means we want to mask out all but a circle in the center of the rectangular video clip. I accomplish this by creating a traveling mask. The mask is a drawing in the canvas. Since I want to place the video element on the canvas element, and also position a shape created by drawing a path on top of the image drawn from the video clip, I use CSS directives to make both video and canvas be positioned using absolute positioning. I want the Reverse button to be on top of the canvas. These directives do the trick:

```
#vid {position:absolute; display:none; }
#canvas {position:absolute; z-index:10; top:0px; left:0px;}
#revbtn {position:absolute; z-index:20; }
```

A way to remember how the layering works is to think of the z-axis as coming out of the screen. Elements set at higher values are on top of elements set at lower values. The `top` and `left` properties of the canvas are each set to 0 pixels to position the upper-left corner of the canvas in the upper-left corner of the window.

■ **Note** When the z-index is referenced or modified in JavaScript, its name is `zIndex`. Hopefully, you appreciate why the name *z-index* would not work: the hyphen (-) would be interpreted as a minus operator.

The video element is set in the style directive to have no display. This is because as an element by itself, it is not supposed to show anything. Instead, the content of the current frame is drawn to the canvas using the following statement:

```
ctx.drawImage(v,ballx, bally, videow,videoh);
```

The `ballx` and `bally` values are initialized in the `init` functions and incremented as described in the last section. The width and height of the video clip have been modified to be appropriate for the window size.

One way to understand this is to imagine that the video is being played somewhere offscreen and the browser has access to the information so it can extract the current frame to use in the `drawImage` method.

Movable Video Element

The videobounceE application moves the actual video element on the document. The video element is not drawn on the canvas, but is a distinct element in the HTML document. However, I need to make sure that the mask, which is drawn on the canvas, is always in the right place with respect to the video element. I need to code the style directives to make sure that the video is under the canvas, which in turn is under the Reverse button. A critical step is to set the positioning to be absolute for all three elements (video, canvas, and button) and position the canvas so that it is located with its upper-left corner in the upper-left corner of the window. This is critical for positioning the video element and mask, as we shall explore later. The style directives are

```
#vid {position:absolute; display:none; z-index: 1; }
#canvas {position:absolute; z-index:10; top:0px; left:0px;}
#revbtn {position:absolute; z-index:20;}
```

Moving a video element around requires making the video visible and starting the playing of the video. It also requires positioning. The video element is positioned through references to `style.left` and `style.top`. Furthermore, the settings for the `left` and `top` attributes must be in the form of a character string representing a number followed by the string `"px"`, standing for pixels. The following code

```
v.style.left = String(ballx)+"px";
v.style.top = String(bally)+"px";
v.play();
v.style.visibility = "visible";
v.style.display = "block";
```

is executed in the init function. Notice also that the initial position of the video is changed to the initial ballx and bally values. The numeric values need to be converted to strings, and then the "px" needs to be concatenated to the ends of the strings. This is because HTML/JavaScript assumes that style attributes are strings. I write the same code for setting the video element's top and left properties to the values corresponding to ballx and bally in the drawscene function. The statements that replace the ctx.drawImage statement are

```
v.style.left = String(ballx)+"px";
v.style.top = String(bally)+"px";
```

All the code for both videobounceC and videobounceE will be listed with comments in the "Building the Application and Making It Your Own" section.

Looping Video

You may have noticed that the video tag has the attribute setting loop="loop". This indicates that the video is to loop—that is, start over again—each time the playing of the clip reaches the end. At the time of writing, this does not work for Firefox, so I use the statement

```
v.addEventListener("ended",restart,false);
```

to set up an event to invoke the indicated function when the ended event occurs. The false parameter means that the event should not be bubbled to any other application. It's unlikely that another application is listening for this event, but it doesn't hurt to stop the bubbling action. I defined the function called restart.

```
function restart() {
        v.currentTime=0;
         v.play();
}
```

Traveling Mask

The objective of the mask is to mask out—that is, cover up—all of the video except for a circle in the center. The style directives ensure that I can use the same variables—namely ballx and bally—to refer to the video and mask in both situations: video drawn and video element moved. So now the question is how to make a mask that is a rectangular donut with a round hole.

I accomplish this by writing code to draw two paths and filling them in with white. Since the shape of the mask can be difficult to visualize, I have created two figures to show you what it is. Figure 3-8 shows the outline of the two paths.

Figure 3-8. *Outline of paths for the mask*

Figure 3-9 shows the outline and the paths filled in.

Figure 3-9. *Paths for the mask after a fill and a stroke*

Now, the actual path only has the fill, and the fill color is white. You need to imagine these two white shapes traveling along on top of the video. The effect of the mask is to cover up most of the video clip. The parts of the canvas that have no paint on them, so to speak, are transparent, and the video clip content shows through. Putting it another way, the canvas is on top of the video element, but it is equivalent to a sheet of glass. Each pixel that has nothing drawn in it is transparent.

The code drawing the masks is the same for both video drawn on canvas (videobounceC) and video element moving on the screen (videobounceE). The first path starts at the upper-left corner, and then goes over, down to the midway point, and finally back left. The path then is a semicircular arc. The last parameter indicating the sense of the arc is **true** for counterclockwise. The path continues with a line to the left edge and then back up to the start. The second path starts in the middle of the left edge, proceeds down to the lower-left corner, goes to the lower-right corner, moves up to the middle of the right side, and then moves to the left. The arc this time has **false** as the value of the parameter for direction, indicating the arc is clockwise. The path ends where it started.

```
ctx.beginPath();
ctx.moveTo(ballx,bally);
ctx.lineTo(ballx+videow,bally);
ctx.lineTo(ballx+videow,bally+.5*videoh);
ctx.lineTo(ballx+.5*videow+maskrad, bally+.5*videoh);
ctx.arc(ballx+.5*videow,bally+.5*videoh,maskrad,0,Math.PI,true);
ctx.lineTo(ballx,bally+.5*videoh);
ctx.lineTo(ballx,bally);
ctx.fill();
```

```
ctx.moveTo(ballx,bally+.5*videoh);
ctx.lineTo(ballx,bally+videoh);
ctx.lineTo(ballx+videow,bally+videoh);
ctx.lineTo(ballx+videow,bally+.5*videoh);
ctx.lineTo(ballx+.5*videow+maskrad,bally+.5*videoh);
ctx.arc(ballx+.5*videow,bally+.5*videoh,maskrad,0,Math.PI,false);
ctx.lineTo(ballx,bally+.5*videoh);
ctx.fill();
```

You can follow along the coding with my "English'" description to see how it works.

By the way, my initial attempt was to draw a path consisting of a four-sided shape representing the outer rectangle and then a circle in the middle. This worked for some browsers, but not others.

For the videobounceC application, the mask is on top of the video drawn on canvas because the two white filled-in paths are drawn after the drawImage statement draws a frame from the video. I achieve the same effect in the videobounceE application by specifying the z-index of the video element to be 0 and the z-index of the canvas to be 10. Remember that the z-axis is the axis that comes out of the screen. Higher values are closer to us and on top of lower values. The canvas with the z-index set to 10 is on top of the video element with the z-index set to 0. The next chapter, which demonstrates a spotlight moving on top of a map from Google Maps, will feature changing the z-index using JavaScript.

User Interface

The user interface for both versions of the videobounce project only includes one action for the user: the user can reverse the direction of travel. The button is defined by an element in the body:

```
<button id="revbtn" onClick="reverse();">Reverse </button><br/>
```

The effect of the onClick setting is to invoke the function named reverse. This function is defined to change the signs of the horizontal and vertical displacements:

```
function reverse() {
        ballvx = -ballvx;
        ballvy = -ballvy;
}
```

There is one important consideration for any user interface. You need to make sure it is visible. This is accomplished by the following style directive:

```
#revbtn {position:absolute; z-index:20; }
```

The z-index places the button on top of the canvas, which in turn is on top of the video.

Having explained the individual HTML5, CSS, and JavaScript features that can be used to satisfy the critical requirements for bouncing video, I'll now show the code in the two videobounce applications along with the code used to show the trajectory in Figure 3-2.

Building the Application and Making It Your Own

The two applications for simulating the bouncing of a video clip ball in a two-dimensional box contain similar code, as does the program that produced the picture of the trajectory. A quick summary of the applications follows. The video applications are summarized by the following:

1. `init`: initialization, including adapting to fit the window and setting up the timed event for invoking `drawscene`

2. `drawscene`:

   a. Erase the canvas.

   b. Determine new location of video (virtual ball) using `moveandcheck`.

   c. Either draw the image from video at a specified location on the canvas or reposition the video element to a specified position.

   d. Draw paths on canvas to act as a mask to the video.

   e. Draw the box.

3. `moveandcheck`: Check if the virtual ball will hit any wall. If so, change the appropriate displacement value.

The trajectory function also uses `init` and `moveandcheck`, but has a simpler `drawscene` function:

1. Determine the new location of the circle (virtual ball) using `moveandcheck`.

2. Draw a path that consists of a circle and draw the circle using fill and then stroke.

3. Draw the box.

The function describing the invoked/called by and calling relationships (shown in Table 3-1) are the same for all the applications.

Table 3-1. *Functions in the Bouncing Video Projects*

Function	Invoked/Called By	Calls
`init`	Invoked by action of the `onLoad` attribute in the `<body>` tag	
`drawscene`	Invoked by action of the `setInterval` command issued in `init`	`moveandcheck`
`moveandcheck`	Invoked in `drawscene`	
`reverse`	Invoked by action of `onClick` in the button	
`restart`	Invoked by action of `addEventListener` in `init` (not present in `videobounceTrajectory`)	

Table 3-2 shows the code for the videobounceC application, which draws the current frame of the video on the canvas at set intervals of time.

Table 3-2. Complete Code for the VideobounceC Application

Code Line	Description
`<!DOCTYPE html>`	Header
`<html>`	Opening `html` tag
`<head>`	Opening head tag
`<title>Video bounce</title>`	Complete title
`<meta charset="UTF-8">`	Meta element
`<style>`	Opening style
`#vid {position:absolute; display:none; }`	Set up positioning of video; set display to none; video element never appears
`#canvas {position:absolute; z-index:10; top:0px; left:0px;}`	Set positioning to absolute and position to be upper-left corner; set z-index so it is under the Reverse button
`#revbtn {position:absolute; z-index:20; }`	Set positioning to absolute and z-index so it is over the canvas
`</style>`	Close style
`<script type="text/javascript">`	Opening script tag
`var ctx;`	Used to hold canvas context, used for all drawing
`var cwidth ;`	Used to hold canvas width
`var cheight ;`	Used to hold canvas height
`var ballrad = 50;`	Set ball radius
`var ballx = 50;`	Initial horizontal coordinate for ball
`var bally = 60;`	Initial vertical coordinate for ball
`var maskrad;`	Used for mask radius
`var ballvx = 2;`	Initial ball horizontal displacement

Code Line	Description
`var ballvy = 4;`	Initial ball vertical displacement
`var v;`	Will hold video element
`function restart() {`	Function header for restart
`v.currentTime=0;`	Reset place in video to the start
`v.play();`	Play video
`}`	Close **restart** function
`function init(){`	Function header for **init**
`canvas1 = document.getElementById('canvas');`	Set reference for canvas
`ctx = canvas1.getContext('2d');`	Set reference for canvas context
`canvas1.width = window.innerWidth;`	Set canvas width to match current window width
`cwidth = canvas1.width;`	Set variable
`canvas1.height = window.innerHeight;`	Set canvas height to match current window height
`cheight = canvas1.height;`	Set variable
`v = document.getElementById("vid");`	Set reference to video element
`v.addEventListener("ended",restart,false);`	Set up event handling when video ends; done because **loop** attribute setting in element header does not work in Firefox browser
`v.width = Math.min(v.videoWidth/3,.5*cwidth);`	Set video width
`v.height = Math.min(v.videoHeight/3,.5*cheight);`	Set video height
`videow = v.width;`	Set variable
`videoh = v.height;`	Set variable

Code Line	Description
`ballrad = Math.min(50,.5*videow,.5*videoh);`	Modify `ballrad` if there is a very small video
`maskrad = .4*Math.min(videow,videoh);`	Set `maskrad` based on video dimensions
`ctx.lineWidth = ballrad;`	Set line width for drawing the box
`ctx.strokeStyle ="rgb(200,0,50)";`	Set color to reddish
`ctx.fillStyle="white";`	Set fill style for mask to be white
`v.play();`	Start video
`setInterval(drawscene,50);`	Set up timed event
`}`	Close `init` function
`function drawscene(){`	Function header for `drawscene`
`ctx.clearRect(0,0,cwidth,cheight);`	Erase canvas
`moveandcheck();`	Check if next move is at a wall, and if so, adjust displacements and position; otherwise, just make the move
`ctx.drawImage(v,ballx, bally, videow,videoh);`	Draw image from video at indicated position
`ctx.beginPath();`	Start the path for the top half of the mask
`ctx.moveTo(ballx,bally);`	Move to starting point
`ctx.lineTo(ballx+videow,bally);`	Move over horizontally
`ctx.lineTo(ballx+videow,bally+.5*videoh);`	Move down to halfway
`ctx.lineTo(ballx+.5*videow+maskrad, bally+.5*videoh);`	Move in to the start of where the opening will be
`ctx.arc(ballx+.5*videow,bally+.5*videoh,maskrad,0, Math.PI,true);`	Make semicircular arc

Code Line	Description
`ctx.lineTo(ballx,bally+.5*videoh);`	Move to the left
`ctx.lineTo(ballx,bally);`	Move to start
`ctx.fill();`	Fill in the white top of the mask
`ctx.moveTo(ballx,bally+.5*videoh);`	Move to start the bottom of the mask; move to point midway down on the left
`ctx.lineTo(ballx,bally+videoh);`	Move down to the lower left
`ctx.lineTo(ballx+videow,bally+videoh);`	Move over to the right corner
`ctx.lineTo(ballx+videow,bally+.5*videoh);`	Move up to the middle on the right
`ctx.lineTo(ballx+.5*videow+maskrad,bally+.5*videoh);`	Move in to the start of the hole in the mask
`ctx.arc(ballx+.5*videow,bally+.5*videoh,maskrad,0,Math.PI,false);`	Make semicircular arc
`ctx.lineTo(ballx,bally+.5*videoh);`	Move to the right
`ctx.fill();`	Fill in the white bottom of the mask
`ctx.strokeRect(0,0,cwidth,cheight);`	Draw the box
`}`	Close `drawscene` function
`function moveandcheck() {`	Header for `moveandcheck` function
`var nballx = ballx + ballvx+.5*videow;`	Set up trial values for x
`var nbally = bally +ballvy+.5*videoh;`	Set up trial values for y
`if (nballx > cwidth) {`	Compare to right wall, on a hit
`ballvx =-ballvx;`	Change sign of the horizontal displacement
`nballx = cwidth;`	Set trial value to be exactly at the right wall

Code Line	Description
`}`	Close clause
`if (nballx < 0) {`	Compare to left wall, on a hit
`    nballx = 0;`	Set trial value to be exactly at the left wall
`    ballvx = -ballvx;`	Change sign of the horizontal displacement
`}`	Close clause
`if (nbally > cheight) {`	Compare to bottom wall, on a hit
`    nbally = cheight;`	Set trial value to exact height
`    ballvy =-ballvy;`	Change the sign of the vertical displacement
`}`	Close clause
`if (nbally < 0) {`	Compare to top wall on a hit
`   nbally = 0;`	Change trial value to be exactly at the top wall
`   ballvy = -ballvy;`	Change the sign of the vertical displacement
`}`	Close clause
`ballx = nballx-.5*videow;`	Set `ballx` using trial value, and offset to be the upper-left corner, not the center
`bally = nbally-.5*videoh;`	Set `bally` using the trial value, and offset to be the upper-left corner, not the center
`}`	Close `moveandcheck` function
`function reverse() {`	Function header for the button action
`    ballvx = -ballvx;`	Change sign of horizontal displacement

Code Line	Description
`   ballvy = -ballvy;`	Change sign of vertical displacement
`}`	Close reverse function
`</script>`	Closing script tag
`</head>`	Closing head tag
`<body onLoad="init();">`	Opening body tag; set up call to `init`
`<video id="vid" loop="loop" preload="auto">`	Video element header
`<source src="joshuahomerun.mp4" type='video/mp4;` `codecs="avc1.42E01E, mp4a.40.2"'>`	Source for the mp4 video
`<source src="joshuahomerun.webmvp8.webm"` `type='video/webm; codec="vp8, vorbis"'>`	Source for the WEBM video
`<source src="joshuahomerun.theora.ogv" type='video/ogg;` `codecs="theora, vorbis"'>`	Source for the OGG video
`Your browser does not accept the video tag.`	Message for noncompliant browsers
`  </video>`	Close video tag
`<button id="revbtn" onClick="reverse();">Reverse` `</button> `	Button for viewer to reverse direction
`<canvas id="canvas" >`	Opening canvas tag
`This browser doesn't support the HTML5 canvas` `element.`	Message for noncompliant browsers
`</canvas>`	Closing canvas tag
`</body>`	Closing body tag
`</html>`	Closing html tag

The second version of this application moves the video element as opposed to drawing the current frame of the video on the canvas. My research indicates that this may use less computer resources when it is executing. All versions have much in common, and I will point this out by only commenting on the lines that are different.

Table 3-3. *Complete Code for the VideobounceE Program*

Code Line	Description
`<!DOCTYPE html>`	
`<html>`	
`<head>`	
`<title>Video bounce</title>`	
`<meta charset="UTF-8">`	
`<style>`	
`#vid {position:absolute; display:none; z-index: 1;`	Need to set positioning and z-index because display setting will be changed to make element visible
`}`	End directive
`#canvas {position:absolute; z-index:10; top:0px; left:0px;}`	This will be on top of video and under button
`#revbtn {position:absolute; z-index:20;}`	
`</style>`	
`<script type="text/javascript">`	
`var ctx;`	
`var cwidth ;`	
`var cheight ;`	
`var ballrad = 50;`	
`var ballx = 80;`	Starting point is arbitrary
`var bally = 80;`	Starting point is arbitrary
`var maskrad;`	
`var ballvx = 2;`	

Code Line	Description
`var ballvy = 4;`	
`var v;`	
`function restart() {`	
`  v.currentTime=0;`	
`  v.play();`	
`}`	
`function init(){`	
`  canvas1 = document.getElementById('canvas');`	
`  ctx = canvas1.getContext('2d');`	
`  canvas1.width = window.innerWidth;`	
`  cwidth = canvas1.width;`	
`  canvas1.height = window.innerHeight;`	
`  cheight = canvas1.height;`	
`  window.onscroll = function () {`	
`      window.scrollTo(0,0);`	
`    };`	
`  v = document.getElementById("vid");`	
`  v.addEventListener("ended",restart,false);`	
`  v.width = Math.min(v.videoWidth/3,.5*cwidth);`	
`  v.height = Math.min(v.videoHeight/3,.5*cheight);`	
`  videow = v.width;`	
`  videoh = v.height;`	

Code Line	Description
`ballrad = Math.min(50,.5*videow,.5*videoh);`	
`maskrad = .4*Math.min(videow,videoh);`	
`ctx.lineWidth = ballrad;`	
`ctx.strokeStyle ="rgb(200,0,50)";`	
`ctx.fillStyle="white";`	
`v.style.left = String(ballx)+"px";`	
`v.style.top = String(bally)+"px";`	
`v.play();`	
`v.style.display = "block";`	Make video element visible
`setInterval(drawscene,50);`	
`}`	
`function drawscene(){`	
`ctx.clearRect(0,0,cwidth,cheight);`	
`moveandcheck();`	
`v.style.left = String(ballx)+"px";`	Position video horizontally
`v.style.top = String(bally)+"px";`	Position video vertically
`ctx.beginPath();`	
`ctx.moveTo(ballx,bally);`	
`ctx.lineTo(ballx+videow,bally);`	
`ctx.lineTo(ballx+videow,bally+.5*videoh);`	
`ctx.lineTo(ballx+.5*videow+maskrad, bally+.5*videoh);`	

Code Line	Description
`ctx.arc(ballx+.5*videow,bally+.5*videoh,maskrad,0,` `Math.PI,true);`	
`ctx.lineTo(ballx,bally+.5*videoh);`	
`ctx.lineTo(ballx,bally);`	
`ctx.fill();`	
`ctx.moveTo(ballx,bally+.5*videoh);`	
`ctx.lineTo(ballx,bally+videoh);`	
`ctx.lineTo(ballx+videow,bally+videoh);`	
`ctx.lineTo(ballx+videow,bally+.5*videoh);`	
`ctx.lineTo(ballx+.5*videow+maskrad,bally+.5*videoh);`	
`ctx.arc(ballx+.5*videow,bally+.5*videoh,maskrad,0,` `Math.PI,false);`	
`ctx.lineTo(ballx,bally+.5*videoh);`	
`ctx.fill();`	
`ctx.strokeRect(0,0,cwidth,cheight);   // box`	
`}`	
`function moveandcheck() {`	
`var nballx = ballx + ballvx;`	Trial value
`var nbally = bally +ballvy;`	Trial value
`if ((nballx+videow) > cwidth) {`	Add total width and compare
`ballvx =-ballvx;`	Change sign of horizontal displacement
`nballx = cwidth-videow;`	Set to exact position

79

Code Line	Description
`}`	
`if (nballx < 0) {`	
`    nballx = 0;`	
`    ballvx = -ballvx;`	
`}`	
`if ((nbally+videoh) > cheight) {`	Compare total length
`    nbally = cheight-videoh;`	Set to exact position
`    ballvy =-ballvy;`	Change sign of vertical displacement
`}`	
`if (nbally < 0) {`	
`    nbally = 0;`	
`    ballvy = -ballvy;`	
`}`	
`ballx = nballx;`	Set to trial position, possibly adjusted
`bally = nbally;`	Set to trial position, possibly adjusted
`}`	
`function reverse() {`	
`    ballvx = -ballvx;`	
`    ballvy = -ballvy;`	
`}`	
`</script>`	
`</head>`	

Code Line	Description
`<body onLoad="init();" >`	
`<video id="vid" loop="loop" preload="auto">`	
`<source src="joshuahomerun.webmvp8.webm"` `type='video/webm; codec="vp8, vorbis"'>`	
`<source src="joshuahomerun.mp4" type='video/mp4;` `codecs="avc1.42E01E, mp4a.40.2"'>`	
`<source src="joshuahomerun.theora.ogv" type='video/ogg;` `codecs="theora, vorbis"'>`	
`Your browser does not accept the video tag.`	
`</video>`	
`<button id="revbtn" onClick="reverse();">Reverse` `</button> `	
`<canvas id="canvas" >`	
`This browser doesn't support the HTML5 canvas element.`	
`</canvas>`	
`</body>`	
`</html>`	

I made the `trajectory` function by modifying the `drawscene` to videobounceC. Since I wanted the circle to be similar in size to the masked video clip, I added an `alert` statement temporarily to the videobounceC function after the video width and height were set, and ran the program using those values:

```
v.width = Math.min(v.videoWidth/3,.5*cwidth);
v.height = Math.min(v.videoHeight/3,.5*cheight);
alert("width "+v.width+" height "+v.height);
```

I then used the values, 106 and 80, to be the `videow` and `videoh` values in the trajectory program. The complete code, with the changed lines annotated, is shown in Table 3-4. Note that the main difference between this program and the first two is the missing lines.

Table 3-4. *Complete code for VideobounceTrajectory Program*

Code Line	Description
`<!DOCTYPE html>`	
`<html>`	
`<head>`	
`<title>Video bounce</title>`	
`<meta charset="UTF-8">`	
`<style>`	
`#canvas {position:absolute; z-index:10; top:0px; left:0px;}`	
`#revbtn {position:absolute; z-index:20; }`	
`</style>`	
`<script type="text/javascript">`	
`var ctx;`	
`var cwidth ;`	
`var cheight ;`	
`var ballrad = 50;`	
`var ballx = 50;`	
`var bally = 60;`	
`var ballvx = 2;`	
`var ballvy = 4;`	
`function init(){`	
`    canvas1 = document.getElementById('canvas');`	

Code Line	Description
`ctx = canvas1.getContext('2d');`	
`canvas1.width = window.innerWidth;`	
`cwidth = canvas1.width;`	
`canvas1.height = window.innerHeight;`	
`cheight = canvas1.height;`	
`videow= Math.min(106,.5*cwidth);`	Use values of actual video width
`videoh = Math.min(80,.5*cheight);`	Use values of actual video height
`ballrad = Math.min(50,.5*videow,.5*videoh);`	
`maskrad = .4*Math.min(videow,videoh);`	
`ctx.lineWidth = ballrad;`	
`ctx.fillStyle= "white";`	
`ctx.strokeStyle ="rgb(200,0,50)";`	
`ctx.strokeRect(0,0,cwidth,cheight);`	
`setInterval(drawscene,50);`	
`}`	
`function drawscene(){`	
`moveandcheck();`	
`ctx.beginPath();`	Begin path for circle
`ctx.moveTo(ballx+.5*videow+maskrad, bally+.5*videoh);`	Move to point on circle at right
`ctx.arc(ballx+.5*videow,bally+.5*videoh,maskrad,0, 2*Math.PI,true);`	Draw circle
`ctx.lineWidth=1;`	Set line width

Code Line	Description
`ctx.fill();`	Fill in (this will be white)
`ctx.stroke();`	Set red stroke (outline)
`ctx.lineWidth= ballrad;`	Set line width for the box
`ctx.strokeRect(0,0,cwidth,cheight);`	Draw the box
`}`	
`function moveandcheck() {`	
`    var nballx = ballx + ballvx+.5*videow;`	
`    var nbally = bally +ballvy+.5*videoh;`	
`    if (nballx > cwidth) {`	
`        ballvx =-ballvx;`	
`        nballx = cwidth;`	
`    }`	
`    if (nballx < 0) {`	
`        nballx = 0;`	
`        ballvx = -ballvx;`	
`    }`	
`    if (nbally > cheight) {`	
`        nbally = cheight;`	
`        ballvy =-ballvy;`	
`    }`	
`    if (nbally < 0) {`	
`        nbally = 0;`	

Code Line	Description
`    ballvy = -ballvy;`	
`  }`	
`  ballx = nballx-.5*videow;`	
`  bally = nbally-.5*videoh;`	
`}`	
`function reverse() {`	
`  ballvx = -ballvx;`	
`  ballvy = -ballvy;`	
`}`	
`</script>`	
`</head>`	
`<body onLoad="init();">`	
`<button id="revbtn" onClick="reverse();">Reverse </button> `	
`<canvas id="canvas" >`	
`This browser doesn't support the HTML5 canvas element.`	
`</canvas>`	
`</body>`	
`</html>`	

Making the Application Your Own

The first way to make this application your own is to use your own video. You do need to find something that is acceptable when displayed as a small circle. As mentioned earlier, you need to produce versions using the different video codecs. A next step is adding other user interface actions, including changing the horizontal and vertical speeds, as was done in the bouncing ball projects in *The Essential Guide to*

HTML5. Another set of enhancements would be to add video controls. Video controls can be part of the video element, but I don't think that would work for a video clip that needs to be small and is moving! However, you could implement your own controls with buttons modeled after the Reverse button. For example, the statement

```
v.pause();
```

does pause the video.

The attribute `v.currentTime` can be referenced or set to control the position within the video clip. You saw how the range input type works in Chapter 1, so consider building a slider input element to adjust the video.

You may decide you want to change my approach to adapting to the window dimensions. One alternative is to change the video clip dimensions to maintain the aspect ratio. Another alternative is to change the video dimensions all the time. This means that the video dimensions and the canvas directions will be in proportion all the time. Yet another alternative, though I think this will be disconcerting, is to make reference to the window dimensions at each time interval and make changes in the canvas, and possibly the video, each time. There is an event that can be inserted into the body tag:

```
<body onresize="changedims();" ... >
```

This coding assumes that you have defined a function named `changedims` that includes some of the statements in the current `init` function to extract the `window.innerWidth` and `window.innerHeight` attributes to set the dimensions of the canvas and the video.

More generally, the objective of this chapter is to show you ways to incorporate video into your projects in a dynamic fashion, both in terms of position on the screen and timing. In particular, it is possible to combine playing of video with drawings on a canvas for exciting effects.

Screen savers exist in which the screen is filled up by a bouncing object similar to the trajectory program. You can change the `drawscene` function to produce different shapes. Also, as I mentioned before, you can apply the techniques explained in *The Essential Guide to HTML5* to provide actions by the viewer. You can refer to Chapter 1 in this book for the use of a range input (slider). Yet another possibility is to provide the viewer a way to change the color of the circle (or other shape you design) using the input type of color. The Opera browser provides a color-picker option.

Testing and Uploading the Application

As has been mentioned, but is worth repeating, you need to acquire a suitable video clip. At the time of writing this book, you then need to use a program such as Miro to produce the WEBM, mp4, and OGG versions because browsers recognize different video encodings (codecs). This situation may change. Again, if you are content with implementing this for just one browser, you can check which video encoding works for that browser and just prepare one video file. The video files and the `html` file need to be in the same folder on your computer and in the same folder on your server if and when you upload this application to your server account. Alternatively, you can use a complete web address or the correct relative address in the source elements.

Summary

In this chapter, you learned different ways to manipulate video. These included the following:

- Drawing the current frame of video as an image onto a canvas
- Repositioning of a video element on the screen by changing the `left` and `top` style attributes
- Using style directives to layer a video, a canvas, and a button
- Creating a moving mask on a canvas
- Acquiring information on the dimensions of the window to adapt an application to different situations

The next chapter will show you how to use the Google Maps Application Programming Interface (API) in an HTML5 project. The project will involve using a canvas and changing the z-index so that the canvas is alternatively under and over the material produced by Google Maps.

CHAPTER 4

Map Maker: Combining Google Maps and the Canvas

In this chapter, you will learn how to do the following:

- Use the Google Maps API to display a map at a specific location

- Draw graphics on a canvas using transparency (also known as the alpha or opacity level) and a customized cursor icon

- Provide a graphical user interface (GUI) to your users by combining the use of Google Maps and HTML5 features by managing the events and the z-index levels

- Calculate the distance between two geographical locations

Introduction

The project for this chapter is an application involving a geographic map. Many applications today involve the use of an Application Programming Interface (API) provided by another person or organization. This chapter will be an introduction to the use of the Google Maps API, and is the first of three chapters using the Google Maps JavaScript Version 3 API. Figure 4-1 shows the opening screen.

Base location (small red x)
Change base location:
○ Friends of ED, NYC
○ Purchase College
○ Illinois Institute of Technology
[CHANGE]

Figure 4-1. *Opening screen of map spotlight project*

Notice the small red (hand-drawn) x located just above and to the left of SoHo. When deciding on map markers, you face a trade-off. A smaller marker is more difficult to see. A larger and/or more intricate marker is easier to see but blocks more of the map or distracts from the map. The *x* marks a neighborhood in lower Manhattan. It is the address of the friends of ED publishers. For this program, it is the initial base location. The base location is used to calculate distances.

Moving the mouse over the map is shown in Figure 4-2.

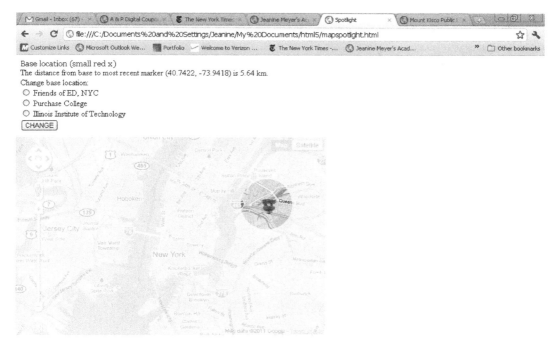

Figure 4-2. *Shadow/spotlight over map*

Notice the shadow and spotlight combination now on the map. Most of the map is covered by a semitransparent shadow. You need to trust me that this screenshot was taken when I had moved the mouse over the map. There is a circle around the mouse position in which the original map shows through. The cursor is not the standard, default cursor but one I created using a small image representing a compact fluorescent lightbulb.

The text on the screen shows the distance from the base to the last spot on the map I clicked to be 5.64 kilometers. The marker for all such locations is a hand-drawn *x*. The latitude and longitude of this location is indicated in parentheses.

The general GUI features provided by Google Maps are available to the users of this project. This includes a vertical slider that controls the scale of the presentation. Figure 4-3 demonstrates the result of using that slider to zoom in. It is possible to zoom in even further.

Base location (small red x)

The distance from base to most recent marker (40.7422, -73.9418) is 5.64 km.

Change base location:

○ Friends of ED, NYC

○ Purchase College

○ Illinois Institute of Technology

[CHANGE]

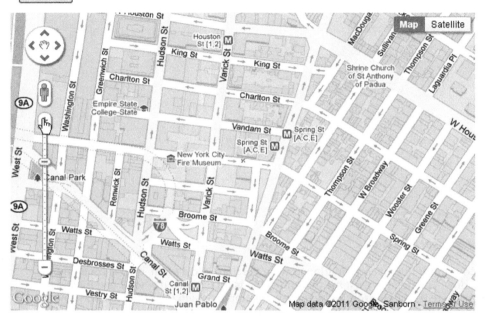

Figure 4-3. *Zoomed in to street level*

It also is possible to pan the map by clicking the hand in the upper-left corner and then virtually grabbing the mouse by pressing down on the mouse button and pulling. Figure 4-4 shows the effects of zooming out and moving north. The screen shows the shadow/spotlight again.

Base location (small red x)
The distance from base to most recent marker (41.2365, -73.6977) is 62.39 km.
Change base location:

○ Friends of ED, NYC
○ Purchase College
○ Illinois Institute of Technology

[CHANGE]

Figure 4-4. *Zooming out and moving north*

The program provides a way to change the base location. There are three choices: the location of the publisher, friends of ED, in New York City; Purchase College (where I teach), located in Purchase, New York, which is north of New York City; and Illinois Institute of Technology (where my son teaches), located in Chicago, Illinois. The interface for making this selection is a set of radio buttons—only one button can be selected at a time—and a button labeled CHANGE to be clicked when the user/viewer/visitor decides to make a change. Figure 4-5 shows the results of making a change to Purchase College. Notice the hand-drawn red *x* marking the base location and the text at the top of the page indicating the new base location by name.

Base location (small red x) is Purchase College/SUNY
Change base location:

○ Friends of ED, NYC
◉ Purchase College
○ Illinois Institute of Technology

[CHANGE]

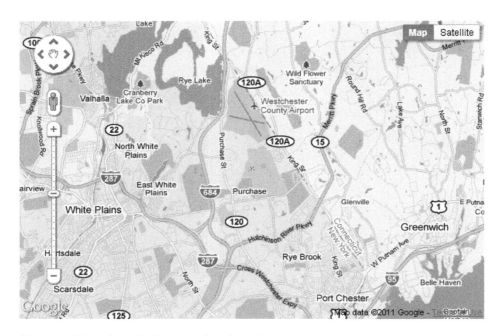

Figure 4-5. *Purchase College new base location*

Next, I switch to Illinois Institute of Technology in Chicago, Illinois, as the base by clicking the third radio button. The result is shown in Figure 4-6.

Base location (small red x) is Illinois Institute of Technology
Change base location:
○ Friends of ED, NYC
○ Purchase College
◉ Illinois Institute of Technology
[CHANGE]

Figure 4-6. *Base at Illinois Institute of Technology in Chicago*

Again, notice the small red *x* indicating the base location and the text at the top of the screen with the name of the new base location.

The location of each base is determined by the latitude and longitude values for each of the three values that I have determined. My code is not "asking" Google Maps to find these locations by name. You may get different results if you type the terms "Purchase College, NY" and "Illinois Institute of Technology" into Google or Google Maps. To make this application your own, you would decide on a set of base locations and look up the latitude and longitude values. I will suggest ways to do this in the next section.

Just in case you are curious, zooming out to the farthest out position on the zoom/scale produces what is shown in Figure 4-7. This projection exhibits what is called the Greenland problem. Greenland is not bigger than Africa, but actually about 1/14 times the size.

Base location (small red x)
The distance from base to most recent marker (40.6855, -74.0935) is 8.7 km.
Change base location:

○ Friends of ED, NYC
○ Purchase College
○ Illinois Institute of Technology

[CHANGE]

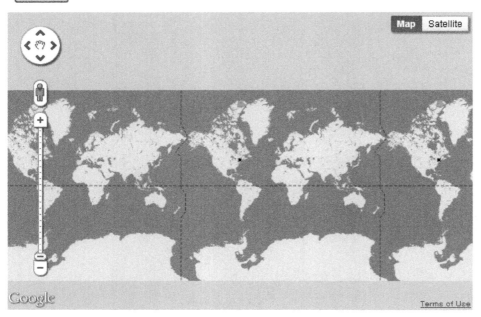

Figure 4-7. *Farthest-out view of map*

Figure 4-8 shows the map at close to the closest-in limit. The map has also been changed to the satellite view using the buttons in the upper-right corner.

Base location (small red x) is Friends of ED, NYC
The distance from base to most recent marker (40.6855, -74.0935) is 8.7 km.
Change base location:

⦿ Friends of ED, NYC
◯ Purchase College
◯ Illinois Institute of Technology

[CHANGE]

Figure 4-8. *Zoomed in to where city blocks can be detected*

Notice that the slider on the left is about four notches above the closest setting. Lastly, Figure 4-9 shows the map zoomed in to the limit. This is essentially at the building level, at least for Manhattan.

Base location (small red x) is Friends of ED, NYC
The distance from base to most recent marker (40.7257, -74.0049) is 0.01 km.
Change base location:
⦿ Friends of ED, NYC
○ Purchase College
○ Illinois Institute of Technology
[CHANGE]

Figure 4-9. *Zoomed in all the way*

By using the interface to zoom out and pan and zoom in again, I can determine the distance from any of the base locations to any other location in the world! I also can use this application to determine latitude and longitude values of any location. You need to know the latitude and longitude for changing or adding to the list of base locations and for determining locations for the project in Chapter 5. I review latitude and longitude in the next section.

Google Maps by itself is an extremely useful application. This chapter and the next two demonstrate how to bring that functionality into your own application. That is, we combine the general facilities of Google Maps with anything, or almost anything, we can develop using HTML5 and JavaScript.

Latitude & Longitude and Other Critical Requirements

The most fundamental requirement for this project, and the ones in the next two chapters, is an understanding of the coordinate system for geography. Just as a coordinate system is required for specifying points on a canvas or positions on the screen, it is necessary to use a system for places on planet earth. The latitude and longitude system has been developed and standardized over the last several hundred years. The values are angles, with latitude indicating degrees from the equator and longitude indicating degrees from the Greenwich prime meridian in the United Kingdom. The latter is an arbitrary choice that became standard in the late 1800s. There is a northern hemisphere bias here: latitude values go from 0 degrees at the equator to 90 degrees at the North Pole and –90 degrees at the South Pole. Similarly, longitude values are positive going east from the Greenwich prime meridian and negative going west. Latitudes are parallel to the equator and longitudes are perpendicular. Latitudes are often called parallels and typically appear as horizontal lines, and longitudes are called meridians and typically appear as verticals. This orientation is arbitrary, but fairly solidly established.

I will use decimal values, which is the default displayed in Google Maps, but you will see combinations of degree, minute (1/60 of a degree), and second (1/60 of a minute). It is not necessary that you memorize latitude longitude values, but it is beneficial to develop some intuitive sense of the system. You can do this by doing what I call "going both ways." First, identify and compare latitude longitude values for places you know, and second, pick values and see what they are. For example, the base values for my version of the project are as follows:

- [40.725592,–74.00495, "friends of ED, NYC"]

- [41.04796,–73.70539, "Purchase College/SUNY"]

- [41.878928,–87.641926, "Illinois Institute of Technology"]

The first thing to notice is that the latitude values are fairly close and the longitude values are negative and not quite so close. The friends of ED office in New York City is within 1 degree of latitude and 1 degree of longitude of Purchase College. The distance according to Google Maps is 27.4 miles. The longitude value for Illinois Institute of Technology is more negative, indicating that it's more westerly than the two New York State locations. This all makes sense, but you need to take the time to think it through.

There are many ways to find the latitude and longitude of a specific location. You can use Google Maps as follows:

1. Invoke Google Maps (go to `www.google.com` and click Maps or go to `http://.maps.google.com`).

2. At the upper right, click the gear icon for a drop-down menu. Click the Maps Labs option. A window will appear titled Google Maps Labs. Scroll down to the LatLng Marker option and click the circle next to Enable. If you sign in, all settings will remain in force the next time you sign in. Save and close the window.

3. Type in the location you are interested in into the location field.

4. Right/Ctrl+click the location to get a drop-down menu, as shown in Figure 4-10.

5. Click Drop LatLng marker to get the result shown in Figure 4-11.

Figure 4-10. *Getting latitude longitude values in Google Maps*

After choosing the Drop LatLng Marker option, you will see the latitude and longitude values in a small box, as shown in Figure 4-11.

Figure 4-11. *Box showing latitude and longitude*

Another option is to use Wolfram Alpha (www.wolframalpha.com), as shown in Figure 4-12, which provides a way to determine latitude and longitude values as well as many other things.

Figure 4-12. Results of query on Wolfram Alpha

Notice the format of the results. This is the degree/minute/second format, with N for north and W for west. When I click the "Show decimal" button, the program displays what is shown in Figure 4-13.

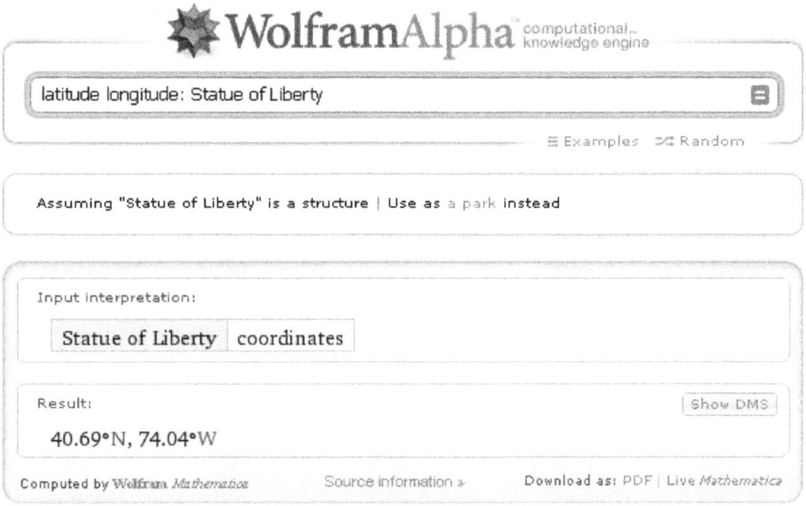

Figure 4-13. Decimal results for query to Wolfram Alpha

Notice that the longitude still appears with W for West as opposed to the negative value given by Google Maps.

Doing what I call "going in the opposite direction," you can put latitude and longitude values into Google Maps. Figure 4-14 shows the results of putting in 0.0 and 0.0. It is a point in the ocean south of Ghana. This is a point on the equator *and* on the Greenwich prime meridian.

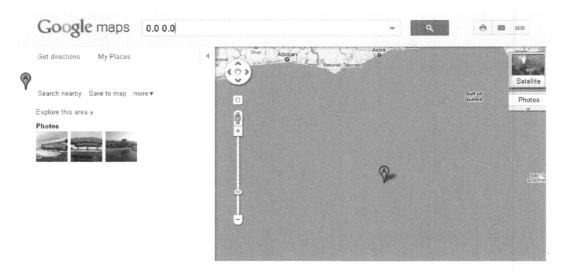

Figure 4-14. *The equator at the Greenwich prime meridian*

I tried to find a place in England on the Greenwich prime meridian and produced the result shown in Figure 4-15 when guessing at the latitude of 52.0 degrees.

Figure 4-15. *Results near a place on the Greenwich prime meridian*

The A marker indicates the closest place in the Google database to the requested location. I used the Drop LatLng marker option to reveal the exact latitude and longitude values.

The critical requirements for this project start off with the task of bringing Google Maps into a HTML5 application using specified latitude and longitude values. An additional requirement is producing the shadow/spotlight combination on top of the map to track the movements of the mouse. I also require a change from the default cursor for the mouse to something of my own choosing.

Next, I added a requirement to drop markers on the map, but again, with graphical icons that I picked, not the upside-down teardrop that is standard in Google Maps. The teardrop marker is nice enough, but my design objective was to be different to show you how to incorporate your own creativity into an application.

Beyond the graphics, I wanted the users to be able to make use of the Google Maps devices and any GUI features I built using HTML5. This all required managing events set up by the Google Maps API and events set up using HTML5 JavaScript. The responses to events that I wanted to make the user interface included the following:

- Tracking mouse movement with the shadow/spotlight graphic

- Responding to a click by placing an *x* on the map

- Retaining the same response to the Google Maps interface (slider, panning buttons, panning by grabbing the map)

- Treating the radio buttons and CHANGE button in the appropriate manner

Google Maps provides a way to determine distances between locations. Since I wanted to set up this project to work in terms of the base location, I needed a way to calculate distances directly.

These are the critical requirements for the map spotlight project. Now I will explain the HTML5 features I used to build the project. The objective is to use Google Maps features and JavaScript features, including events, and not let them interfere with each other. You can use what you learn for this and other projects.

HTML5, CSS, and JavaScript Features

The challenges for the map-maker project are bringing in the Google Map and then using the map and canvas and buttons together in terms of appearance and in the operation of the GUI. I'll describe the basic Google Maps API and then explain how HTML5 features provide the partial masking and the event handling.

Google Maps API

The Google Maps JavaScript API Version 3 Basics has excellent documentation located at `http://code.google.com/apis/maps/documentation/javascript/basics.html`. You do not need to refer to it right now, but it will help you if and when you decide to build your own project. It will be especially helpful in producing applications for mobile devices.

Most APIs are presented as a collection of related objects, each object having attributes (also known as properties) and methods. The API also may include events and a method for setting up the event. This is the situation with the Google Maps API. The important objects are `Map`, `LatLng`, and `Marker`. The method to set up an event is `addListener`, and this can be used to set up a response to clicking a map.

The Google Maps API is brought into your HTML5 document with a script element:

```
<script type="text/javascript" charset="UTF-8"↵
 src="http://maps.google.com/maps/api/js?sensor=false"></script>
```

I will discuss the script tag again, specifically the `sensor=false` setting, in Chapter 6.

The next step—and this could be all you need if all you want is to bring in a Google Map—is to set up a call to the `Map` constructor method. Pseudocode for this is

```
map = new google.maps.Map(place you are going to put the map, associative array with options);
```

Note that there is no harm is making the variable have the name `map`.

Let's take up the two parameters one at a time. The place to put the map could be a div defined in the body of the HTML document. However, I chose to create the div dynamically. I did this using code in an `init` function invoked in the usual way, by setting the `onLoad` attribute in the body statement. I also wrote code to create a canvas element inside the div. The code is

```
        candiv = document.createElement("div");
        candiv.innerHTML = ("<canvas id='canvas' width='600' height='400'>No canvas↵
</canvas>");
        document.body.appendChild(candiv);
        can = document.getElementById("canvas");
                pl = document.getElementById("place");
                ctx = can.getContext("2d");
```

`can`, `pl`, and `ctx` are global variables, each available for use by other functions.

■ **Note** Though I try to use the language "bring access to Google Maps into the HTML document," I am guilty of describing a function that "makes" a map. The Google Maps connection is a dynamic one in which Google Maps creates what are termed "tiles to be displayed."

The second parameter to the Map method is an associative array. An associative array has named elements, not indexed elements. The array for the Map method can indicate the zoom level, the center of the map, and the map type, among other things. The zoom level can go from 0 to 18. Level 0 is what is shown in Figure 4-7. Level 18 could show buildings. The types of maps are ROADMAP, SATELLITE, HYBRID, and TERRAIN. These are indicated using constants from the Google Maps API. The center is given by a value of type LatLng, constructed, as you may expect, using decimal numbers representing latitude and longitude values. The use of an associative array means that we don't have to follow a fixed order for parameters, and default settings will be applied to any parameter we omit.

The start of my makemap function follows. The function is called with two numbers indicating the latitude and longitude on which to center the map. My code constructs a LatLng object, sets up the array holding the specification for the map, and then constructs the map—that is, constructs the portal to Google Maps.

```
function makemap(mylat,mylong) {
        var marker;
        blatlng = new google.maps.LatLng(mylat,mylong);

myOptions = {
        zoom: 12,
                center: blatlng,
                mapTypeId: google.maps.MapTypeId.ROADMAP
        };
map = new google.maps.Map(document.getElementById("place"), myOptions);
```

The Map method constructs access to Google Maps starting with a map with the indicated options in the div with the ID place. The makemap function continues, placing a marker at the center of the map. This is done by setting up an associative array as the parameter for the Marker method. The icon marker will be an image I created using an image of my own design, a drawn red *x*.

```
marker = new google.maps.Marker({
 position: blatlng,
 title: "center",
 icon: rxmarker,
 map: map });
```

There is one more statement in the makemap function, but I will explain the rest later.

Canvas Graphics

The graphic that we want to move with the mouse over the map is similar to the mask used in Chapter 3 to turn the rectangular video clip into a circular video clip. Both masks can be described as resembling a rectangular donut: a rectangle with a round hole. We draw the graphics for the shadow/spotlight using two paths, just like the mask for the video in the previous chapter. There are two distinct differences, however, between the two situations:

- The exact shape of this mask varies. The outer boundary is the whole canvas, and the location of the hole is aligned with the current position of the mouse. The hole moves around.

- The color of the mask is not solid paint, but a transparent gray.

The canvas starts out on top of the Google Map. I accomplish this by writing style directives that set the z-index values:

```
canvas {position:absolute; top: 165px; left:0px; z-index:100;}
#place {position:absolute; top: 165px; left: 0px; z-index:1;}
```

The first directive refers to all canvas elements. There is only one in this HTML document. Recall that the z-axis comes out of the screen toward the viewer, so higher values are on top of lower values. Note also that we use `zIndex` in the JavaScript code and `z-index` in the CSS. The JavaScript parser would treat the – sign as a minus operator, so the change to `zIndex` is necessary. I will need to write code that changes the zIndex to get the event handling that I want for this project.

Figure 4-16 shows one example of the shadow mask drawn on the canvas. The canvas is over the map in terms of the z-index, and the mask is drawn with a gray color that is transparent so the map underneath is visible.

Figure 4-16. Shadow/spotlight on one place on the map

Figure 4-17 shows another example of the shadow mask drawn on the same map. This came about because of movement of the mouse by the user.

Base location (small red x) is Friends of ED, NYC
The distance from base to most recent marker (40.7257, -74.0047) is 0.03 km.
Change base location:
⦿ Friends of ED, NYC
○ Purchase College
○ Illinois Institute of Technology

[CHANGE]

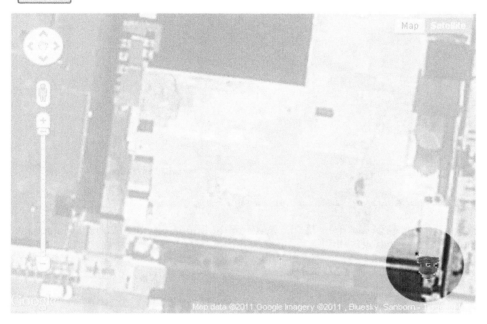

Figure 4-17. *Shadow mask over another position on the map*

Several topics are interlinked here. Let's assume that the variables mx and my hold the position of the mouse cursor on the canvas. I will explain how later in this chapter. The function drawshadowmask will draw the shadow mask. The transparent gray that is the color of the mask is defined in a variable I named grayshadow and constructed using the built-in function rgba. The rgba stands for red-green-blue-alpha. The alpha refers to the transparency/opacity. A value of 1 for alpha means that the color is fully opaque: solid. A value of 0 means that it is fully transparent—the color is not visible. Recall also that the red, green, and blue values go from 0 to 255, and the combination of 255, 255, and 255 would be white. This is a time for experimentation. I decided on the following setting for the gray/grayish/ghostlike shadow:

```
var grayshadow = "rgba(250,250,250,.8)";
```

The function `drawshadowmask` makes use of several variables that are constants—they never change. A schematic indicating the values is shown in Figure 4-18.

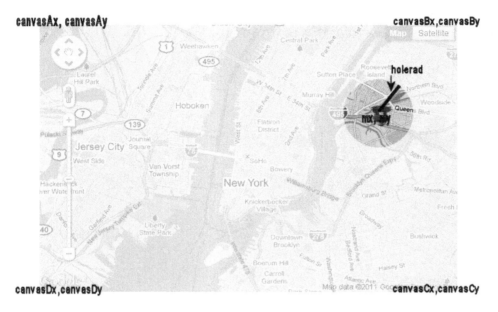

Figure 4-18. *Schematic with variable values indicated for mask*

The mask is drawn in two parts as was done for the mask for the bouncing video. You may look back to Figure 3-8 and Figure 3-9. The coding is similar:

```
function drawshadowmask(mx,my) {
   ctx.clearRect(0,0,600,400);
   ctx.fillStyle = grayshadow;
   ctx.beginPath();
   ctx.moveTo(canvasAx,canvasAy);
   ctx.lineTo(canvasBx,canvasBy);
   ctx.lineTo(canvasBx,my);
   ctx.lineTo(mx+holerad,my);
   ctx.arc(mx,my,holerad,0,Math.PI,true);
   ctx.lineTo(canvasAx,my);
   ctx.lineTo(canvasAx,canvasAy);
   ctx.closePath();
   ctx.fill();
   ctx.beginPath();
   ctx.moveTo(canvasAx,my);
   ctx.lineTo(canvasDx,canvasDy);
   ctx.lineTo(canvasCx,canvasCy);
   ctx.lineTo(canvasBx,my);
   ctx.lineTo(mx+holerad,my);
   ctx.arc(mx,my,holerad,0,Math.PI,false);
```

```
    ctx.lineTo(canvasAx,my);
    ctx.closePath();
    ctx.fill();
}
```

Now we move on to the red lightbulb.

Cursor

The cursor—the small graphic that moves on the screen when you move the mouse—can be set in the style element or in JavaScript. There are several built-in choices for the graphic (e.g., crosshair, pointer), and we also can refer to our own designs for a custom-made cursor, which is what I demonstrate in this project. I included the statement

```
can.onmousedown = function () { return false; } ;
```

in the `init` function to prevent a change to the default cursor when pressing down on the mouse. This may not be necessary since the default may not be triggered.

To change the cursor for moving the mouse to something that conveyed a spotlight, I created a picture of a red compact fluorescent lightbulb and saved it in the file `light.gif`. I then used the following statement in the function `showshadow`. The `showshadow` function has been set as the event handler for `mousemove`:

```
can.style.cursor = "url('light.gif'), pointer";
```

to indicate that JavaScript should use that address for the image for the cursor when on top of the `can` element. Furthermore, if the file 'light.gif' is not available, the statement directs JavaScript to use the built-in pointer icon. This is similar to the way that fonts can be specified with a priority listing of choices. The variable `can` has been set to reference the canvas element. The cursor will not be used when the canvas has been pushed under the Google Map, as will be discussed in the next section.

Events

The handling of events—namely mouse events, but also events for changing the slider on the Google Map or clicking the radio buttons—seemed the most daunting when I started work on this project. However, the actual implementation turned out to be straightforward. In the `init` function, I write code to set up event handling for movement of the mouse, mouse button down, and mouse button up, all regarding the canvas element:

```
    can.onmousedown = function () { return false; } ;
    can.addEventListener('mousemove',showshadow,true);
    can.addEventListener('mousedown',pushcanvasunder,true);
    can.addEventListener("mouseout",clearshadow,true);
```

The `true` value for the third parameter indicates that this event is to *bubble*, meaning that it is to signal other listeners. However, more work was needed to achieve the event handling I wanted for this project. I will explain the three functions and then go on to describe one more event.

The `showshadow` function, as indicated previously, calls the `drawshadowmask` function. I could have combined these two functions, but dividing tasks into smaller tasks generally is a good practice. The `showshadow` function determines the mouse position, makes an adjustment so the lightbulb base is at the center of the spotlight, and then makes the call to `drawshadowmask`:

```
function showshadow(ev) {
   var mx;
   var my;
   if ( ev.layerX || ev.layerX == 0) {
       mx= ev.layerX;
       my = ev.layerY;
       }
  else if (ev.offsetX || ev.offsetX == 0) {
       mx = ev.offsetX;
       my = ev.offsetY;
       }
   can.style.cursor = "url('light.gif'), pointer";
   mx = mx+10;
   my = my + 12;
   drawshadowmask(mx,my);
}
```

Now I needed to think what I wanted to do when the user pressed down on the mouse. I decided that I wanted the shadow to go away and the map to be displayed in its full brightness. In addition to the appearance of things, I also wanted the Google Maps API to resume control. A critical reason for wanting the Google Maps API to take over is that I wanted to place a marker on the map, as opposed to the canvas, to mark a location. This is because I wanted the marker to move with the map, and that would be very difficult to do by drawing on the canvas. I would need to synchronize the marker on the canvas with panning and zooming of the map. Instead, the API does all this for me. In addition, I needed the Google Maps API to produce latitude and longitude values for the location.

The way to put Google Maps back in control, so to speak, was to "push the canvas under." The function is

```
function pushcanvasunder(ev) {
       can.style.zIndex = 1;
       pl.style.zIndex = 100;
}
```

The operation of pushing the canvas under or bringing it back on top is not instantaneous. I am open to suggestions on (1) how to define the interface and (2) how to implement what you have defined. There is room for improvement here.

One more situation to take care of is what I want to occur if and when the user moves the mouse off from the canvas? The mouseout event is available as something to be listened for, so I wrote the code setting up the event (see the can.addEventListener statements shown above) to be handled by the clearshadow function. The clearshadow function accomplishes just that: clearing the whole canvas, including the shadow:

```
function clearshadow(ev) {
       ctx.clearRect(0,0,600,400);
}
```

In the function that brings in the Google Map, I set up an event handler for mouseup for maps.

```
listener = google.maps.event.addListener(map, 'mouseup', function(event) {
                       checkit(event.latLng);
                       });
```

The call to addListener, a method that is part of the Google Maps API as opposed to JavaScript proper, sets up the call to the checkit function. The checkit function is invoked using an attribute of the event object as a parameter. As you can guess, event.latLng is the latitude and longitude values at the position of the mouse when the mouse button was released on the map object. The checkit function will use those values to calculate the distance from the base location and to print out the values along with the distance on the screen. The code invokes a function I wrote that rounds the values. I did this to avoid displaying a value with many significant digits, more than is appropriate for this project. The Google Maps API marker method provides a way to use an image of my choosing for the marker, this time a black ,hand-drawn *x*, and to include a title with the marker. The title is recommended to make applications accessible for people using screen readers, though I cannot claim that this project would satisfy anyone in terms of accessibility. It is possible to produce the screen shown in Figure 4-19.

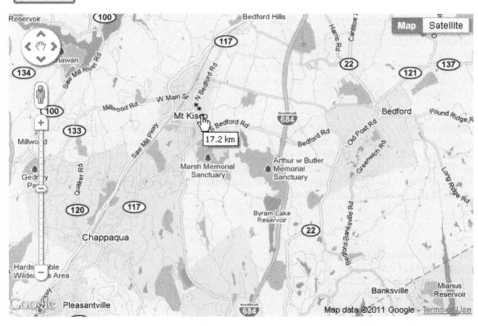

Figure 4-19. Title indicating distance shown on map

The checkit function, called with a parameter holding the latitude and longitude value, follows:

```
function checkit(clatlng) {
    var distance = dist(clatlng,blatlng);
    distance = round(distance,2);
    var distanceString = String(distance)+" km";
    marker = new google.maps.Marker({
    position: clatlng,
    title: distanceString,
    icon: bxmarker,
    map: map });
    var clat = clatlng.lat();
    var clng = clatlng.lng();
    clat = round(clat,4);
    clng = round(clng,4);
    document.getElementById("answer").innerHTML   =
 "The distance from base to most recent marker ("+clat+", "+clng+") is "+String(distance)↵
 +" km.";
    can.style.zIndex = 100;
    pl.style.zIndex = 1;
}
```

Notice that the last thing that the function does is put the canvas back on top of the map.

The CHANGE button and the radio buttons are implemented using standard HTML and JavaScript. The form is produced using the following HTML coding:

```
<form name="f" onSubmit=" return changebase();">
 <input type="radio" name="loc" /> friends of ED, NYC<br/>
 <input type="radio" name="loc" /> Purchase College<br/>
 <input type="radio" name="loc" /> Illinois Institute of Technology<br/>
<input type="submit" value="CHANGE">
</form>
```

The function changebase is invoked when the submit button, labeled CHANGE, is clicked. The changebase function determines which of the radio buttons was checked and uses the Locations table to pick up the latitude and longitude values. It then makes a call to makemap using these values for parameters. This way of organizing data is called *parallel structures*: the locations array elements correspond to the radio buttons. The last statement sets the innerHTML of the header element to display text, including the name of the selected base location.

```
function changebase() {
        var mylat;
        var mylong;
        for(var i=0;i<locations.length;i++) {
                if (document.f.loc[i].checked) {
                        mylat = locations[i][0];
                        mylong = locations[i][1];
                        makemap(mylat,mylong);
                        document.getElementById("header").innerHTML =
                                "Base location (small red x) is "+locations[i][2];
                }
        }
        return false;
}
```

Calculating Distance and Rounding Values for Display

Google Maps, as many of us know, provides information on distances and even distinguishes between walking and driving. For this application, I needed more control on specifying the two locations for which I wanted the distance calculated, so I decided to develop a function in JavaScript. Determining the distance between two points, each representing latitude and longitude values, is done using the spherical law of cosines. My source was www.movable-type.co.uk/scripts/latlong.html. Here is the code:

```
function dist(point1, point2) {
  var R = 6371; // km
  // var R =  3959; // miles
  var lat1 = point1.lat()*Math.PI/180;
  var lat2 = point2.lat()*Math.PI/180 ;
  var lon1 = point1.lng()*Math.PI/180;
  var lon2 = point2.lng()*Math.PI/180;
  var d = Math.acos(Math.sin(lat1)*Math.sin(lat2) +
  Math.cos(lat1)*Math.cos(lat2) *
  Math.cos(lon2-lon1)) * R;
    return d;
  }
```

■ **Caution**   I don't include many comments in the code because I include the tables with each line annotated. However, comments are important. I strongly recommend leaving the comments on km and miles in the dist function so you can adjust your program as appropriate. Alternatively, you could display both values or give the user a choice.

The last function is for rounding values. When a quantity is dependent on a person moving a mouse, you shouldn't display a value to a great number of decimal places. However, we should keep in mind that latitude and longitude represent big units. I decided I wanted the distances to be shown with two decimal places and the latitude and longitude with four.

The function I wrote is quite general. It takes two parameters, one the number num and the other places, indicating how many decimal places to take the value. You can use it in other circumstances. It rounds up or down, as appropriate, by adding in the value I call the *increment* and then calculating the biggest integer not bigger than the value. So

- round(9.147,2) will produce 9.15; and

- round(9.143, 2) will produce 9.14.

The way the code works is first to determine what I term the *factor*, 10 raised to the desired number of places. For 2, this will be 100. I then calculate the increment. For two places, this will be 5 / 100 * 10, which is 5 / 1,000, which is .005. My code does the following:

1. Adds the increment to the original number

2. Multiplies the result by the factor

113

3. Calculates the largest whole number not bigger than the result (this is called the floor)—producing a whole number

4. Divides the result by the factor

The code follows:

```
function round (num,places) {
        var factor = Math.pow(10,places);
        var increment = 5/(factor*10);
        return Math.floor((num+increment)*factor)/factor;
}
```

I use the round function to round off distances to two decimal places and latitude and longitude to four decimal places.

■ **Tip**   JavaScript has a method called toFixed that essentially performs the task of my round. If num holds a number—say, 51.5621—then num.toFixed() will produce 51 and num.toFixed(2) will produce 51.56. I've read that there can be inaccuracies with this method, so I chose to create my own function. You may be happy to go with toFixed() in your own applications, though.

With the explanation of the relevant HTML5 and Google Maps API features, we can now put it all together.

Building the Application and Making It Your Own

The map spotlight application sets up the combination of Google Maps functionality with HTML5 coding. A quick summary of the application is the following:

1. init: Initialization, including bringing in the map (makemap) and setting up mouse events with handlers: showshadow, pushcanvasunder, clearshadow

2. makemap: Brings in a map and sets up event handling, including the call to checkit

3. showshadow: Invokes drawshadowmask

4. pushcanvasunder: Enables events the on map

5. checkit: Calculates distance, adds a custom marker, and displays distance and rounded latitude and longitude

The function table describing the invoked/called by and calling relationships (Table 4-1) is the same for all the applications.

Table 4-1. *Functions in the Map Maker Project*

Function	Invoked/Called By	Calls
init	Invoked by action of the onLoad attribute in the <body> tag	makemap
pushcanvasunder	Invoked by action of addEventListener called in init	
clearshadow	Invoked by action of addEventListener called in init	
showshadow	Invoked by action of addEventListener called in init	drawshadowmask
drawshadowmask	Called by showshadow	
makemap	Called by init	
checkit	Called by action of addEventListener called in makemap	round, dist
round	Called by checkit (three times)	
dist	Called by checkit	
changebase	Called by action of onSubmit in <form>	makemap

Table 4-2 shows the code for the Map Maker application, named mapspotlight.html.

Table 4-2. *Complete Code for the mapspotlight.html Application*

Code Line	Description
<!DOCTYPE html>	Header
<html>	Opening html tag
<head>	Opening head tag
<title>Spotlight </title>	Complete title
<meta charset="UTF-8">	Meta tag
<style>	Opening of style element
header {font-family:Georgia,"Times New Roman",serif;	Set fonts for the heading
font-size:16px;	Font size

Code Line	Description
`display:block; }`	Line breaks before and after
`canvas {position:absolute; top: 165px; left:0px;`	Style directive for the single canvas element: position slightly down the page
`z-index:100;}`	Initial setting for canvas is on top of map
`#place {position:absolute; top: 165px; left: 0px;`	Style directive for the div holding the Google Map; position exactly the same as the canvas
`z-index:1;}`	Initial setting to be under canvas
`</style>`	Close style element
`<script type="text/javascript" charset="UTF-8" src="http://maps.google.com/maps/api/js?sensor=false"></script>`	Bring in the external script element holding the Google Maps API; no attempt to use sensing for geolocation
`<script type="text/javascript" charset="UTF-8">`	Opening script tag
`var locations = [`	Define set of base locations
`[40.725592,-74.00495, "Friends of ED, NYC"],`	Latitude, longitude name for friends of ED
`[41.04796,-73.70539,"Purchase College/SUNY"],`	. . . Purchase College
`[41.878928, -87.641926,"Illinois Institute of Technology"]`	. . . Illinois Institute of Technology
`];`	Close array of locations
`var candiv;`	Used to hold div holding the canvas
`var can;`	Reference canvas element

Code Line	Description
`var ctx;`	Reference context of canvas; used for all drawing
`var pl;`	Reference the div holding the Google Map
`function init() {`	Function header for `init`
`  var mylat;`	Will hold latitude value
`  var mylong;`	Will hold longitude value
`  candiv = document.createElement("div");`	Create a div
`  candiv.innerHTML = ("<canvas id='canvas' width='600' height='400'>No canvas </canvas>");`	Set its contents to be a canvas element
`  document.body.appendChild(candiv);`	Add to the body
`  can = document.getElementById("canvas");`	Set reference to the canvas
`  pl = document.getElementById("place");`	Set reference to the div holding the Google Map
`  ctx = can.getContext("2d");`	Set the context
`  can.onmousedown = function () { return false; } ;`	Prevents change of cursor to default
`    can.addEventListener('mousemove',showshadow,true);`	Set event handling for mouse moving
`   can.addEventListener('mousedown',pushcanvasunder,true);`	Set event handling for pushing down on mouse button
`    can.addEventListener("mouseout",clearshadow,true);`	Set event handling for moving mouse off of the canvas
`  mylat = locations[0][0];`	Set the latitude to be the latitude of the 0th location

Code Line	Description
`mylong = locations[0][1];`	Set the longitude to be the longitude of the 0th location
`makemap(mylat,mylong);`	Invoke function to make a map (bring in Google Maps at specified location)
`}`	Close `init` function
`function pushcanvasunder(ev) {`	Header for `pushcanvas` function, called with parameter referencing the event
`can.style.zIndex = 1;`	Push canvas down
`pl.style.zIndex = 100;`	Set map div up
`}`	Close `pushcanvasunder` function
`function clearshadow(ev) {`	Header for `clearshadow` function, called with parameter referencing the event
`ctx.clearRect(0,0,600,400);`	Clear canvas (erase shadow mask)
`}`	Close `clearshadow` function
`function showshadow(ev) {`	Header for showshadow function, called with parameter referencing the event
`var mx;`	Will be used to hold horizontal position of mouse
`var my;`	Will be used to hold vertical position of mouse
`if ( ev.layerX || ev.layerX == 0) {`	Does this browser use `layerX`?

Code Line	Description
`mx = ev.layerX;`	If so, use it to set `mx` . . .
`my = ev.layerY;`	. . . and `my`
`} else if (ev.offsetX || ev.offsetX == 0) {`	Try `offsetX`
`mx = ev.offsetX;`	If so, use it to set `mx` . . .
`my = ev.offsetY;`	. . . and `my`
`}`	Close clause
`can.style.cursor = "url('light.gif'), pointer";`	Set up cursor to be `light.gif` if available, otherwise pointer
`mx = mx+10;`	Make rough correction to make center of light at base of lightbulb horizontally and . . .
`my = my + 12;`	. . . vertically
`drawshadowmask(mx,my);`	Invoke `drawshadowmask` function at the modified (mx,my)
`}`	Close `showshadow` function
`var canvasAx = 0;`	Constant for mask: Upper-left x
`var canvasAy = 0;`	Upper-left y
`var canvasBx = 600;`	Upper-right x
`var canvasBy = 0;`	Upper-right y
`var canvasCx = 600;`	Lower-right x
`var canvasCy = 400;`	Lower-right y
`var canvasDx = 0;`	Lower-left x

Code Line	Description
`var canvasDy = 400;`	Lower-left y
`var holerad = 50;`	Constant radius for hole in shadow (radius of spotlight)
`var grayshadow = "rgba(250,250,250,.8)";`	Color for faint shadow; note alpha of .8
`function drawshadowmask(mx,my) {`	Header for `drawshadowmask` function; parameters hold center of donut hole
`ctx.clearRect(0,0,600,400);`	Erase whole canvas
`ctx.fillStyle = grayshadow;`	Set color
`ctx.beginPath();`	Start first (top) path
`ctx.moveTo(canvasAx,canvasAy);`	Move to upper-left corner
`ctx.lineTo(canvasBx,canvasBy);`	Draw over to upper-right corner
`ctx.lineTo(canvasBx,my);`	Draw to vertical point specified by my parameter
`ctx.lineTo(mx+holerad,my);`	Draw over to the left to edge of hole
`ctx.arc(mx,my,holerad,0,Math.PI,true);`	Draw semicircular arc
`ctx.lineTo(canvasAx,my);`	Draw to left side
`ctx.lineTo(canvasAx,canvasAy);`	Draw back to start
`ctx.closePath();`	Close path
`ctx.fill();`	Fill in
`ctx.beginPath();`	Start of second (lower) path
`ctx.moveTo(canvasAx,my);`	Start at point on left side indicated by my parameter

Code Line	Description
`ctx.lineTo(canvasDx,canvasDy);`	Draw to lower-left corner
`ctx.lineTo(canvasCx,canvasCy);`	Draw to lower-right corner
`ctx.lineTo(canvasBx,my);`	Draw to point on right edge
`ctx.lineTo(mx+holerad,my);`	Draw to left to edge of hole
`ctx.arc(mx,my,holerad,0,Math.PI,false);`	Draw semicircular arc
`ctx.lineTo(canvasAx,my);`	Draw to right edge
`ctx.closePath();`	Close path
`ctx.fill();`	Fill in
`}`	Close `drawshadowmask` function
`var listener;`	Variable set by `addListener` call; *not used again*
`var map;`	Holds map
`var blatlng;`	Holds base latitude longitude object
`var myOptions;`	Holds associative array used for map
`var rxmarker = "x1.png";`	Holds file name for red *x* image
`var bxmarker = "bx1.png";`	Holds file name for black *x* image
`function makemap(mylat,mylong) {`	Header for `makemap` function; parameters hold location of center of the map
`  var marker;`	Will hold marker created for center

Code Line	Description
`blatlng = new google.maps.LatLng(mylat,mylong);`	Build a `LatLng` object (special data type for the API)
`myOptions = {`	Set associative array
`zoom: 12,`	Zoom setting (can be 0 to 18)
`center: blatlng,`	Center
`mapTypeId: google.maps.MapTypeId.ROADMAP`	Type of map
`};`	Close `myOptions` array
`map = new google.maps.Map(document.getElementById("place"), myOptions);`	Invoke the API to bring in a map at indicated place
`marker = new google.maps.Marker(`	Place marker in center of map; `marker` method takes an associative array as its parameter
`{`	Start of associative array
`position: blatlng,`	Set the position
`title: "center",`	Set the title
`icon: rxmarker,`	Set the icon
`map: map`	Set the map named parameter to the variable named map
`}`	Close the associative array which is the parameter to the call to Marker
`);`	Close the call to `Marker`
`listener = google.maps.event.addListener(`	Set up event handling (the three following parameters)
`map,`	The object, namely the map

Code Line	Description
`'mouseup',`	The specific event
`function(event) {`	An autonomous function (defined directly as a parameter in addListener)
`checkit(event.latLng);`	Calling `checkit` with the indicated latitude longitude object
`}`	Close the function definition
`);`	Close the call to `addListener`
`}`	Close the `makemap` function
`function checkit(clatlng) {`	Function header for `checkit`; called with the latitude longitude object
`var distance = dist(clatlng,blatlng);`	Invoke `dist` function to calculate distance between the clicked position and the base
`distance = round(distance,2);`	Round the value
`var distanceString = String(distance)+" km";`	Set `distanceString` to be the display
`marker = new google.maps.Marker(`	Invoke the `Marker` method, which takes an associative array as its parameter
`{`	Start of associative array
`position: clatlng,`	Set position
`title: distanceString,`	Set title
`icon: bxmarker,`	Set icon to be black *x*

Code Line	Description
`map: map`	Set map element of associative array to the value of the variable named map
`}`	Close associative array
`);`	Close call to **Marker** method
`var clat = clatlng.lat();`	Extract the latitude value
`var clng = clatlng.lng();`	Extract the longitude value
`clat = round(clat,4);`	Round value to 4 decimal places
`clng = round(clng,4);`	Round value to 4 decimal places
`document.getElementById("answer").innerHTML  =`	Set up text on screen . . .
`"The distance from base to most recent marker ("` `+ clat+", "+clng+") is "+String(distance) +" km.";`	. . . to be calculated and formatted information
`can.style.zIndex = 100;`	Set canvas to be on top
`pl.style.zIndex = 1;`	Set pl (holding map) to be underneath
`}`	Close **checkit** function
`function round (num,places) {`	Header for function to round values
`var factor = Math.pow(10,places);`	Determine factor from number of places
`var increment = 5/(factor*10);`	Determine the increment to round up or down
`return Math.floor((num+increment)*factor)/factor;`	Do calculation
`}`	Close **round** function

Code Line	Description
`function dist(point1, point2) {`	Function header for `dist` (distance) function

`// spherical law of cosines,`
`// from`
`// http://www.movable- type.co.uk/scripts/latlong.html`
	Attribution for my source. This is standard mathematics

`var R = 6371; // km`	Factor used to produce answer in kilometers
`// var R = 3959; // miles`	Commented out, but keep just in case you want to give answer in miles
`var lat1 = point1.lat()*Math.PI/180;`	Convert value to radians
`var lat2 = point2.lat()*Math.PI/180 ;`	Convert value to radians
`var lon1 = point1.lng()*Math.PI/180;`	Convert value to radians
`var lon2 = point2.lng()*Math.PI/180;`	Convert value to radians
`var d =`	Calculation . . .
`Math.acos(Math.sin(lat1)*Math.sin(lat2) +` `Math.cos(lat1)*Math.cos(lat2) * Math.cos(lon2-lon1)) * R;`	Use trigonometry to determine distance
`return d;`	Return result
`}`	Close `dist` function
`function changebase() {`	Header for `changebase` function
`var mylat;`	Will hold new base location latitude
`var mylong;`	Will hold new base location longitude
`for(var i=0;i<locations.length;i++) {`	`for` loop to determine which radio button is checked

Code Line	Description
`if (document.f.loc[i].checked) {`	Is this one checked?
`mylat = locations[i][0];`	If so, set `mylat`
`mylong = locations[i][1];`	Set `mylong`
`makemap(mylat,mylong);`	Invoke `makemap`
`document.getElementById("header").` `innerHTML = "Base location (small red x) is "+locations[i][2];`	Change text in header to show the name
`}`	Close `if true` clause
`}`	Close `for` loop
`return false;`	Return `false` to present refresh
`}`	Close function
`</script>`	Closing script tag
`</head>`	Closing head tag
`<body onLoad="init();">`	Opening body tag; include `onLoad` to invoke `init`
`<header id="header">Base location (small red x) </header>`	Semantic header element
`<div id="place" style="width:600px; height:400px"></div>`	Div to hold Google Maps
`<div id="answer"></div>`	Div to hold information on clicked locations
`Change base location:  `	Text
`<form name="f" onSubmit=" return changebase();">`	Start of form for changing base
`<input type="radio" name="loc" /> Friends of ED, NYC `	Radio button choice
`<input type="radio" name="loc" /> Purchase College `	Radio button choice

Code Line	Description
`<input type="radio" name="loc" /> Illinois Institute of Technology `	Radio button choice
`<input type="submit" value="CHANGE">`	The button to make the change
`</form>`	Closing form tag
`</body>`	Closing body tag
`</html>`	Closing `html` tag

You need to decide on your set of base locations. Again, there is nothing special about three. If your base list is too large, you may consider using `<optgroup>` to produce a drop-down list. In any case, you need to define a set of locations. Each location has two numbers—latitude and longitude—and a string of text comprising the name. This text is repeated in the HTML coding in the form.

Testing and Uploading the Application

This project consists of the HTML file and three image files. For my version of the project, the image files were the lightbulb, `light.gif`; the red *x*, `rxmarker.png`; and the black *x*, `bxmarker.png`. There is nothing special about these image file types. You can use whatever you like. It could be argued that my *x* markers are too tiny, so think about your customers when deciding on what to do.

This application does require you to be online to test since that is the only way to make contact with Google Maps.

Summary

In this chapter, you learned how to do the following:

- Use the Google Maps API
- Combine Google Maps with canvas graphics
- Produce a GUI that includes Google Maps events and HTML5 events
- Draw using the alpha setting controlling transparency/opacity
- Change to a custom-made cursor
- Calculate distances between geographic points
- Round off decimal values for suitable display

The next chapter describes another project using Google Maps. You will learn how to build an application in which you can associate a picture, a video clip, or a picture-and-audio-clip combination with specific geographic locations, and display and play the specified media when a user clicks at or near the locations on a map.

CHAPTER 5

Map Portal: Using Google Maps to Access Your Media

In this chapter, you will explore the following:

- Using the Google Maps API to play and display video, audio, and images

- Creating HTML5 markup dynamically

- Separating the program from descriptions of content

- Building a geography game

Introduction

The projects in this chapter make use of the Google Maps API as a way to play video, display images, or play audio *and* display an image, all based on geographic locations. You can use these projects as models to build a study of a geographic area, report on a business or vacation trip, or create a geography quiz. I will describe three distinct applications. For all three applications, I have acquired media, such as video files, audio files, and image files, and I have defined in code an association between the files and specific geographic locations. To give you an idea of what I mean, for my projects, associations between a target location (which is given in latitude and longitude coordinates in the code) and media are shown in Table 5-1.

Table 5-1. *Outline of Content*

Description of Location	Media
Purchase College	Video from robotics class
Mount Kisco	Picture of Esther and an audio file of her playing piano
Dixon, Illinois	Picture of Aviva
Statue of Liberty, New York City	Video of fireworks

All three applications proceed smoothly with the different types of media. This is due to the features of HTML5 and, I say modestly, my programming. The media files are separate and the same for all three applications. It still is recommended that you supply multiple video and audio formats to make sure your application will work in the different browsers. The media types recognized by browsers may change so that fewer types are required, but this is not the case at this time.

The first application, consisting of one HTML file, named `mapvideos.html`, invites the viewer to click the map. If the click is close enough to one of the targeted locations, the viewer either sees the corresponding image, sees the corresponding video playing, or both sees the corresponding image and hears the corresponding audio file. The program handles all three types of media and media combinations.

The second application appears to the viewer to be the same as the first, but there is an important difference in the implementation. This application consists of two `html` files: `mapmediabase.html` and `mediacontent.js`. The `mediacontent.js` file holds the information describing the specific media content of the application. The `mapmediabase.html` program brings in the `mediacontent.js` file and creates during runtime what is necessary to replicate the first application.

I include both the first and second application because the first one is easier to understand, since all the information is in one place. When you develop your own applications, you can try to go straight to an implementation that separates coding from content, but don't feel too bad if you don't.

The third application is a quiz. Like the second, it consists of two files: `mapmediaquiz.html` and `mediaquizcontent.js`. The `mediaquizcontent.js` file contains information connecting the media to the locations and also contains the text for the questions.

The three applications have much of the same coding. The process of creating the second and third applications will show you how to scale up your applications by separating the details of a specific set of media (or other things) from the bulk of the programming.

Figure 5-1 shows the opening screen for the first application.

Click on map.

Figure 5-1. Opening screen

Figure 5-2 shows what happens when I click the screen on the Purchase College campus. A video clip appears and starts playing. You also can see "Lego robot" in the title position.

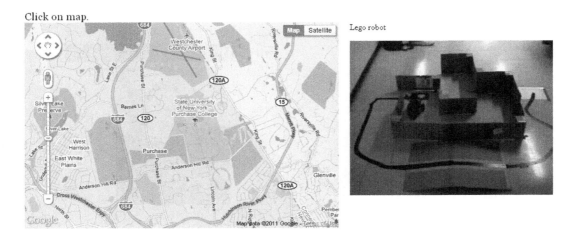

Figure 5-2. Result of clicking at Purchase College

Figure 5-3 shows the result of clicking the screen, but not sufficiently close to any of the target locations. Notice that I have panned the map, moving it to the north.

Click on map.

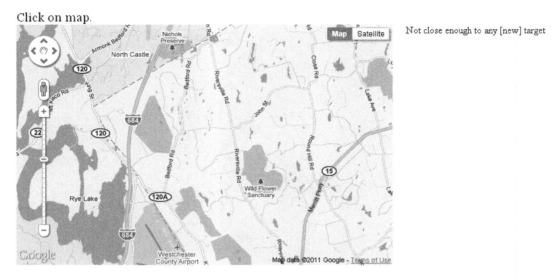

Not close enough to any [new] target

Figure 5-3. *Click not close to any target*

Figure 5-4 shows the result of my clicking near enough to Mt. Kisco to get a reward. I needed to move further north to get to Mt. Kisco. Notice also the audio control, providing a way to pause and resume playing and also change the speaker volume. The controls for audio (and video) will be different in the different browsers, but the functionality is the same.

Click on map.

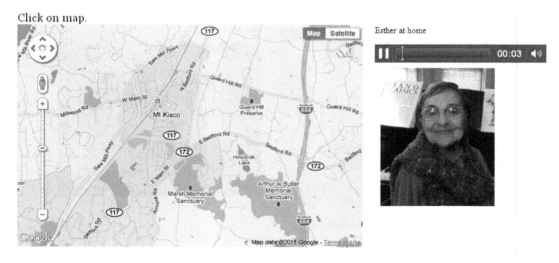

Esther at home

Figure 5-4. *Image-and-audio combination*

Because I know where the locations are, I know to zoom out to get to the next location. Figure 5-5 shows the results of using the Google Maps interface to accomplish this. The audio track continues playing and I still see the picture.

Figure 5-5. Zooming out in preparation for a pan south

Figure 5-6 shows the result of moving the map to the south and then zooming in to the location of the Statue of Liberty, the targeted location for the fireworks video clip.

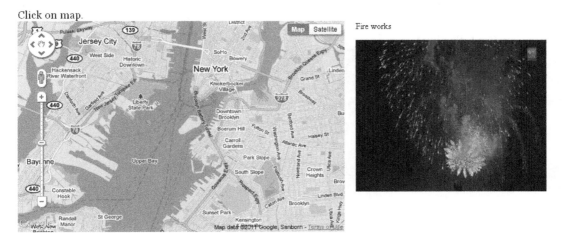

Figure 5-6. Clicking Liberty Island after panning and zooming in

Again, I know where the pictures are, so I zoom out, pan to the west of Chicago, and click the small town of Dixon, Illinois. Figure 5-7 shows the image I expected.

Click on map.

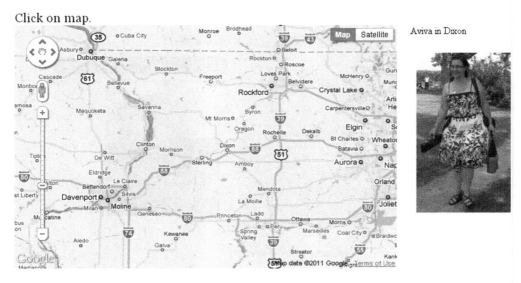

Aviva in Dixon

Figure 5-7. Panning to the west and zooming in to Dixon, Illinois

It actually took some work (to be explained later) to make the second application resemble the first with respect to layout.

Now I will show screenshots for the third application, the quiz. Figure 5-8 shows the opening screen.

Where does Grandma Esther live?

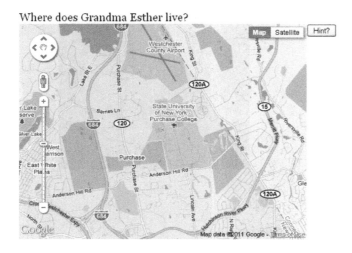

Title will be placed here.

Figure 5-8. Opening screen of quiz

The question is, Where does Grandma Esther live? The player must click close to the location associated with this question. You might be able to guess the answer from the previous screenshots. Figure 5-9 shows an incorrect response. I just clicked the map near Purchase College.

Where does Grandma Esther live?

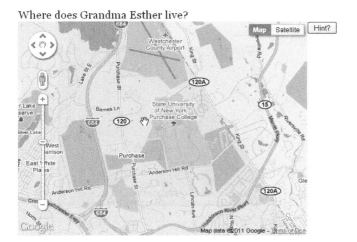

Not close enough to the answer.

Figure 5-9. *Incorrect response*

I know the answer, and furthermore, how to get to it on the map. I move the map north to Mt. Kisco and click there. Figure 5-10 shows the familiar image and the audio control. Piano music is playing.

Show the Lego robot navigating a maze.

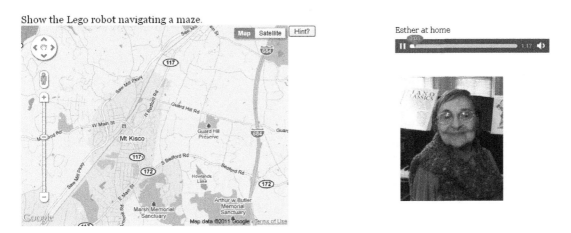

Esther at home

Figure 5-10. *A correct answer is given, so the image is shown and the audio is played, and the next question is given.*

Notice that the screen shows the next question as soon as the last one is answered correctly.

When designing a game such as this one, it is best to take pity on a player when they don't know the answer. I provide the Hint? button, though it goes beyond just giving a hint. Skipping ahead, I will get the next two questions correct, and then I will need help on finding Dixon, Illinois. Figure 5-11 shows the prompt.

Find where Aviva played the flute.

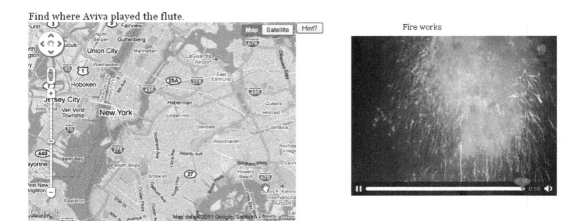

Figure 5-11. Prompt concerning flute playing

If I click the Hint? button, the application will bring in a new map, centered at the desired location. Figure 5-12 shows the screen.

Find where Aviva played the flute.

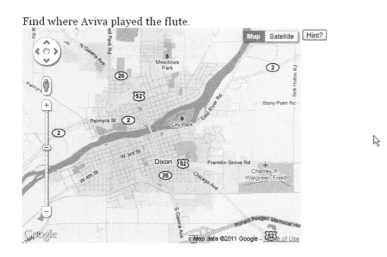

Figure 5-12. Map centered on Dixon, Illinois

It is still necessary to click the map, hopefully on or near the red *x*, to complete the question. You may say that there are better ways of hinting—such as supplying specifically chosen text holding the name of the place—and I won't argue with you. This is what I decided to do.

With this introduction, I'll go on to discuss the project history and the critical requirements.

Project History and Critical Requirements

A senior at Purchase College had collected and made video clips and photographs about the ethnic neighborhoods of Queens, New York, and wanted a way to present the work. The Google Maps API and the new facilities in HTML5 seemed perfect for the task. Keep in mind that the student only needed a way to present the work on a computer she set up at the senior project show, so the issue of noncompliant browsers was not a concern. The critical requirements include what is supplied by the Google Maps API. As you learned in the previous chapter, we can write code to access a map centered at a specified geographic location, set at an initial zoom level, and showing views of roads or satellite or terrain or a hybrid. In addition, the API provides a way to respond to the event of the viewer clicking the map. We need a way to define specific locations to be compared with the location corresponding to the viewer's click.

My first system for the student just used video and images. I later decided to add the image-and-audio combination. The critical requirement for the application is displaying and playing the designated media at the correct time *and* stopping and removing the media when appropriate, such as when it is time for the next presentation.

After developing the initial project, I thought of changes. The first one was the addition of the image-and-audio combination. I decided I did not want audio just by itself. The next change was to separate the specific content from the general coding. This, in turn, required a way to create markup for video and audio elements dynamically.

I always like games and lessons, and it seemed like a natural step to build an application with questions or prompts that the viewer—now best described as player or student. The player gives the answer by finding the right position on the map. Both the general application and the quiz application have a requirement to define a tolerance with respect to the answers. The viewer/player/student cannot be expected to click exactly on the correct spot.

When testing the quiz, I realized I needed some way to help the player get past a particularly difficult question. Because I am a teacher, I decided to show the player the answer, rather than just skipping the question. However, as I indicated earlier, you may be able to devise a better way to produce hints.

Games should have some randomness feature, so I decided to shuffle the questions, though I did this somewhat later in the process.

Having described the critical requirements, the next section will contain explanation of the specific HTML5 features that can be used to build the projects.

HTML5, CSS, and JavaScript Features

Like the map maker project in Chapter 4, these projects are implemented by combining the use of the Google Maps API with features of HTML5. The combination for this project is not as tricky. The map stays on the left side of the window and the media is presented on the right. I will review quickly how to get access to a map and how to set up the event handling, and then go on to the HTML5, CSS, and JavaScript features for satisfying the rest of the critical requirements.

Google Maps API for Map Access and Event Handling

Access to the Google Maps API requires a script element with reference to an external file. For this application, I used

```
<script type="text/javascript" charset="UTF-8"⏎
 src="http://maps.google.com/maps/api/js?sensor=false"></script>
```

I set up the map using a function I named makemap. It has two parameters: two decimal numbers that represent the latitude and longitude values:

```
function makemap(mylat, mylong)
```

The global variables zoomlevel, holding a number from 0 to 18, and xmarker, holding the address of an image file, are set before the function makemap is invoked.

The code to bring in a map is an invocation of the google.maps.Map constructor method. It takes two parameters. The first is the location in the HTML document where the map is to appear. I set up a div with ID place in the body of the document:

```
<div id="place" style="float: left;width:50%; height:400px"></div>
```

The second parameter is an associative array. The following three statements set up the location at which the map is centered as a Google Maps latitude/longitude object, create the associative array myOptions, and invoke the Map constructor:

```
blatlng = new google.maps.LatLng(mylat,mylong);
myOptions = {
        zoom: zoomlevel,
        center: blatlng,
            mapTypeId: google.maps.MapTypeId.ROADMAP
        };
map = new google.maps.Map(document.getElementById("place"), myOptions);
```

For completeness sake, here are screenshots with other settings for the map type. These are TERRAIN, HYBRID, and SATELLITE. Figure 5-13 shows the results of requesting the setting showing the terrain—that is, colors indicating elevations, water, park, and human-constructed areas:

```
mapTypeId: google.maps.MapTypeId.TERRAIN
```

Click on map.

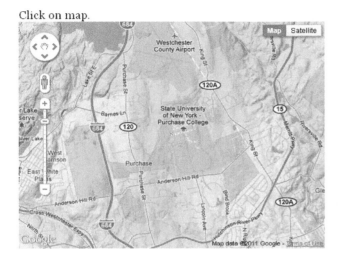

Title will be placed here.

Figure 5-13. *TERRAIN map type*

Figure 5-14 shows the results of requesting the HYBRID view, combining satellite and road map imagery.

```
mapTypeId: google.maps.MapTypeId.HYBRID
```

Click on map.

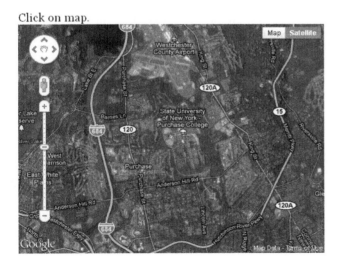

Title will be placed here.

Figure 5-14. *HYBRID map type*

By the way, the hybrid map is what is produced by clicking the Satellite option on the interface. Figure 5-15 shows the results of requesting SATELLITE images.

```
mapTypeId: google.maps.MapTypeId.SATELLITE
```

Click on map.

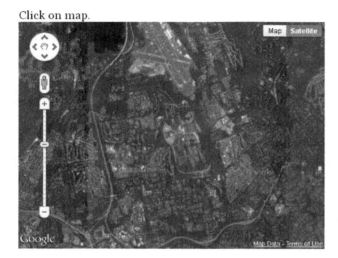

Title will be placed here.

Figure 5-15. SATELLITE map type

Lastly, you may have an application in which you do not want the viewer to change the map. You can prevent the user from changing the map by disabling the default interface with the use of an additional option in the `myOptions` array. Note the comma after ROADMAP.

```
mapTypeId: google.maps.MapTypeId.ROADMAP,
disableDefaultUI: true
```

Figure 5-16 shows the results.

Click on map.

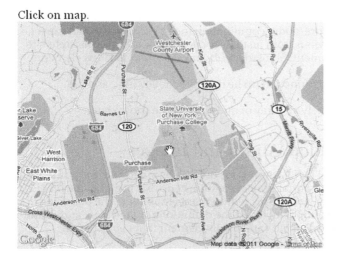

Title will be placed here.

Figure 5-16. *Map interface removed*

There are two more operations for makemap to carry out. A custom marker is placed on the map at the indicated center location and event handling is set up for clicking the map:

```
marker = new google.maps.Marker({
        position: blatlng,
        title: "center",
        icon: xmarker,
      map: map });
listener = google.maps.event.addListener(map, 'click', function(event) {
                    checkit(event.latLng);
                    });
```

The xmarker value references an Image object that has its src set to an external file named x1.png.

Project Content

The portal projects all present media connected to a map location. My projects use three types of media: video, picture, and pictureaudio. Note: these are my terms for the three types I have chosen to include in the project. The content of the portal projects is specified using an array I named content. Each element of the array is itself an array five or six elements. The first four elements are the same for all the types: the latitude, longitude, title, and type. The fifth or the fifth and the sixth point to the specific media elements. The array

```
content = [
[41.19991,-73.72353,"Esther at home","pictureaudio",esther,aud1],
[41.05079,-73.70448,"Lego robot ","video",vid1],
[40.68992,-74.04460,"Fire works ","video",vid2],
[41.8442,-89.480,"Aviva in Dixon","picture",aviva]
];
```

specifies four locations, starting with a picture/audio combination, followed by two videos, followed by one picture. The element in the array for the picture/audio combination includes, as you would expect, two additional pieces of information. It is not obvious from just this section of code, but esther refers to an Image element and aud1 refers to an audio element. Similarly, vid1 and vid2 refer to video elements, and aviva refers to another Image element.

The content array is referenced by the checkit function (to be described following), and the appropriate media are presented.

The quiz project has additional content, namely an array of questions, to be shown later.

Presentation and Removal of Video, Audio and Images

I assume you have a basic understanding of the HTML5 features for presenting video and audio and for drawing images from files on the canvas. The map portal projects require code that presents the media on demand (i.e., making the media appear and go away). This requirement is similar to the bouncing video of Chapter 3. In the basic mapvideos application, I included the definitions of the video, audio, and canvas elements in the body element of the document, all within a div element that I specified as floating to the right:

```
<div style="float: right;width:38%;height:400px">
<div id="answer">Title will be placed here.</div>
<p>   </p>
<video id="maze" preload="auto" controls="controls" width="400">
<source src="maze.mp4" type='video/mp4; codecs="avc1.42E01E, mp4a.40.2"'>
<source src="maze.theora.ogv" type='video/ogg; codecs="theora, vorbis"'>
<source src="maze.webmvp8.webm" type='video/webm; codec="vp8, vorbis"'>
Your browser does not accept the video tag.
</video>
<video id="fire" preload="auto" controls="controls">
<source src="sfire3.mp4" type='video/mp4; codecs="avc1.42E01E, mp4a.40.2"'>
<source src="sfire3.theora.ogv" type='video/ogg; codecs="theora, vorbis"'>
<source src="sfire3.webmvp8.webm" type='video/webm; codec="vp8, vorbis"'>
Your browser does not accept the video tag.
</video>
<audio id="mpiano" controls="controls" preload="preload">
<source src="estherT.ogg" type="audio/ogg" />
<source src="estherT.mp3" type="audio/mpeg" />
<source src="estherT.wav" type="audio/wav" />
</audio>
<canvas id="canvas" width="300" height="300" >
Your browser doesn't recognize canvas
</canvas>
</div>
```

Notice that I did not use the loop attribute in the <video> tag, nor did I put in a call to addEventListener to a function to restart the video, based on the assumption that loop is not recognized by some browsers. This is because the video controls are visible, and if the viewer wants to replay the video, he or she can do it.Similarly, the viewer can re-play the audio clip.

In the style element, I put directives to make all video not display, and for the positioning to be relative:

```
video {display:none; position:relative;
}
audio {display:none; position:relative;}
```

I did not have to do something analogous for the canvas. The canvas is always present, but if nothing has been drawn on it or it has been cleared, then nothing is visible.

The critical coding for presenting the media is in a `switch` statement within the `checkit` function. The `bestyet` variable holds the index of the element in the `content` array that is the closest to the location where the viewer/player clicked the map. If it has been determined to be close enough, then it will proceed with displaying the picture and playing the video or audio.

```
switch (content[bestyet][3]) {
        case "video":
            answer.innerHTML=content[bestyet][2];
            v = content[bestyet][4];
            v.style.display="block";
            v.currentTime = 0;
            v.play();

            break;
        case "picture":
        case "pictureaudio":
            answer.innerHTML=content[bestyet][2];
            ctx.drawImage(content[bestyet][4],10,10);
            if (content[bestyet][3]=="picture") {
                    break;}
            else {
            audioel = content[bestyet][5];
            audioel.style.display="block";
            audioel.currentTime = 0;
            audioel.play();
            break;
            }

        }
```

Changing the display style to `"block"` has the effect of displaying the video or audio controls. Assigning 0 to the `currentTime` means that the video or audio will play from the start. You can make use of `currentTime` to produce other effects—for example, playing different parts of a long audio or video clip.

There is one more piece of coding that is required. This is removing the last-viewed content: stopping the video or audio, and stopping the display. The code to do this must take account of the chance that there is nothing to remove. The code is

```
            if (v != undefined) {
        v.pause();
        v.style.display = "none";
    }
    if (audioel != undefined) {
        audioel.pause();
        audioel.style.display = "none";
    }
     ctx.clearRect(0,0,300,300);
```

Note that there is no harm in clearing the canvas even if there was nothing drawn on it. There would be an error in the statement **v.pause();** if **v** was not set. For the quiz project, I put this code into its own function, which I named **eraseold**, because removing the old material needs to be done at two different places in the code.

Distances and Tolerances

The calculation of distance between two latitude/longitude points was described in the previous chapter. The issue to be explained here concerns how to make comparisons of distances. For the portal application, I need to write code to determine the location specified in the **content** array that is closest to the position the viewer clicked. I do this using a **for** loop. As is typical in these "best so far" calculations, I start off the process by computing the distance to the 0th (i.e., the first) element in the **content** array. This is the best so far. The **for** loop then proceeds, starting with index 1.

```
function checkit(clatlng) {
      var i;
      var latlnga =new google.maps.LatLng(content[0][0],content[0][1]);
      var bestyet = 0;
      var closestdistance = dist(clatlng,latlnga);
      var distance;
      for (i=1;i<content.length;i++) {
            latlnga = new google.maps.LatLng(content[i][0],content[i][1]);
            distance = dist(clatlng,latlnga);
            if (distance < closestdistance) {
                  closestdistance = distance;
                  bestyet = i;
            }
      }
```

When the **for** loop is complete, **bestyet** holds the index to the best yet, meaning the closest, and **closestdisatnce** holds the distance to that element, which has been determined to be the closest (smallest) distance.

I then need to write code that checks if that element—the one with index named in **bestyet**—is close enough to proceed. In gaming and other applications, the term *tolerance* or *margin* are used. You can't expect a person to click exactly on a location. That is not possible when the units are pixels, and it definitely isn't possible when the units are latitude and longitude and the exact point may not be available to the user under the current zoom level. The variable **maxdistance** holds the value that I choose to use for this test. Here is the rest of the **checkit** function (without repeating the whole **switch** statement):

```
      if (distance < maxdistance) {
      marker = new google.maps.Marker({
            position: clatlng,
            title: content[bestyet][2],
            icon: xmarker,
            map: map });
      switch (content[bestyet][3]) {
         ...
      }
      }
```

```
        else {
                answer.innerHTML="Not close enough to any [new] target";
        }

}
```

Regular Expressions

Regular expressions are a powerful facility for describing patterns of character strings (text) for checking and for manipulation. It is a whole language for specifying patterns. For example, to give you a flavor of this large topic, the pattern

`/^5[1-5]\d{2}-?\d{4}-?\d{4}-?\d{4}$/`

can be used detect MasterCard numbers. These numbers start with 51 to 55, followed by two more digits, and then three groups of four digits. This pattern accepts the dashes, but does not require them. The ^ symbol means the pattern must be present at the start of the string, and the $ means it must go to the end of the string. The forward slashes (/) are delimiters for the pattern and the backslashes are escape characters. Interpreting this pattern starting at the start goes as follows:

- ^: Start at the start of the string.

- 5: Pattern must contain a 5.

- [1-5]: Pattern must contain one of the numbers 1, 2, 3, 4, or 5.

- \d{2}: Pattern must contain exactly two digits.

- -?: Pattern must contain 0 or 1 -.

- \d{4}: Pattern must contain exactly four digits.

- -?: Pattern must contain 0 or 1 -.

- \d{4}: Pattern must contain exactly four digits.

- -?: Pattern must contain 0 or 1 -.

- \d{4}: Pattern must contain exactly four digits.

- $: End of string.

MasterCard numbers must obey other rules as well, and you can do the research to find out how to verify them further. Don't worry, we'll be using a much simpler regular expression (also known as a *regex*) than that.

The use of regular expressions predates HTML. Regular expressions can be used in forms to specify the format of the input. For this application, we will use the `replace` method for strings to find all instances of a specific small piece of text within a long string and replace it with something else. One of the statements I use is

`videomarkup = videomarkup.replace(/XXXX/g,name);`

What this does is find all occurrences (this is what the g does) of the string XXXX and replace them with the value of the variable name.

I could and probably should have made even more use of regular expressions to verify the data defining the content of the applications. Maybe that's something you want to experiment with in your own applications.

External Script File

For this project and the one in the previous chapter, I demonstrated the use of a script element to bring in an external script file, namely the Google Maps API. You can also use this facility to bring in your own external file. My goal is to put all the specific content relating to my project in its own file. For the `mapmediabase` case, this is a file I named `mediacontent.js`. It follows in its entirety:

```
var base= [41.04796,-73.70539,"Purchase College/SUNY"];
var zoomlevel = 13;
var precontent = [
    [41.19991,-73.72353,"Esther at home","pictureaudio","estherT","esther.jpg"],
    [41.05079,-73.70448,"Lego robot ","video","maze"],
    [40.68992,-74.04460,"Fire works ","video","sfire3"],
    [41.8442,-89.480,"Aviva in Dixon","picture","avivadixon.jpg"]
    ];
var maxdistance = 5;
```

■ **Tip**   The next step could be putting the information on the media content in a database.

The `base`, `zoomlevel`, and `maxdistance` variables are all what they seem. The base is the initial center point for the map. The zoom level specifies the initial zoom. I say *initial* because the user can use the Google Maps controls to pan or zoom in or out. The `maxdistance` is the number I use to check if the user clicks close enough to one of the locations. You will need to determine what the appropriate distance is for your application.

I simply moved the variable declarations from the other document into what will be the external, content-specific document. I must admit that I forgot about `zoomlevel` and `maxdistance`, and only moved them after thinking about what other projects might be. For example, you may decide to build a project with a very different zoom level. Maybe you want your player to distinguish at the city block level, in which case the maximum distance might be 1 kilometer or less.

The `precontent` array resembles but is not the same as the `content` array. What is different is that the fields that now have `"estherT"`, `"esther.jpg"`, `"maze"`, `"sfire3"`, and `"avivadixon.jpg"` are used to create HTML5 elements or JavaScript elements. Once these are created, then references can be inserted in a `content` array. For this to work, I needed to change the names of the video and the audio files so that the video element coding and the audio element coding all fit a pattern.

For the mapmediaquiz application, I needed to add the questions. I could have added another element to the inner arrays of the `precontent` array, but decided against since that would require changes in the coding. Instead, I defined another array called `questions`. This is called *parallel structures* and is a common technique.

■ **Note**   At some point, the right decision may be to stop using straight JavaScript arrays, including the use of parallel structures, and make use of XML or a database. I didn't think it was called for in this application, but I could be wrong. Note that the use of databases does provide a way to hide the data.

```
var base= [41.04796,-73.70539,"Purchase College/SUNY"];
var zoomlevel = 13;
var precontent = [
    [41.19991,-73.72353,"Esther at home","pictureaudio","estherT","esther.jpg"],
    [41.05079,-73.70448,"Lego robot ","video","maze"],
    [40.68992,-74.04460,"Fire works ","video","sfire3"],
    [41.8442,-89.480,"Aviva in Dixon","picture","avivadixon.jpg"]
    ];
var questions = [
  "Where does Grandma Esther live?",
  "Show the Lego robot navigating a maze.",
  "Where are great fireworks?",
  "Find where Aviva played the flute."
];
var maxdistance = 10;
```

The external scripts are brought into the main document using a script element. For the mapmediabase program, this is

```
<script type="text/javascript" src="mediacontent.js"> </script>
```

and for mapmediaquiz, this is

```
<script type="text/javascript" src="mediaquizcontent.js"> </script>
```

Now I will explain how to use the precontent information to build what is required to make the projects work.

Dynamic Creation of HTML5 Markup and Positioning

The external script statements bring in the information for the base and the quiz applications. Now is the time to explain how the information is used. In both cases, the init function will invoke a function I named loadcontent. This function calls makemap to make a map at the indicated base location.

```
makemap(base[0],base[1]);
```

The content array starts off as an empty array.

```
var content = [];
```

By the way, this is different from

```
var content;
```

Your code needs to make content an array.

It then uses a for loop to iterate over all the elements of precontent. The start of the for loop adds the *i*th element of precontent to the content array.

```
for (var i=0;i<precontent.length;i++) {
                content.push(precontent[i]);
                name = precontent[i][4];
```

The next line is the header of a `switch` statement using as the condition the element of the inner arrays that indicates the type.

```
switch (precontent[i][3]) {
```

For `video` and `pictureaudio`, the code creates a div element and positions it so that it floats to the right. It then places inside the div element the right markup for video or audio. What is that markup? I have what I will describe as dummy strings that have XXXX where the actual names of the video or audio files would go. These strings are

```
var videotext1 = "<video id=\"XXXX\" preload=\"auto\" controls=\"controls\"↵
 width=\"400\"><source src=\"XXXX.mp4\" type=\'video/mp4; codecs=\"avc1.42E01E,↵
 mp4a.40.2\"\'>";
var videotext2="<source src=\"XXXX.theora.ogv\" type=\'video/ogg; codecs=\"theora,↵
 vorbis\"\'><source src=\"XXXX.webmvp8.webm\" type=\'video/webm; codec=\"vp8, vorbis\"\'>";
var videotext3="Your browser does not accept the video tag.</video>";
var audiotext1="<audio id=\"XXXX\" controls=\"controls\" preload=\"preload\"><source↵
 src=\"XXXX.ogg\" type=\"audio/ogg\" />";
var audiotext2="<source src=\"XXXX.mp3\" type=\"audio/mpeg\" /><source src=\"XXXX.wav\"↵
 type=\"audio/wav\" /></audio>";
```

I divided the strings into sets of three and two just to make it easier for me to check. Notice the use of the backslash (\) It tells JavaScript to use the next symbol as is, and not interpret it as a special operator for regular expressions. This is how the quotation marks inside the screen get carried over to be part of the HTML.

My approach required that I make sure that the names of the video and audio files follow this pattern. This meant that the mp4 files all needed to contain just the name and no internal dots.

I write code using the regular expression function replace to take information out of the `precontent` array and put it in the strings in as many places as necessary. The `switch` statement in its entirety is

```
switch (precontent[i][3]) {
                case "video":
                        divelement= document.createElement("div");
                        divelement.style = "float: right;width:30%;";
                        videomarkup = videotext1+videotext2+videotext3;
                        videomarkup = videomarkup.replace(/XXXX/g,name);
                        divelement.innerHTML = videomarkup;
                        document.body.appendChild(divelement);
                        videoelementreference = document.getElementById(name);
                        content[i][4] = videoelementreference;
                        break;
                case "pictureaudio":
                        divelement = document.createElement("div");
                        divelement.style = "float: right;width:30%;";
                        audiomarkup = audiotext1+audiotext2;
                        audiomarkup = audiomarkup.replace(/XXXX/g,name);
                        divelement.innerHTML = audiomarkup;
                        document.body.appendChild(divelement);
                        audioreference = document.getElementById(name);
```

```
                savedimagefilename = content[i][5];
                content[i][5] = audioreference;
                imageobj = new Image();
                imageobj.src= savedimagefilename;
                content[i][4] = imageobj;
                break;
        case "picture":
                imageobj = new Image();
                imageobj.src= precontent[i][4];
                content[i][4] = imageobj;
                break;
        }
```

Notice that the `pictureaudio` case does some juggling to create the content element with references to the newly created audio element and the Image element.

However, this was not quite enough to ensure that the video and audio end up on the right-hand side for all browsers. That is, it worked for some but not others. I decided to position the audio and video exactly—that is, in absolute terms. This required the following CSS in the style element for all video and audio elements:

```
video {display:none; position:absolute; top: 60px; right: 20px; }
audio {display:none; position:absolute; top: 60px; right: 20px;}
```

The position of the audio is for the audio controls.

Hint Button

You can tell from my coding that I was ambivalent about whether to provide a hint or help a player who had given up. In the body element, I included

```
<button onClick="giveup();">Hint? </button>
```

The `giveup` function creates a new map. That is, it uses the `makemap` function to construct access to a different Google Map in the same place. It also erases the old media and puts directions into the answer element.

```
function giveup() {
        makemap(content[nextquestion][0],content[nextquestion][1]);
        eraseold();
        answer.innerHTML="Click at red x to finish this question.";
}
```

Shuffling

I added a shuffle step to mix up the order of questions. More exactly, the program shuffles the `content` array and the `questions` array, keeping the items in parallel. The shuffle algorithm I used is the same Fisher-Yates algorithm demonstrated in Chapter 10 of *The Essential Guide to HTML5*. See also `http://eli.thegreenplace.net/2010/05/28/the-intuition-behind-fisher-yates-shuffling/` for an explanation on how the shuffling works.

This algorithm determines a random location for each element. Since I need to keep the two arrays in parallel, the same swap operation must be made for each array. In the code that follows, you see that it is determined that the s and i elements are to change locations. Two variables, hold and holdq, are the extra places used in the swap operation.

```
function shufflecontent() {
        var i=content.length-1;
        var s;
        var hold;
        var holdq;
        while(i>0) {
                s = Math.floor(Math.random()*(i+1));
                hold = content[s];
                content[s]=content[i];
                content[i] = hold;
                holdq = questions[s];
                questions[s]=questions[i];
                questions[i] = holdq;
                i--;
        }
}
```

With this explanation of the various parts, I'll go on in the next section to describe the three applications.

Building the Application and Making It Your Own

The first and critical step in making the application your own is to decide on the content. You can choose to not implement the first application, mapvideos, which has the content hard-coded, so to speak, with all the other coding. Again, I included it because I wrote it first and it is the easiest to understand. I strongly believe that most people would develop something like it, and then possibly decide to separate content from coding. You may go straight to mapmediabase or mapmediaquiz if you like.

The Mapvideos Application

The mapvideos application sets up the combination of Google Maps functionality with HTML5 coding for video, audio, and pictures on canvas. The canvas is not on top of the map. A quick summary of the application follows:

1. init: Performs initialization, including invoking makemap for bringing in the map. The init function constructs the content array using data constructed as references to elements in the body.

2. makemap: Brings in a map and sets up event handling, including the call to checkit.

3. checkit: Compares the clicked location with the locations described in the content array. If one is close enough, then the associated media is shown and played.

4. dist: Computes the distance between two locations.

Table 5-2 outlines the functions in the mapvideos project. The function table describing the invoked/called by and calling relationships is similar for all the applications.

Table 5-2. *Functions in the Mapvideos Portal Project*

Function	Invoked/Called By	Calls
init	Invoked by action of the onLoad attribute in the <body> tag	makemap
makemap	Invoked by init	
checkit	Invoked by addListener call in makemap	dist
dist	Invoked by checkit	

Table 5-3 shows the code for the original portal application, mapvideos.html.

Table 5-3. *Complete Code for the Mapvideos Portal Application*

Code Line	Description
`<!DOCTYPE html>`	Doctype for HTML5
`<html>`	html tag
`<head>`	Head tag
`<title>Clickable map </title>`	Complete title element
`<meta charset="UTF-8">`	Meta tag, standard for HTML5
`<style>`	Style tag
`header {font-family:Georgia, "Times New Roman",serif;`	Set styling for the header, a semantic element; the font family makes Georgia the first choice, with Times New Roman a fallback, and the default serif the next fallback choice of fonts
`font-size:20px;`	Fairly big font
`display:block;`	Set line breaks before and afterward

`}`	Close style directive
`video {display:none; position:relative; }`	Style directive for video
`audio {display:none; position:relative;}`	Style directive for audio; note that this is for the controls
`</style>`	Closing style tag
`<script type="text/javascript" charset="UTF-8" src="http://maps.google.com/maps/api/js?sensor= false"></script>`	Script element bringing in Google Maps API
`<script type="text/javascript" charset="UTF-8">`	Starting script tag
`var maxdistance = 5;`	Set `maxdistance` to be 5, a value I decided was appropriate; a click needed to be within 5 kilometers of one of the targets to be considered close enough
`var listener;`	Placeholder for call of `addListener`
`var map;`	Variable holding the current map
`var myOptions;`	Variable for the associative array holding the options for a call to the `Map` constructor
`var ctx;`	Variable holding the context of the canvas
`var blatlng;`	Variable holding the constructed latitude/longitude object for the base location
`var esther = new Image();`	Variable holding an Image object
`esther.src = "esther.jpg";`	Set the `src` of this Image object to the file address
`var aviva = new Image();`	Variable holding an Image object
`aviva.src = "avivadixon.jpg";`	Set the `src` of this Image object to the file address
`var vid1;`	Set in `init` to one of the video elements
`var vid2;`	Set in `init` to one of the video elements

`var aud1;`	Set in `init` to the audio element
`var content;`	Declared here as global variable; will be set in `init`
`var answer;`	Will be set in `init` to reference a div in the body
`var v;`	reference to current (last) video
`var audioel;`	Reference to current (last) audio
`var base= [41.04796,-73.70539,` `"Purchase College/SUNY"];`	Variable set to the base for my project
`function init() {`	Function header for `init`

`  ctx =`
`document.getElementById("canvas").getContext('2d`
`');`
	Set `ctx` for use in drawing on canvas

`  makemap(base[0],base[1]);`	Invoke `makemap`
`  answer = document.getElementById("answer");`	Set answer
`  vid1 = document.getElementById("maze");`	Set `vid1` for one of the video elements
`    vid2 = document.getElementById("fire");`	Set `vid2` for the other video element
`  aud1 = document.getElementById("mpiano");`	Set `aud1` for the audio element
`  content = [`	Set the setting of the `content` array
`  [41.19991,-73.72353,"Esther at` `home","pictureaudio",esther,aud1],`	Info for the Esther picture audio combination
`  [41.05079,-73.70448,"Lego robot` `","video",vid1],`	Info for the Lego robot video
`  [40.68992,-74.04460,"Fire works` `","video",vid2],`	Info for the Fireworks video
`  [41.8442,-89.480,"Aviva in` `Dixon","picture",aviva]`	Info for the Aviva picture
`  ];`	End of `content` array

`}`	Close `init` function
`var xmarker = "x1.png";`	Set file address for marker on the map
`function makemap(mylat,mylong) {`	Header for `makemap` function; map to be centered (mylat,mylong)
`var marker;`	Holds the constructed marker
`blatlng = new google.maps.LatLng(mylat,mylong);`	Set the latitude/longitude object
`myOptions = {`	Start to set up the `options` array
`zoom: 13,`	Zoom set at constant, arrived at after experimenting
`center: blatlng,`	Center at blatlng
`mapTypeId: google.maps.MapTypeId.ROADMAP`	Roadmap type
`};`	Close myOptions array
`map = new google.maps.Map(document.getElementById("place"), myOptions);`	Invoke constructor to bring in the Google Maps

`marker = new google.maps.Marker({`
`          position: blatlng,`
`          title: "center",`
`          icon: xmarker,`
`          map: map });`
	Mark center

`listener = google.maps.event.addListener(map, 'click', function(event) {`	Set up event handling for clicking the map
`checkit(event.latLng);`	The function checkit is invoked with the latLng attribute of the event as the parameter
`});`	Close call to bring in map
`}`	Close `makemap` function
`function checkit(clatlng) {`	Header for `checkit` function
`var i;`	Used for indexing

`var latlnga =new` `google.maps.LatLng(content[0][0],content[0][1]);`	Build latitude/longitude object from first element of content
`var bestyet = 0;`	Will point to the index determined to be the best (closest) so far
`var closestdistance =` `dist(clatlng,latlnga);`	Calculate distance to the first element
`var distance;`	Used to hold distance
`for (i=1;i<content.length;i++) {`	Set up iteration over content, starting at the second (index = 1) element
`latlnga = new` `google.maps.LatLng(content[i][0],content[i][1]);`	Build latitude/longitude object
`distance =` `dist(clatlng,latlnga);`	Calculate distance
`if (distance < closestdistance)` `{`	Compare to the closest so far; if this one is less. . .
`closestdistance =` `distance;`	. . . then replace previous candidate for closest distance . . .
`bestyet = i;`	. . .. and previous index
`}`	Close *if* true clause
`}`	Close *for* loop
`distance =` `Math.floor((closestdistance+.005)*100)/100;`	Set distance; note that formatting not needed at this stage; may choose to use in the future
`if (v != undefined) {`	Check if there was a previous video
`v.pause();`	Pause it
`v.style.display = "none";`	Remove from display
`}`	Close if previous video clause
`if (audioel != undefined) {`	Check if previous audio

`audioel.pause();`	Pause it
`audioel.style.display = "none";`	Erase controls for last audio played
`}`	Close `if` audio clause
`ctx.clearRect(0,0,300,300);`	Clear canvas
`if (distance < maxdistance) {`	Is this distance close enough?

`marker = new google.maps.Marker({`
`    position: clatlng,`
`    title: content[bestyet][2],`
`    icon: xmarker,`
`    map: map });`
	Mark the target position on the map; note that this is the target location, not the click location

`switch (content[bestyet][3]) {`	Determine what type of media this is
`case "video":`	For `video`
`answer.innerHTML=content[bestyet][2];`	Display the title
`v = content[bestyet][4];`	Set `v` to be the video
`v.style.display="block";`	Make the video element visible (The previous setting of style.display was "none".)
`v.currentTime = 0;`	Set the video time to zero to start playback at the beginning; this restarts the video, just in case it has starting playing before
`v.play();`	Play the video
`break;`	Leave the `switch` statement
`case "picture":`	For `picture`
`case "pictureaudio":`	For `pictureaudio`
`answer.innerHTML=content[bestyet][2];`	Display the title
`ctx.drawImage(content[bestyet][4],10,10);`	Draw the image on the canvas

`if` `(content[bestyet][3]=="picture") {`	If it is picture . . .
`break;}`	. . . leave the switch
`else {`	Else (for the picture/audio combination)
`audioel = content[bestyet][5];`	Set `audioel` to be the audio element
`audioel.style.display="block";`	Display the audio—that is, the controls
`audioel.currentTime = 0;`	Set time to zero
`audioel.play();`	Play the audio
`break;`	Leave the switch
`}`	Close the `picture` or `pictureaudio` clause
`}`	Close the switch
`}`	Close the `if close enough` clause
`else {`	Else
`answer.innerHTML="Not close` `enough to any [new] target";`	Display message that click was not close enough to anything
`}`	Close clause
`}`	Close `checkit` function
`function dist(point1, point2) {`	Header for `dist`-between-two-points function
`var R = 6371; // km`	Factor used for kilometers (the radius of the earth)
`// var R =  3959; // miles`	Comment in code; leave in just in case you want to switch to miles
`var lat1 = point1.lat()*Math.PI/180;`	Change to radians
`var lat2 = point2.lat()*Math.PI/180 ;`	Change to radians
`var lon1 = point1.lng()*Math.PI/180;`	Change to radians

`var lon2 = point2.lng()*Math.PI/180;`	Change to radians
`var d = Math.acos(Math.sin(lat1)*Math.sin(lat2)` `+` `Math.cos(lat1)*Math.cos(lat2) *` `Math.cos(lon2-lon1)) * R;`	Calculation based on spherical law of cosines
`return d;`	Return result
`}`	Close `dist` function
`</script>`	Closing script tag
`</head>`	Closing head tag
`<body onLoad="init();">`	Body tag, invoked `init`
`<header id="header">Click on map.</header>`	Header for the page
`<div id="place" style="float: left;width:60%;height:400px"></div>`	Set up div to float to the left; this will be the place for the map
`<div style="float: right;width:38%;height:400px">`	Set up div to float to the right; it holds the answer and the media (video, audio, and canvas)
`<div id="answer">Title will be placed here.</div>`	Place for the titles (i.e., text about the location and the media)
`<p> </p>`	Spacing
`<video id="maze" preload="auto" controls="controls" width="400">`	Video tag
`<source src="maze.mp4" type='video/mp4; codecs="avc1.42E01E, mp4a.40.2"'>`	Possible source
`<source src="maze.theora.ogv" type='video/ogg; codecs="theora, vorbis"'>`	Possible source
`<source src="maze.webmvp8.webm" type='video/webm; codec="vp8, vorbis"'>`	Possible source
`Your browser does not accept the video tag.`	Standard text for noncompliant browsers
`</video>`	Closing video tag

`<video id="fire" preload="auto" controls="controls">`	Video tag
`<source src="sfire3.mp4" type='video/mp4; codecs="avc1.42E01E, mp4a.40.2"'>`	Possible source
`<source src="sfire3.theora.ogv" type='video/ogg; codecs="theora, vorbis"'>`	Possible source
`<source src="sfire3.webmvp8.webm" type='video/webm; codec="vp8, vorbis"'>`	Possible source
`Your browser does not accept the video tag.`	Standard text for noncompliant browsers
`</video>`	Closing video tag
`<audio id="mpiano" controls="controls" preload="preload">`	Audio tag
`<source src="estherT.ogg" type="audio/ogg" />`	Possible source
`<source src="estherT.mp3" type="audio/mpeg" />`	Possible source
`<source src="estherT.wav" type="audio/wav" />`	Possible source
`</audio>`	Closing tag
`<canvas id="canvas" width="300" height="300" >`	Canvas tag
`Your browser doesn't recognize canvas`	Standard text for noncompliant browsers
`</canvas>`	Closing canvas tag
`</div>`	Closes div that floated from the right
`</body>`	Closing body tag
`</html>`	Closing html tag

The Mapmediabase Application

The next application, `mapmediabase.html`, recreates the first application, but uses a separate file for the content. You can easily make this one your own by changing the content. You need to obtain the latitude/longitude coordinates for your locations. To do so, you can use the `mapspotlight.html` application covered in the last chapter, you can use Google Maps directly, you can use Wolfram Alpha, or you can look them up in an atlas. A quick summary of the application follows:

1. `init`: Performs initialization, including the call to `loadcontent`.

2. `loadcontent`: Uses the variables, most significantly the `precontent` array included in the external script element, to create new markup for the media. It also invokes `makemap`.

3. `makemap`: Brings in the map and sets up event handling, including the call to `checkit`.

4. `checkit`: Compares the clicked location with the locations described in the `content` array. If one is close enough, then the associated media is shown and played.

5. `dist`: Computes the distance between two locations.

Table 5-4 outlines the functions in the second portal application. The function table describing the invoked/called by and calling relationships for the `mapmediabase.html` application is similar for all the applications.

Table 5-4. *Functions in the Second Portal Application*

Function	Invoked/Called By	Calls
init	Invoked by action of the onLoad attribute in the <body> tag	makemap
makemap	Invoked by init	
checkit	Invoked by addListener call in makemap	dist
dist	Invoked by checkit	
loadcontent	Invoked by init	

Table 5-5 shows the code for the second portal application, named `mapmediabase.html`. Please look back at the "External Script File" section to see the code (all the variable declarations) for the contents of `mediacontent.js`.

Table 5-5. *Complete Code for the Second Portal Application*

Code Line	Description
`<!DOCTYPE html>`	
`<html>`	
`<head>`	
`<title>Clickable map </title>`	
`<meta charset="UTF-8">`	
`<style>`	
`header {font-family:Georgia,"Times New Roman",serif;`	
`font-size:20px;`	
`display:block;`	
`}`	
`video {display:none; position:absolute; top: 60px; right: 20px; }`	Required to get video to be on the right
`audio {display:none; position:absolute; top: 60px; right: 20px;}`	Required to get audio controls to be on the right
`canvas {position:relative; top:60px}`	
`#answer {position:relative; font-family:Georgia, "Times New Roman", Times, serif; font-size:16px;}`	
`</style>`	
`<script type="text/javascript" charset="UTF-8" src="http://maps.google.com/maps/api/js?sensor=false"> </script>`	
`<script type="text/javascript" src="mediacontent.js"> </script>`	Bring in the specific content
`<script type="text/javascript" charset="UTF-8">`	

Code Line	Description
`var listener;`	
`var map;`	
`var myOptions;`	
`var ctx;`	
`var blatlng;`	
`var content = [];`	
`var answer;`	
`var v;`	
`var audioel;`	
`var videotext1 = "<video id=\"XXXX\" preload=\"auto\" controls=\"controls\" width=\"400\"><source src=\"XXXX.mp4\" type=\'video/mp4; codecs=\"avc1.42E01E, mp4a.40.2\"\'>";`	The first dummy (template) text to be used to create markup for video element
`var videotext2="<source src=\"XXXX.theora.ogv\" type=\'video/ogg; codecs=\"theora, vorbis\"\'><source src=\"XXXX.webmvp8.webm\" type=\'video/webm; codec=\"vp8, vorbis\"\'>";`	The second piece of dummy text to be used to create markup for video element
`var videotext3="Your browser does not accept the video tag.</video>";`	The third piece of dummy text to be used to create markup for video element
`var audiotext1="<audio id=\"XXXX\" controls=\"controls\" preload=\"preload\"><source src=\"XXXX.ogg\" type=\"audio/ogg\" />";`	The first piece of dummy text to be used to create markup for audio element
`var audiotext2="<source src=\"XXXX.mp3\" type=\"audio/mpeg\" /><source src=\"XXXX.wav\" type=\"audio/wav\" /></audio>";`	The second piece of dummy text to be used to create markup for audio element
`function init() {`	
`  ctx = document.getElementById("canvas").getContext('2d');`	
`    answer = document.getElementById("answer");`	

Code Line	Description
`loadcontent();`	Invoke `loadcontent` to perform the rest of the initialization
`}`	
`function loadcontent() {`	Header for `loadcontent` function
`var divelement;`	Used to hold dynamically created div
`makemap(base[0],base[1]);`	Bring in the map
`var videomarkup;`	Used to hold the text string for the video element HTML markup
`var videoelementreference;`	Used to hold the reference to the newly created video element
`var audiomarkup;`	Used to hold the text string for the audio element HTML markup
`var audioelementreference;`	Used to hold the reference to the newly created audio element
`var imageobj;`	Used to hold the newly created Image object
`var name;`	Used to hold the name
`var savedimagefilename;`	Needed to hold the image file name because slot in inner array is overwritten
`for (var i=0;i<precontent.length;i++) {`	Iterate over the precontent items
`content.push(precontent[i]);`	Add the item (itself an array) to the `content` array

Code Line	Description
`name = precontent[i][4];`	Extract the name
`switch (precontent[i][3]) {`	Switch over the different types (`video`, `picture`, `pictureaudio`)
`case "video":`	For the `video` case
`divelement= document.createElement("div");`	Create a new container div
`divelement.style = "float: right;width:30%;";`	Style it to float to the right (though this does not work in all browsers)
`videomarkup = videotext1+videotext2+videotext3;`	Create the whole HTML markup for video elements
`videomarkup = videomarkup.replace(/XXXX/g,name);`	Change **XXXX** to the name given in precontent
`divelement.innerHTML = videomarkup;`	Set the constructed text to be the HTML within the div
`document.body.appendChild(divelement);`	Add the div to the body
`videoelementreference = document.getElementById(name);`	Obtain a reference to the created video element
`content[i][4] = videoelementreference;`	Put this value into the `content` array
`break;`	Leave switch
`case "pictureaudio":`	For the `pictureaudio` case
`divelement = document.createElement("div");`	Create a new container div
`divelement.style = "float: right;width:30%;";`	Style it to float to the right (though this does not work in all browsers)
`audiomarkup = audiotext1+audiotext2;`	Create the whole HTML markup for audio elements

Code Line	Description
`audiomarkup = audiomarkup.replace(/XXXX/g,name);`	Change the XXXX to the name given in precontent
`divelement.innerHTML = audiomarkup;`	Set the constructed text to be the HTML within the div
`document.body.appendChild(divelement);`	Add the div to the body
`audioreference = document.getElementById(name);`	Obtain a reference to the created audio element
`savedimagefilename = content[i][5];`	Save the file name
`content[i][5] = audioreference;`	Overwrite that position to be the reference to the audio
`imageobj = new Image();`	Create a new Image object
`imageobj.src= savedimagefilename;`	Set its src to be the file name
`content[i][4] = imageobj;`	Set the content item to be the Image object
`break;`	Leave the switch
`case "picture":`	In the case of picture
`imageobj = new Image();`	Create a new Image object
`imageobj.src= precontent[i][4];`	Set its src to be the file name
`content[i][4] = imageobj;`	Set the content item to be the Image object
`break;`	Leave the switch (not strictly necessary, because it is the last one, but leave in just in case new media types are added)
`        }`	Close switch
`    }`	Close for loop
`}`	Close loadcontent function

Code Line	Description
`var xmarker = "x1.png";`	Image for marker on map
`function makemap(mylat,mylong) {`	
`    var marker;`	
`  blatlng = new google.maps.LatLng(mylat,mylong);`	
`myOptions = {`	
`        zoom: zoomlevel,`	Pick up this value from the external file
`    center: blatlng,`	
`    mapTypeId: google.maps.MapTypeId.ROADMAP,`	
`    };`	
`map = new google.maps.Map(document.getElementById("place"), myOptions);`	
`marker = new google.maps.Marker({`	
`    position: blatlng,`	
`    title: "center",`	
`    icon: xmarker,`	
`    map: map });`	
`    listener = google.maps.event.addListener(map, 'click', function(event) {`	
`    checkit(event.latLng);`	
`    });`	
`}`	
`function checkit(clatlng) {`	

Code Line	Description
`var i;`	
`var latlnga =new` `google.maps.LatLng(content[0][0],content[0][1]);`	
`var bestyet = 0;`	
`var closestdistance = dist(clatlng,latlnga);`	
`var distance;`	
`for (i=1;i<content.length;i++) {`	
`latlnga = new` `google.maps.LatLng(content[i][0],content[i][1]);`	
`distance = dist(clatlng,latlnga);`	
`if (distance < closestdistance) {`	
`closestdistance = distance;`	
`bestyet = i;`	
`}`	
`}`	
`distance = Math.floor((closestdistance+.005)*100)/100;`	
`if (distance<maxdistance) {`	

`marker = new google.maps.Marker({`
`        position: clatlng,`
`        title: content[bestyet][2],`
`        icon: xmarker,`
`        map: map });`	

`if (v != undefined) {`	
`v.pause();`	
`v.style.display = "none";`	

Code Line	Description
`}`	
`if (audioel != undefined) {`	
`audioel.pause();`	
`audioel.style.display = "none";`	
`}`	
`switch (content[bestyet][3]) {`	
`case "video":`	
`answer.innerHTML=content[bestyet][2];`	
`ctx.clearRect(0,0,300,300);`	
`v = content[bestyet][4];`	
`v.style.display="block";`	
`v.currentTime = 0;`	
`v.play();`	
`break;`	
`case "picture":`	
`case "pictureaudio":`	
`answer.innerHTML=content[bestyet][2];`	
`ctx.clearRect(0,0,300,300);`	
`ctx.drawImage(content[bestyet][4],10,10);`	
`if (content[bestyet][3]=="picture") {`	
`break;}`	
`else {`	

Code Line	Description
audioel = content[bestyet][5];	
audioel.style.display="block";	
audioel.currentTime = 0;	
audioel.play();	
break;	
}	
}	
}	
else {	
answer.innerHTML= "Not close enough to any [new] target.";	
}	
}	
function dist(point1, point2) {	
var R = 6371; // km	
// var R = 3959; // miles	
var lat1 = point1.lat()*Math.PI/180;	
var lat2 = point2.lat()*Math.PI/180 ;	
var lon1 = point1.lng()*Math.PI/180;	
var lon2 = point2.lng()*Math.PI/180;	
var d = Math.acos(Math.sin(lat1)*Math.sin(lat2) + Math.cos(lat1)*Math.cos(lat2) * Math.cos(lon2-lon1)) * R;	
return d;	

Code Line	Description
`}`	
`</script>`	
`</head>`	
`<body onLoad="init();">`	
`<header id="header">Click on map.</header>`	
`<div id="place" style="float: left;width:50%;` `height:400px"></div>`	
`<div style="float: right;width:30%;height:400px">`	
`<div id="answer">Title will be placed here.</div>`	
`<p> </p>`	
`<canvas id="canvas" width="300" height="300" >`	
`Your browser doesn't recognize canvas`	
`</canvas>`	
`</div>`	
`</body>`	
`</html>`	

The Quiz Application

The third and last application for this chapter was a quiz. The implementation was built on the second application. It makes use of an external script file. Look back at the "External Script File" section for the contents. A quick summary of the application follows:

1. init: Performs initialization, including the call to loadcontent.

2. loadcontent: Uses the variables, most significantly the **precontent** array included in the external script element, to create new markup for the media. It also invokes makemap. The **questions** array does not need any more work.

3. `makemap`: Brings in the map and sets up event handling, including the call to `checkit`.

4. `shufflecontent`: Shuffles the `content` and `questions` arrays (keeping them in correspondence).

5. `asknewquestion`: Displays the questions.

6. `checkit`: Compares the clicked location with the location for this question.

7. `dist`: Computes the distance between two locations.

8. `giveup`: Brings in a new map centered at the location for the current question.

9. `eraseold`: Removes any currently showing video, audio, or picture.

Table 5-6 outlines the functions in the quiz application. The function table describing the invoked/called by and calling relationships for the `mapmediabase.html` application is similar for all applications.

Table 5-6. *Functions in the Quiz Application*

Function	Invoked/Called By	Calls
init	Invoked by action of the onLoad attribute in the <body> tag	loadcontent, asknewquestion
makemap	Invoked by init	
checkit	Invoked by addListener call in makemap	dist, asknewquestion
dist	Invoked by checkit	
loadcontent	Invoked by init	
asknewquestion	Invoked by init and checkit	
eraseold	Invoked by checkit and giveup	
giveup	Invoked by action of button	eraseold

Table 5-7 shows the code for the quiz application, with comments for new or changed statements.

Table 5-7. *Include Table Caption*

Code Line	Description
`<!DOCTYPE html>`	
`<html>`	
`<head>`	
`<title>Map Quiz </title>`	
`<meta charset="UTF-8">`	
`<style>`	
`header {font-family:Georgia,"Times New Roman",serif;`	
`        font-size:20px;`	
`        display:block;`	
`}`	
`video {display:none; position:absolute; top: 60px;` `  right: 20px;`	
`}`	
`audio {display:none; position:absolute; top: 60px;` `  right: 20px;}`	
`canvas {position:relative; top:60px}`	
`#answer {position:relative; font-family:Georgia,` `  "Times New Roman", Times, serif; font-size:16px;}`	
`</style>`	

`<script type="text/javascript" charset="UTF-8"`
`src="http://maps.google.com/maps/api/js?sensor=false">`
`</script>`	

`<script type="text/javascript" src="mediaquizcontent.js">` `  </script>`	Bring in the content in `mediaquizcontent.js`

Code Line	Description
`<script type="text/javascript" charset="UTF-8">`	
`var listener;`	
`var map;`	
`var myOptions;`	
`var ctx;`	
`var blatlng;`	
`var content = [];`	
`var answer;`	
`var v;`	
`var audioel;`	
`var videotext1 = "<video id=\"XXXX\" preload=\"auto\" controls=\"controls\" width=\"400\"><source src=\"XXXX.mp4\" type=\'video/mp4; codecs=\"avc1.42E01E, mp4a.40.2\"\'>";`	
`var videotext2="<source src=\"XXXX.theora.ogv\" type=\'video/ogg; codecs=\"theora, vorbis\"\'><source src=\"XXXX.webmvp8.webm\" type=\'video/webm; codec=\"vp8, vorbis\"\'>";`	
`var videotext3="Your browser does not accept the video tag.</video>";`	
`var audiotext1="<audio id=\"XXXX\" controls=\"controls\" preload=\"preload\"><source src=\"XXXX.ogg\" type=\"audio/ogg\" />";`	
`var audiotext2="<source src=\"XXXX.mp3\" type=\"audio/mpeg\" /><source src=\"XXXX.wav\" type=\"audio/wav\" /></audio>";`	
`var nextquestion = -1;`	The question counter needs to start before the 0th one
`function init() {`	

Code Line	Description
`ctx = document.getElementById("canvas").getContext('2d');`	
`answer = document.getElementById("answer");`	
`header = document.getElementById("header");`	
`loadcontent();`	
`shufflecontent();`	Invoke function to shuffle order of questions
`asknewquestion();`	Invoke function to ask question, thus starting off the quiz
`}`	
`function shufflecontent() {`	Header for shufflecontent function; two arrays will be shuffled
`var i=content.length-1;`	Start off at end
`var s;`	Hold the randomly designated spot
`var hold;`	For holding the content element, itself an array
`var holdq;`	For holding the question element
`while(i>0) {`	Start at the end and work down to zero
`s = Math.floor(Math.random()*(i+1));`	Pick a random position
`hold = content[s];`	Start with the content array; save the sth element
`content[s]=content[i];`	Swap in the ith element
`content[i] = hold;`	Put in the saved element

Code Line	Description
`holdq = questions[s];`	Now, working on the `questions` array, save the *s*th element
`questions[s]=questions[i];`	Swap in the *i*th element
`questions[i] = holdq;`	Put in the saved element
`i--;`	Decrement *i*
`}`	Close `while` loop
`}`	Close `shufflecontent` function
`function asknewquestion() {`	Header for `asknewquestion` function
`nextquestion++;`	Increment the counter
`if (nextquestion<questions.length) {`	If still more questions
`header.innerHTML=questions[nextquestion];`	Show question
`}`	Close the if-still-more-questions clause
`else {`	Else
`header.innerHTML="No more questions.";`	Display no more questions
`}`	Close `else` clause
`}`	Close `asknewquestion` function
`function loadcontent() {`	
`var divelement;`	
`makemap(base[0],base[1]);`	
`var videomarkup;`	
`var videoreference;`	

Code Line	Description
`var audiomarkup;`	
`var audioreference;`	
`var imageobj;`	
`var name;`	
`var savedimagefilename;`	
`for (var i=0;i<precontent.length;i++) {`	
`content.push(precontent[i]);`	
`name = precontent[i][4];`	
`switch (precontent[i][3]) {`	
`case "video":`	
`divelement= document.createElement("div");`	
`videomarkup = videotext1+videotext2+videotext3;`	
`videomarkup = videomarkup.replace(/XXXX/g,name);`	
`divelement.innerHTML = videomarkup;`	
`document.body.appendChild(divelement);`	
`videoreference = document.getElementById(name);`	
`content[i][4] = videoreference;`	
`break;`	
`case "pictureaudio":`	
`divelement = document.createElement("div");`	
`audiomarkup = audiotext1+audiotext2;`	
`audiomarkup = audiomarkup.replace(/XXXX/g,name);`	

Code Line	Description
`divelement.innerHTML = audiomarkup;`	
`document.body.appendChild(divelement);`	
`audioreference = document.getElementById(name);`	
`savedimagefilename = content[i][5];`	
`content[i][5] = audioreference;`	
`imageobj = new Image();`	
`imageobj.src= savedimagefilename;`	
`content[i][4] = imageobj;`	
`break;`	
`case "picture":`	
`imageobj = new Image();`	
`imageobj.src= precontent[i][4];`	
`content[i][4] = imageobj;`	
`break;`	
`}`	
`}`	
`}`	
`var xmarker = "x1.png";`	
`function makemap(mylat,mylong) {`	
`        var marker;`	
`  blatlng = new google.maps.LatLng(mylat,mylong);`	

Code Line	Description
`myOptions = {  zoom: zoomlevel,     center: blatlng,` `mapTypeId: google.maps.MapTypeId.ROADMAP     };`	
`map = new google.maps.Map(document.getElementById("place"),` `myOptions);`	

`marker = new google.maps.Marker({`
`position: blatlng, title: "center", icon: xmarker, map: map`
`});`	

`        listener = google.maps.event.addListener(map, 'click',` `function(event) {`	
`                    checkit(event.latLng);`	
`                });`	
`}`	
`function eraseold() {`	Header for **eraseold** function (same code as in previous example, but now in a function)
`    if (v != undefined) {`	Is there an old **v** defined?
`    v.pause();`	Pause it
`      v.style.display = "none";`	Remove from display
`    }`	Close clause
`    if (audioel != undefined) {`	Is there an old **audioel** defined?
`     audioel.pause();`	Pause it
`     audioel.style.display = "none";`	Erase controls for last audio played
`    }`	Close clause
`    ctx.clearRect(0,0,300,300);`	Clear canvas
`}`	Close **eraseold** function

Code Line	Description
`function checkit(clatlng) {`	
`        var latlnga =new google.maps.LatLng(content[nextquestion][0],content[nextquestion][1]);`	Build the latitude/longitude object for the answer to this question
`    var distance = dist(clatlng,latlnga);`	Compute distance
`  eraseold();`	Invoke the function to erase any media now on display
`if (distance<maxdistance) {`	Was the user's click close enough?
`        marker = new google.maps.Marker({position: latlnga, title: content[nextquestion][2], icon: xmarker, map: map });`	Mark the correct location; function continues as in previous applications
`    switch (content[nextquestion][3]) {`	
`      case "video":`	
`answer.innerHTML=content[nextquestion][2];`	
`        ctx.clearRect(0,0,300,300);`	
`        v = content[nextquestion][4];`	
`        v.style.display="block";`	
`        v.currentTime = 0;`	
`        v.play();`	
`        break;`	
`      case "picture":`	
`      case "pictureaudio":`	
`answer.innerHTML=content[nextquestion][2];`	
`        ctx.clearRect(0,0,300,300);`	

Code Line	Description
`ctx.drawImage(content[nextquestion][4],10,10);`	
`if (content[nextquestion][3]=="picture") {`	
`break;}`	
`else {`	
`audioel = content[nextquestion][5];`	
`audioel.style.display="block";`	
`audioel.currentTime = 0;`	
`audioel.play();`	
`break;`	
`}`	
`}`	
`asknewquestion();`	Ask a new question (only if the user's guess was close enough)
`}`	
`else {`	
`answer.innerHTML= "Not close enough to the answer.";`	
`}`	
`}`	
`function dist(point1, point2) {`	
`var R = 6371; // km`	
`// var R =  3959; // miles`	
`var lat1 = point1.lat()*Math.PI/180;`	

Code Line	Description
`var lat2 = point2.lat()*Math.PI/180 ;`	
`var lon1 = point1.lng()*Math.PI/180;`	
`var lon2 = point2.lng()*Math.PI/180;`	

`var d = Math.acos(Math.sin(lat1)*Math.sin(lat2) +`
`Math.cos(lat1)*Math.cos(lat2) *`
`Math.cos(lon2-lon1)) * R;`	

`return d;`	
`}`	
`function giveup() {`	Header for the `giveup` function
`makemap(content[nextquestion][0],content[nextquestion][1]);`	Bring in new map centered at the answer
`eraseold();`	Erase any old media
`answer.innerHTML="Click at red x to finish this question.";`	Display instructions since player needs to click to proceed; this gives the player a way to indicate that he or she has seen the new map
`}`	
`</script>`	
`</head>`	
`<body onLoad="init();">`	
`<header id="header">Click</header>`	
`<div id="place" style="float: left;width:50%;` `height:400px"></div>`	
`<button onClick="giveup();">Hint? </button>`	Button indicated need for help
`<div style="float: right;width:30%;height:400px">`	

Code Line	Description
`<div id="answer">Title will be placed here.</div>`	
`<p>  </p>`	
`<canvas id="canvas" width="300" height="300" >`	
`Your browser doesn't recognize canvas`	
`</canvas>`	
`</div>`	
`</body>`	
`</html>`	

Testing and Uploading the Application

I described three separate applications in this chapter. The `mapvideos.html` application consists of a single HTML file. The other two applications were each made up of two HTML files: one with the bulk of the coding and the other with the content. In all cases, the coding referenced the media. I used the same video files for the two video clips, the audio files for the single audio clip, and the two image files in all three cases. I used the image of a small hand-drawn *x* to mark locations on the map, instead of the default teardrop shape for markers in Google Maps.

As is the case for the project in the last chapter and the next chapter, this application does require you to be online to test since that is the only way to make contact with Google Maps.

Summary

In this chapter, you continued using the Google Maps API. You learned how to do the following:

- Program Google Maps API event handling to detect if the user was close to locations for which you had video, audio, or images

- Separate the definition of media content from the program itself

- Create HTML5 markup dynamically, using a regular expression to produce the right markup

- Start and stop the display and playing of media

In the next chapter, we will explore the use of geolocation, together with the Google Maps API, HTML5, and JavaScript and php to perform the sending of email.

CHAPTER 6

Where am I: Using Geolocation, the Google Maps API, and PHP

In this chapter, you will learn the following:

- How to use geolocation to determine the location of your users/customers/clients

- About reverse geocoding in the Google Maps API to find the address of a given latitude/longitude

- About the asynchronous nature of certain operations in the Google Maps API

- How to send e-mail by using a server-side function

Introduction

The projects for this chapter involve the Google Maps API, geolocation, and PHP. I will describe two applications: the first just to show geolocation, a facility in which the browser determines the user's location using one of a variety of means. This application lets you find out where the location services think you are and compare it to where you really are. The second application provides a way for the user to generate an e-mail using the geolocation information along with other data and send it to someone. This makes use of a server-side PHP script to send the e-mail, and HTML5 form validation to confirm the e-mail addresses.

The geolocation specification is under development in parallel with HTML5 and is considered a distinct specification. It also is different from Google Maps, though Google Location Services is one of the main sources of geolocation information. An obvious thing to do with the location data is to display a Google Map, but you can do anything you want with the information.

One important feature of the geolocation specification is that the user—that is, the person on the client computer browsing the web page—must give approval for the location to be determined. This is so-called "opt-in." The exact look of the screen varies with the different browsers. The terminology varies: a specific address may want to *know*, to *track*, or to *use*. It is all the same thing. Figure 6-1 shows the opening screen using Firefox.

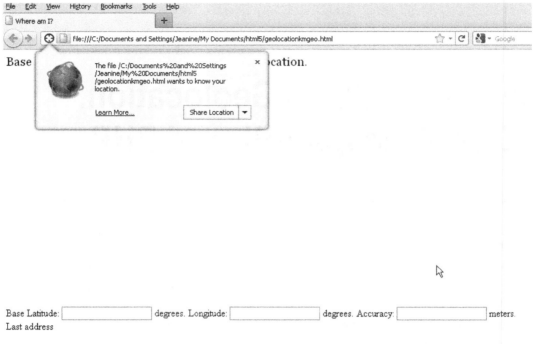

Figure 6-1. *Opening screen with request for permission to share location (Firefox)*

The drop-down menu offers four options: Share Location, Always Share, Never Share, and Not Now. If you choose the first option, when you refresh the screen or return to the page, the program will prompt again for a response.

Notice that other material already appears on the screen from my program. The request for permission is triggered when the code is invoked for the geolocation operation. Figure 6-2 shows the analogous screen in the Opera browser.

Base location (small red x) is your current geolocation.

Base Latitude: [   ] degrees. Longitude: [   ] degrees. Accuracy: [   ] meters.
Last address

Figure 6-2. Opening screen with request for permission to share location (Opera)

Notice that Opera gives the option of remembering the choice for this site. Figure 6-3 shows a follow-on screen that requests another confirmation that the user is opting-in.

Figure 6-3. Additional request from Opera

Figure 6-4 shows the corresponding screen in Chrome. At this point, I had uploaded the application to one of my server accounts. The browser uses the domain name of the account in its query.

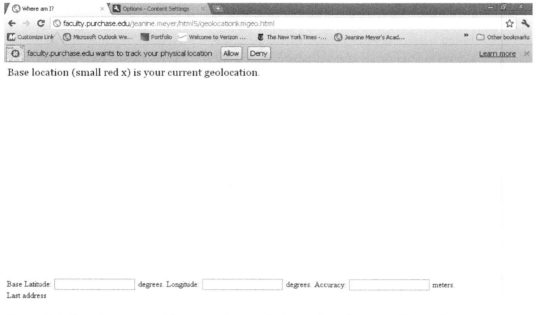

Figure 6-4. Opening screen with request for permission to share location (Chrome)

Figure 6-5 shows the screen for Safari. I returned again to using a file on my local computer.

Base location (small red x) is your current geolocation.

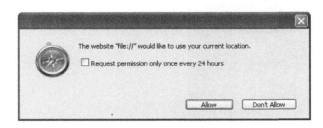

Figure 6-5. Request for permission to share location (Safari)

Notice that Safari provides the user a way to give permission for 24 hours—that is, avoid repeated requests each day. Note that Safari on my desktop PC does not work, and unfortunately hangs up—does nothing—rather than trigger the problem handler when the simplest call is made. I will show where it does work when explaining the different ways that geolocation actually is performed and techniques to use so that the problem handler will be triggered. For now, I note that the variant of Safari running on the iPhone does work. Figure 6-6 shows the permission screen for an iPhone. I wanted to test the other program, so I made use of another server account.

Figure 6-6. Request to share location (iPhone)

There are many variables, which will be explained following, but in my recent experiment around my town, the iPhone returned the most accurate results.

The permission is associated with the browser. For example, clicking "Remember my choice for this site" for Opera will not affect what happens when you use Firefox or any other browser. You also can use the general settings in the browser for all sites. For example, in Firefox, using Tools/Page Info/Permissions, you can choose from among Always Allow, Always Block, and Always Ask, the latter being what is recommended. In Opera, you can right-click (PC) or Ctrl+click (Mac), or choose Edit Site Preferences ➤ Network, to get the same choices. In Chrome, you start by clicking the wrench symbol in the upper right. Then choose Options ➤ Under the Hood ➤ Content Settings, and scroll down to Location. Safari appears to take a different approach. You can click the gear symbol in the upper right and then click Preferences and choose the Security tab. The choices are to allow sites to ask or not give permission at all. The iPhone provides similar options in Settings ➤ General ➤ Location Services.

The geolocation standard is moving its way through the recommendation process in the W3C (see `www.w3.org/2008/geolocation/drafts/API/Implementation-Report.html`). You need to check and keep checking with each browser to determine what features work and how.

So, moving on, what does my program do after being given permission to determine the location? The program, `geolocationkmgeo.html`, uses the returned coordinate values to bring in a Google Map, and uses another service, reverse geocoding, to calculate an address. Figure 6-7 shows the result. The geolocation is termed the *base*.

Base location (small red x) is your current geolocation.

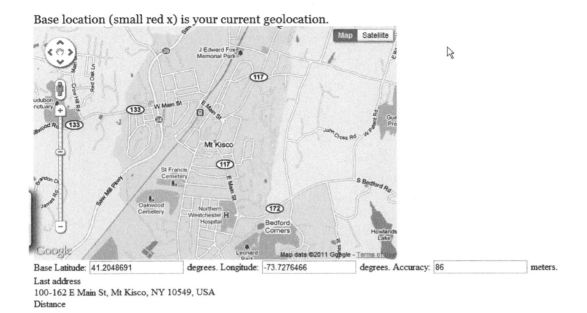

Base Latitude: 41.2048691   degrees. Longitude: -73.7276466   degrees. Accuracy: 86   meters.

Last address
100-162 E Main St, Mt Kisco, NY 10549, USA
Distance

Figure 6-7. *Location found in the basic program*

The reverse geocoding has returned 100-162 E. Main Street, Mt. Kisco, NY 10549, USA for the description of the address with accuracy given as 86 meters. That is fairly accurate for the location of the red *x*. This screenshot was made while using a laptop at the Borders Café (now closed).That fact is significant because, as will be demonstrated, the geolocation itself was fairly accurate The official W3C specification for geolocation supplies little information on how the accuracy is calculated. This project can be used to make your own analysis of how accurate the geolocation is. The user can use the Google Maps interface to zoom and/or pan and then click the screen. This is what I did. A black dot will appear, along with the reverse-geocode address and the distance from the base of the clicked location. This can serve to check out distances to other locations, or calculate the distance from the geolocation to the actual location. Figure 6-8 shows the result of clicking the screen at where I determined I actually was.

Base location (small red x) is your current geolocation.

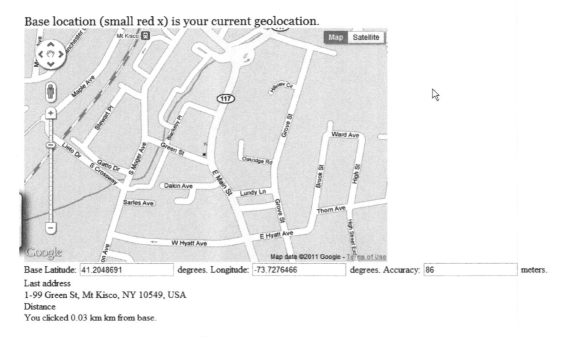

Base Latitude: 41.2048691   degrees. Longitude: -73.7276466   degrees. Accuracy: 86   meters.

Last address

1-99 Green St, Mt Kisco, NY 10549, USA

Distance

You clicked 0.03 km km from base.

Figure 6-8. *Screen showing actual location*

The reverse geocoding is good: we were on Green Street. The program calculates and displays the distance from the base (the red *x*) and where I clicked (the black *x*). The location was .03 kilometers (equivalent to 30 meters). This is within the 86 meter accuracy returned by the geolocation function.

The second application demonstrates how you can use geolocation, reverse-geocode information, and actions you take yourself to compose an e-mail to send to someone else. Of course, many companies offer such services to facilitate meet-ups, promote restaurants, and so on. This application, `geolocationkme-mail.html`, makes use of a small program written in PHP that runs on your server to send e-mail to a person of your choosing. You will need to confirm that this is possible for your server account. This is an extra service that your Internet Service Provider may or may not provide. We'll will return to PHP in Chapter 10.

After agreeing to allow geolocation, the opening screen of the second application is shown (see Figure 6-9).

Base location (small red x) is your current geolocation.

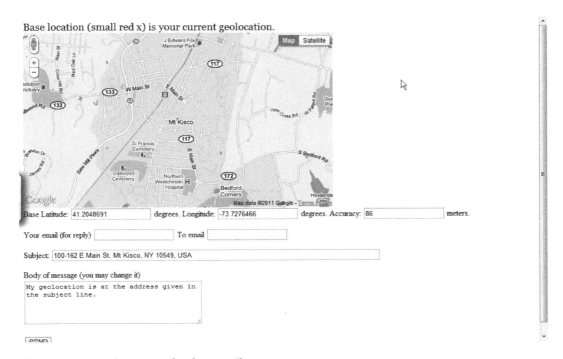

Base Latitude: 41.2048691 ___ degrees. Longitude: -73.7276466 ___ degrees. Accuracy: 86 ___ meters.

Your email (for reply) [_____] To email [_____]

Subject: 100-162 E Main St, Mt Kisco, NY 10549, USA

Body of message (you may change it)

My geolocation is at the address given in
the subject line.

[SEND]

Figure 6-9. *Opening screen for the e-mail program*

Notice that there is a form on display with a place to put From and To e-mail addresses. The subject line has the reverse-geocoding information, and the body of the message refers to the subject line.

Next, I click where I believe I am. This application does require you to be able to find yourself on a map! Figure 6-10 shows the results.

Base location (small red x) is your current geolocation.

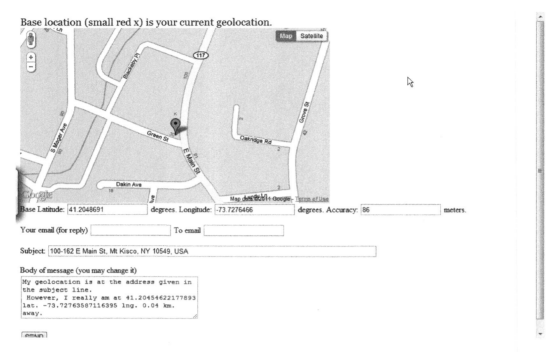

Figure 6-10. After clicking the location, the screen with information in the message body

The clicked location now has the default marker used by Google Maps. This actually was an oversight on my part, but I decided to stick with it to show you that you can use the default upside-down teardrop icon. Notice that the subject line and the body of the e-mail have been filled. Now is the time to put in the From and To addresses. You can also change what is in the body of the e-mail or the subject line. You then click the SEND button. It is not instant, but the message will be sent to your e-mail account. Figure 6-11 shows the message as it appears in my Gmail account.

Figure 6-11. The received e-mail with location information

I am satisfied with how this works, but what I have shown you so far appears to assume that my users/customers/clients will be well behaved and put in proper e-mail addresses. This is a bad assumption to make. To handle this, I declared *form validation* as a requirement for this application. Form validation refers to a set of tests that are done to check if the input is valid. With form validation, if the user neglects to put in anything before hitting the SEND button, the program will present something like what is shown in Figure 6-12 (produced using Chrome).

Figure 6-12. *Message from Chrome when a required field is empty*

If the user puts in something, but that something isn't a valid e-mail address, to the extent that it can be ascertained in terms of format alone, the application will present something like what is shown in Figure 6-13 (also produced using Chrome).

Figure 6-13. *Invalid e-mail address as detected by Chrome*

Other browsers also support similar form validation. Figure 6-14 shows the response produced by Firefox for an empty field.

Figure 6-14. *Message from Firefox when a required field is empty*

Figure 6-15 shows the response produced by Firefox for input that was not the correct format for e-mail.

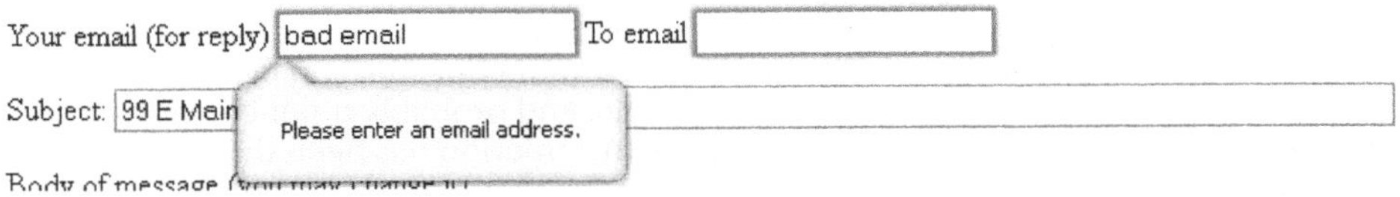

Your email (for reply) bad email   To email
Subject: 99 E Main
          Please enter an email address.
Body of message (you may change it)

Figure 6-15. *Invalid e-mail address as detected by Firefox*

One can argue that it would be better if *all* the form input fields were validated at once, but that could lead to an overcrowded screen. We hope the user gets the message. If not, the messages will be repeated for the To field. The user may wonder about the meaning of the From e-mail field. It does not mean that this message will show up in the SENT folder in the user's e-mail account. What it does is make it possible for the receiver to click Reply.

With this introduction to the projects for this chapter, I'll now provide background on geolocation and other critical requirements for these applications.

Geolocation and Other Critical Requirements

The main requirement for this application concerns geolocation: determining a latitude and longitude position for the client computer. In this section I will give a brief introduction to the wide variety of ways that the task may be accomplished for computers that range from the most mobile smartphone to the most sedentary desktop. The next section will describe the mechanics of how to use position information in HTML5 and JavaScript.

If you have a Global Positioning System (GPS) chip in your car, phone, or tablet computer, the notion of a computer program determining your location is commonplace. A GPS chip uses information from some of the 24 GPS satellites orbiting the earth to determine its location. A single satellite in the sky does not send down the information telling us where we are. Instead, the GPS device on the ground receives signals from multiple satellites. The device uses the current time and the specified time when each signal left the satellite to compute the travel time of each signal. It uses these travel times to compute its distances from the satellites and uses these distances along with the locations of the satellites to make the calculation. Using three satellites determines latitude and longitude; using four determines latitude, longitude, and altitude. Roughly speaking, the determinations are made by calculating the intersection of spheres: two spheres intersect in a circle. The software can make assumptions on the sphere that represents the planet earth, but it may not be accurate, as I know from one time using my car GPS and being "told" I was under the ramp to the Brooklyn Bridge. The local device may use signals from even more satellites, often up to ten, to confirm results. The best GPS applications use information from devices' accelerometers to update their positions during brief interruptions in GPS signal reception, a trick that once was restricted to navigating submarines. A navigation device in a car or an app in a cell phone may also make use of data stored on the device to convert the position into a street address.

So what happens if your computer does not have a GPS chip inside it, or is in a location from which it cannot receive satellite signals, but does have a cell phone radio and is in a cell phone service area? Another way to calculate position is to use the strengths of signals from one or more cell phone towers. Google Location Services and other geolocation applications have determined where many of the towers are and have stored that information in databases. If only a single cell phone tower is in range, a very rough position estimate is the location of that tower. However, if your computer can receive signals from several towers, then it can compute a much better estimate of your position. It uses the towers' different signal strengths instead of GPS satellites' different signal-travel times to compute your position by using known distances from known points.

If your computer has no GPS or cell phone radios but does connect by a short wire to a Wi-Fi radio, then the browser may be able to determine its position using the strengths of signals from other nearby Wi-Fi radios. It turns out that certain companies, such as Google Location Services, have databases with the known position of many, many Wi-Fi hot spots. The location of a Wi-Fi hot spot can be determined even if the hot spot is private and secure. The fact that Google, Apple, and probably other companies collect this information is controversial. One way of collecting the information has been through the vans that travel streets to get the images used for the Google Maps Street View service. Another way is to keep the data used when people use certain apps on their phones and forward it to the companies to add to their databases. In any case, these databases are referenced to provide hot spot positions for the geolocation calculations. Your computer can use the signal strengths of neighboring hot spots to estimate its distances from them, get their locations from the databases, and compute its own position. Of course, its position then goes into the databases for other calculations to use!

■ **Note** Google, Apple, and others claim that data collected is stripped of personal information. I am not sympathetic to companies gathering information secretly. However, we do need to accept that many services are supplied for no explicit, per-use charge. To the adage/cliché, "you get what you pay for," we may add something like, "The crowd or community bears a burden for what we don't pay for."

Lastly, what if your computer has no GPS, cell phone, or Wi-Fi radio? The IP address—the four-number combination that identifies your computer on the Web—is associated with a latitude and longitude value. It does not work well—the positions may be way off--if the computer shares an IP address with many others on a local network. However, this method allows the user of even an isolated computer to benefit from applications knowing the approximate position of the computer. My experience has been that the browsers on my desktop computer did not use Wi-Fi, but used the IP method, or, in the case of Safari, either failed or timed out (see the next section for more on the timeout option). In contrast, browsers on laptops and iPhones and iPads in my house, making use of the Wi-Fi network attached to my desktop computer, did make use of Wi-Fi for geolocation, with much better results.

These are the major technologies for determining position. The geolocation standard under development by the W3C establishes methods, attributes, and events for the use of programmers to access the information, if available.

My projects also make use of reverse geocoding, determining a street address or some sort of descriptive information about the position. Presumably, Google Location Services and other similar services have extensive databases on geographically descriptive terms associated with latitude and longitude values—not each value, certainly, but ranges of values. The HTML5 facility described in the next section provides several results produced by reverse geocoding, and you need to decide what is appropriate for your application. It will be dependent on the region of the country and the world.

Both projects require a response to the user clicking the map. This includes marking the position in a way that persists even when the map is moved or scaled. The projects also calculate the distance from the base location to the marked location.

Sending e-mail requires first of all a way for the user to enter the e-mail address. Sending e-mail is something beyond normal JavaScript processing, so to fulfill this requirement, it will be necessary to do something different—namely, to run a program on the server. Recall the basic mechanism of the Web is that files, including HTML documents, are located on server sites. A browser program, such as Firefox or Opera, runs on what is called the *client computer*—my computer or your computer in our house or at the coffee shop or library. The browser program fetches files from the server and interprets them. To perform a server operation such as sending e-mail, the browser must invoke a program running on the server.

Prior to sending the e-mail, the program needs to get the e-mail addresses, the To address to know where to send the message, and the From address so that reply will work. The program should do some sort of checking to make sure the addresses are valid. You will see that collecting and validating the information is done on the client computer, the one right in front of you or your user. Processing the e-mail and sending it are done by a PHP program running on the server, the computer holding the files for the project.

These are the requirements to build the projects demonstrated in the "Introduction" section. In the next section, I'll describe the HTML5 and PHP features to implement the projects.

HTML5, CSS, JavaScript, and PHP Features

In this section, I will explain the features used to accomplish the requirements for the basic geolocation project and the e-mail project.

Geolocation

The W3C standard for geolocation is independent of how or what service actually supplies the information. It is assumed that the task will take time, so the request is set up as an asynchronous request. The code I wrote to make the request is

```
if (navigator.geolocation) {
  navigator.geolocation.getCurrentPosition(handler, problemhandler, positionopts);
}
else {
  if (document.getElementById("place")) {
    document.getElementById("place").innerHTML = "I'm sorry but geolocation services
 are not supported by your browser";
    document.getElementById("place").style.color = "#FF0000";
  }
}
```

The "Introduction" section showed successful examples of geolocation. At this point, I will show ways to handle problems, which can and do occur, before going on to explain how to use the information.

The condition for the outer `if` tests if `navigator.geolocation` is a recognized object for the browser. If it is *not*, then after checking that a div named `place` exists, the program displays the message starting with "I'm sorry . . ." When I tried this program in an old version of Internet Explorer, I first had to give permission to run any scripts, as shown in Figure 6-16.

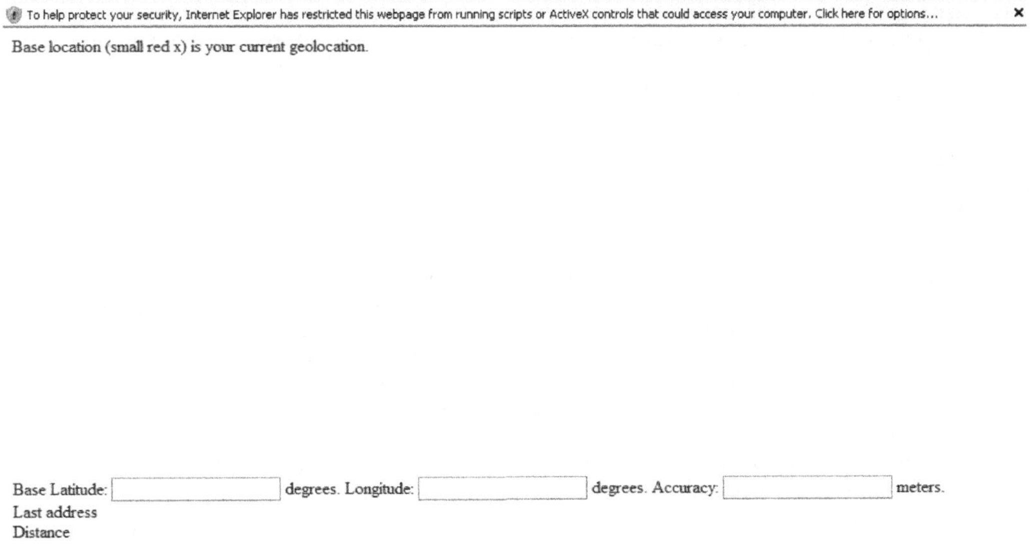

To help protect your security, Internet Explorer has restricted this webpage from running scripts or ActiveX controls that could access your computer. Click here for options…   ✕

Base location (small red x) is your current geolocation.

Base Latitude: [   ] degrees. Longitude: [   ] degrees. Accuracy: [   ] meters.
Last address
Distance

Figure 6-16. Internet Explorer request to run scripts

After I gave permission, Internet Explorer showed that geolocation was not available (see Figure 6-17).

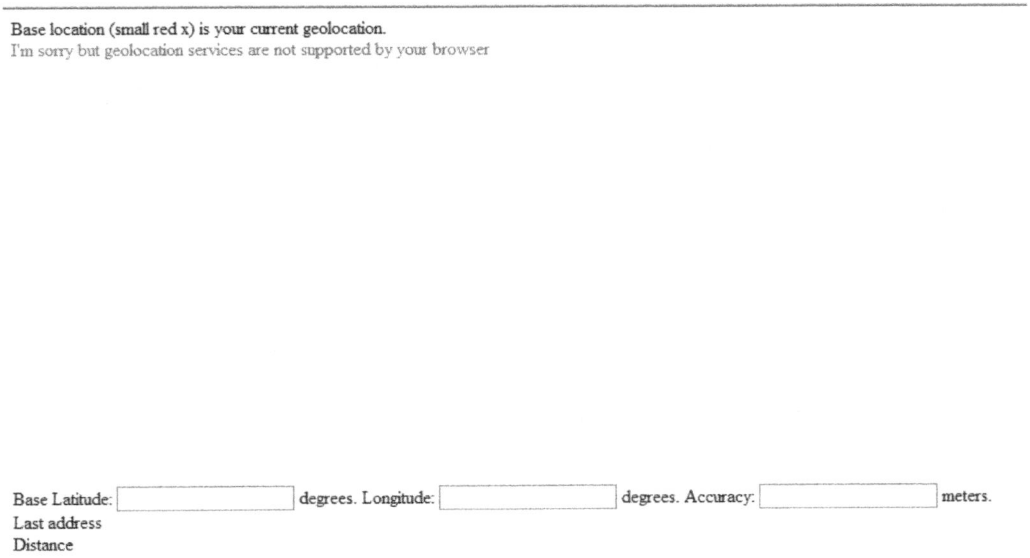

Base location (small red x) is your current geolocation.
I'm sorry but geolocation services are not supported by your browser

Base Latitude: [   ] degrees. Longitude: [   ] degrees. Accuracy: [   ] meters.
Last address
Distance

Figure 6-17. Message on absence of geolocation in old Internet Explorer

If the `navigator.geolocation` object does exist, then my code invokes the `getCurrentPosition` method with three parameters. The first parameter, `handler`, is the name of a function that will be invoked if and when the operation is complete. The second parameter, `problemhandler`, is invoked when there is a problem. The third parameter, `positionopts`, is used to specify options. The setting I used for the options is

```
var positionopts;
positionopts = {
        enableHighAccuracy: true,
        timeout: 10000};
```

The interpretation of the `enableHighAccuracy` setting is not specified by W3C, but the practical implication for now is to use GPS if it is available. When enabled, more process time may be used, and the application as a whole may be slower. Setting this item to `false`, which is the default, also may preserve battery life on the local device. The timeout setting indicates that the time to perform this operation is to be limited to 10,000 milliseconds (10 seconds). There are other option settings, so when you start to use geolocation for production work, do investigate them.

If a problem is detected while performing the geolocation operation, the `problemhandler` function is invoked with a parameter containing a code indicating the nature of the problem. The definition of the `problemhandler` function includes a `switch` statement based on this code.

```
function problemhandler(prob) {
        switch(prob.code) {
        case 1:
        document.getElementById("place").innerHTML = "User declined to share the location↵
 information.";
        break;
        case 2:
        document.getElementById("place").innerHTML = "Errors in getting base location.";
        break;
        case 3:
        document.getElementById("place").innerHTML = "Timeout in getting base location.";
        }

        document.getElementById("header").innerHTML = "Base location needs to be set!";
}
```

Figure 6-18 shows the result of the user denying permission to do geolocation.

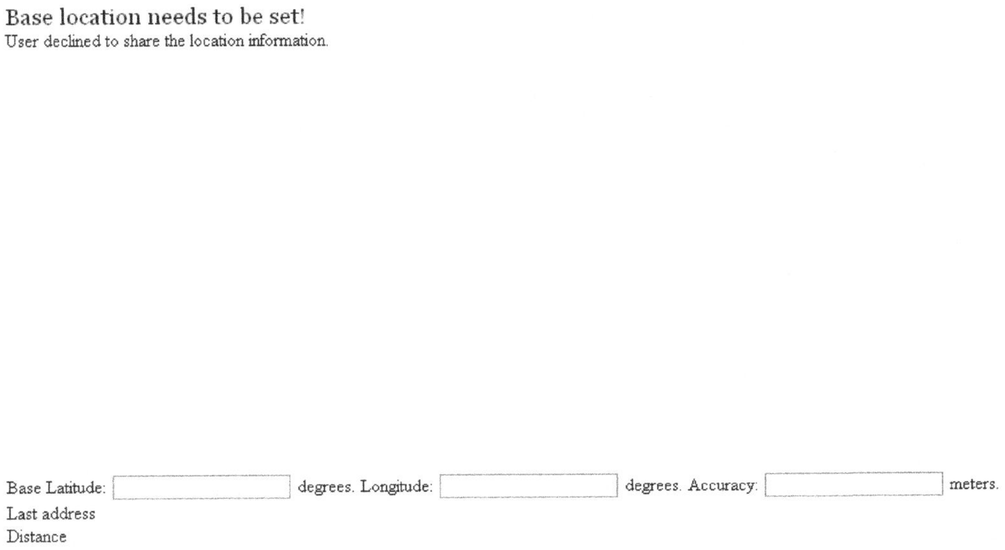

Base location needs to be set!
User declined to share the location information.

Base Latitude: [　　　　　　] degrees. Longitude: [　　　　　　] degrees. Accuracy: [　　　　　　] meters.
Last address
Distance

Figure 6-18. *Result of the user saying no to geolocation*

A subtler problem is the failure to perform the operation in a timely manner. Figure 6-19 shows the situation alluded to earlier concerning using Safari on a desktop computer.

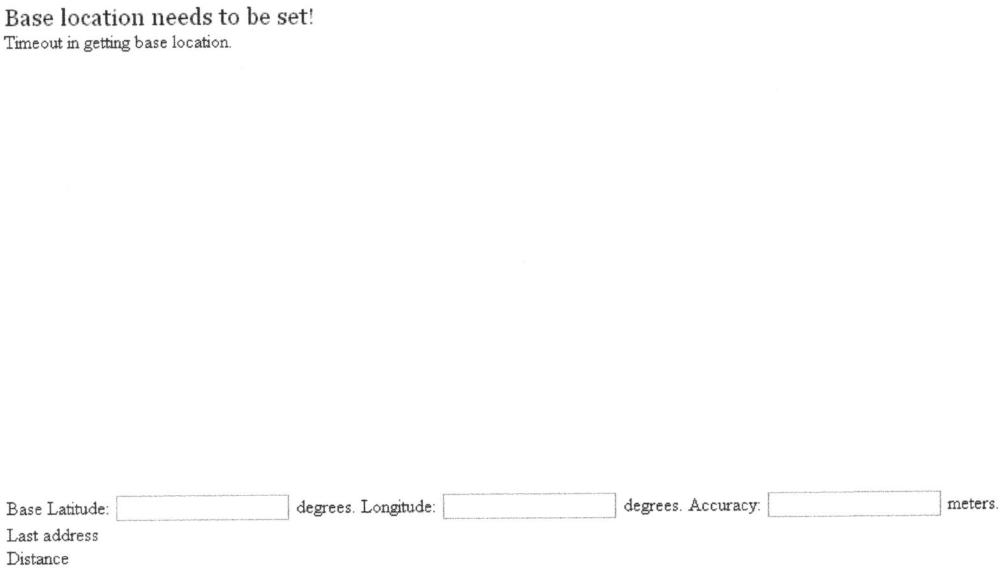

Base location needs to be set!
Timeout in getting base location.

Base Latitude: [　　　　　　] degrees. Longitude: [　　　　　　] degrees. Accuracy: [　　　　　　] meters.
Last address
Distance

Figure 6-19. *Geolocation taking too long*

Let's move on now to the successful case: geolocation has worked. My code has caused the function handler to be invoked with the parameter set by the `getCurrentPosition` method to hold the calculated position information. The code extracts the latitude and longitude values and invokes my `makemap` function, which sets a global variable named `blatlng` and brings in the Google Map. The `makemap` function is essentially the same one used in the projects covered in the last two chapters. A Google Map with the full Google Map interface will appear on the screen. The handler function also displays values and calls `reversegeo`, the topic of the next section. Here is the code for `handler`:

```
function handler(position) {
        var mylat = position.coords.latitude;
        var mylong = position.coords.longitude;
        makemap(mylat,mylong);
        document.coutput.lat.value = mylat;
        document.coutput.lon.value = mylong;
        document.coutput.acc.value = position.coords.accuracy;
        reversegeo(blatlng);
}
```

The `accuracy` value is part of the W3C specification. Its exact meaning is not defined in the standard. One possibility is that it defines the radius of a circle around the returned point within which the actual position will lie. The value returned when I use my desktop PC has been given as 22,000 meters, when in fact the actual location is only 610 meters from the returned location. In any case, , you probably would not share the accuracy information with your user if you were building a production application.

■ **Note** The navigator.geolocation object has other methods and properties. Most notably, there is a `watchPosition` method that sets up monitoring for changes in position or changes in how the position is calculated.

Reverse Geocoding

Reverse geocoding refers to a facility for obtaining description information, such as street addresses, from a latitude/longitude position. Keeping in mind garbage-in/garbage-out, if the original latitude/longitude is in error, then the address returned by a reverse-geolocation operation will also be in error.

The geocode facility I use is part of the Google Maps API, and includes features for obtaining long names, short names, postal codes, and so on. In the `init` function, my code constructs a Geocoder object and sets the variable `geocoder`:

```
geocoder = new google.maps.Geocoder();
```

The `reversegeo` function invokes the `geocode` method of this object. This is an asynchronous operation. That is, the method initiates an operation that takes time. The geocode method starts the task of determining the reverse geocoding. Control moves on to the next statement before the task is complete. Most asynchronous methods work by specifying a function to be invoked when the task is complete. The call to the `geocode` method designates a function. The way I designated the function was to define what is called an *anonymous function* in the method call itself. The function definition in its entirety is the second parameter of the call to `geocode`. The complete `reversegeo` function is shown next.

It essentially is one statement, the call to geocode, which contains within the call the definition of a function.

```
function reversegeo(latlng) {
    geocoder.geocode({'latLng': latlng}, function(results, status) {
      if (status == google.maps.GeocoderStatus.OK) {
      if (results[0]) {
          addressref.innerHTML = results[0].formatted_address;
      } else {
          alert("No results found");
        }
        }
      else {
        alert("Geocoder failed due to: " + status);
      }
    });
}
```

The geocode method can be used to find locations using descriptions (addresses), or for reverse geocoding: determining descriptions from locations. The presence of the 'latlng' coordinate is what indicates that this is a reverse-geocoding operation. My code specifies the latitude/longitude, and geocode returns descriptive information such as a street address.

■ **Note** If instead you specify an address using {'address': locrequest}, where locrequest is a string variable holding an address, then geocode will return the latitude/longitude. This provides a way for you to bring into your application the basic capability of Google Maps.

The results parameter is an array that holds the address information, starting with the most exact and working up. Figure 6-20 shows the alert box produced by this addition to the code:

```
var out = "";
    for (var i=0;i<results.length;i++) {
      out += results[i].formatted_address +"\n";
    }
    alert(out);
```

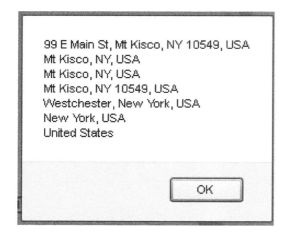

99 E Main St, Mt Kisco, NY 10549, USA
Mt Kisco, NY, USA
Mt Kisco, NY, USA
Mt Kisco, NY 10549, USA
Westchester, New York, USA
New York, USA
United States

OK

Figure 6-20. *The results array from geocoding*

The reason the second and third lines are identical may have to do with the fact that Mt. Kisco is a coterminous village and town. In any case, you may need to run a program with this sort of display to determine what you want to use in your specific application. My examples use `results[0]`. You may decide it is best to use `results[3]`. It is up to you and can be viewed as a situation of precision vs. accuracy.

Clicking the Map

The requirements I have stipulated for these projects allow the user to click the map. As was discussed in the previous two chapters, the Google Maps API provides a way to set up event handling. In the `makemap` function, I include the line

```
listener = google.maps.event.addListener(map, 'click', function(event) {
                    checkit(event.latLng);
                    });
```

The `checkit` function uses the clicked location to make a marker, calculate an address using `reversegeo`, calculate the distance from the base to the clicked location, and display information. In the basic geolocation application, the definition for `checkit` is the following:

```
function checkit(clatlng) {
        var distance = dist(clatlng,blatlng);
        var result;
        distance = Math.floor((distance+.005)*100)/100;
        var distanceString = String(distance);
```

```
        marker = new google.maps.Marker({
                position: clatlng,
                title: distanceString,
                icon: bxmarker,
                map: map });
        markersArray.push(marker);
        reversegeo(clatlng);
    distanceref.innerHTML  = "You clicked "+distanceString+" km from base.";
}
```

The marker used is a custom one, a black *x*. The title, which is what you see if you move the mouse to the marker, is the distance, formatted to be a two-decimal number. The sentence starting with "You clicked . . ." is displayed as part of the body of the document.

The checkit function for the e-mail geolocation project is similar. The objective of this application is to compose an e-mail relating to the user's location; look back to Figure 6-10. The definition of the checkit function for this application uses the default marker and creates a sentence about the distances for the body of the message.

```
function checkit(clatlng) {
        var distance = dist(clatlng,blatlng);
        var result;
        distance = Math.floor((distance+.005)*100)/100;
        var distanceString = String(distance)+" km. away.";
        var newcoords = String(clatlng.lat())+" lat. "+String(clatlng.lng())+" lng.";
        distanceString = newcoords+" "+distanceString;
        marker = new google.maps.Marker({
                position: clatlng,
                title: distanceString,
                map: map });
        document.msg.body.value = document.msg.body.value + " However, I really am↵
 at "+distanceString;
}
```

Checking E-mail Address Input and Invoking PHP to send e-mail

As described in the "Introduction" section, any application involving the sending of e-mails based on user input should attempt to check that the input fits the format for an e-mail address. Fortunately, this is one of the new features of HTML5. The input elements in forms have a type attribute, and one type is e-mail. Standard HTML (4 and earlier) provides a way to specify that submission of the form is to cause invoking of a file on the server. I describe this more in the next section, including the significance of the method setting. The complete form for e-mail follows:

```
<form name="msg" action="sendemailp.php" method="post">
  <p>Your email (for reply)
    <input type="email" name="from" required/>
To email
    <input type="email" name="to" required  />
</p>
```

```
Subject: <input type="text" name="subject" size="100" />
  <p>
    Body of message (you may change it) <br/>
    <TEXTAREA NAME="body" COLS=40 ROWS=5>
My geolocation is at the address given in the subject line.
</TEXTAREA>
        </p>
 <input type="submit" value="SEND" />
</form>
```

This code produces the error checking shown in Figures 6-12 to 6-15 (shown previously), and should be appreciated as removing responsibilities from the programmer.

The action attribute in the form tag specified the php file sendemailp.php. This means that when the form is submitted, assuming the input is valid, the browser will send a message to the server (the computer from which it downloaded the HTML document). The message will be to invoke sendemailp.php. The input data will be passed along. I will now give a brief introduction to php. Chapter 10 on the database project will contain more information.

A Brief Introduction to the PHP Language

The sending of e-mail is a facility provided on servers, not client computers. There are several languages for writing what are called server-side scripts, and PHP is one of them. It is well-maintained and well-documents at www.php.net. You will read more about PHP in the description of a database project in Chapter 10.

The previous section showed how to invoke a PHP script as the result of submission of a form. The form input can be passed to the script in one of two ways: POST and GET. The GET way makes use of what is called the *query string*. The POST way is done using the HTTP headers. I chose to use POST for this example.

The main purpose of a PHP script is to do something on the server, probably using form input from an HTML document, and generate an HTML document to be passed back to the browser for display. It is not the case with the example for this project, but many PHP scripts consist of a mixture of HTML and PHP. The PHP portions are indicated by the delimiters <?php and ?>. The function echo adds its input to the HTML document being created.

A feature of PHP is that variables, built in and programmer defined, start with dollar signs. For example, if the PHP script has been invoked by the action of a form, with the method specified as POST, and the form had an input element named to, then the line

```
$to = $_POST['to'];
```

would access the form input named to and assign it to the variable $to.

As mentioned, PHP scripts compose HTML documents, so a frequent operation is concatenation of strings. The operator in PHP for this is . (dot). The line

```
$headers = "From: " . $_POST['from'];
```

extracts the form input named from and adds it to the literal string "From: " to form a longer string, which is assigned to the variable $headers.

Another feature of PHP, which probably is the strangest to experienced programmers, is that variables can be included in strings. The statement

```
echo("There was a problem: <br>the body is $body,<br> the to is $to,<br> subject is↵
 $subject,<br> headers is $headers.");
```

produces the output shown in Figure 6-21.

There was a problem:

the body is My geolocation is at the address given in the subject line. ,

the to is jeanine.meyer@gmail.com,

subject is 99 E Main St, Mt Kisco, NY 10549, USA,

headers is From: jeanine.meyer@purchase.edu.

Figure 6-21. *Demonstration of PHP echo of composed string*

The values of the variables $body, $to, $subject, and $headers have been extracted and made part of the string. Notice also that the string contains the HTML markup <br>.

The sending of e-mail is fairly straightforward. There is a built-in PHP function, mail, that does the work, using as parameters the To address, the subject, the message body, and any header material. The function returns true if the sending operation was successful and false otherwise. Note that the sending operation can be successful and the recipient e-mail service may still reject the address as being nonexistent. The complete code for sendemailp.php is shown in the next section.

Building the Application and Making It Your Own

You can make these projects your own by combining the geolocation feature with more substantial applications. Knowing where the visitors to your site are located can help personalize the application, and perhaps influence the choice of images. An informal summary/outline of the basic geolocation application follows:

- init: For initialization, including invoking the call for geolocation, which is done asynchronously

- handler *and* problemhandler: For completing the geolocation

- makemap: For bringing in the Google Map

- checkit: For responding to clicks on the map and invoking diste

- reversegeo: For determining an address from a latitude/longitude value

Table 6-1 lists all the functions and indicates how they are invoked and what functions they invoke.

Table 6-1. *Functions in the Basic Geolocation Project*

Function	Invoked/Called By	Calls
init	Invoked by action of the `onLoad` attribute in the `<body>` tag	
handler	Invoked by action of the `getCurrentPosition` call in `init`	makemap, reversegeo
reversegeo	Invoked in `handler`	
problemhandler	Invoked by action of the `getCurrentPosition` call in `init`	
makemap	Invoked by `handler`	
checkit	Invoked by action of `addListener` in `makemap`	dist
dist	Invoked by `checkit`	

Table 6-2 shows the code for the basic application, with comments for each line. Much of this code you have seen in the previous chapters.

Table 6-2. *Complete Code for the Geolocation Project*

Code Line	Description
`<!DOCTYPE html>`	Doctype header for HTML5
`<html>`	html tag
`<head>`	Head tag
`<title>Where am I?</title>`	Complete title element
`<meta charset="UTF-8">`	Meta tag for character sets
`<style>`	Style tag
`header {font-family:Georgia,"Times New Roman",serif;`	Set up formatting for header element, including font choices
`font-size:20px;`	Font size
`display:block;`	Set up line break before and after
`}`	Close style directive

Code Line	Description
`</style>`	Closing tag for style
`<script type="text/javascript" charset="UTF-8" src="http://maps.google.com/maps/api/js?sensor=false"></script>`	Script to bring in Google Map API
`<script type="text/javascript" charset="UTF-8">`	Opening script tag
`var positionopts;`	Set up global variable for options for geolocation
`positionopts = {`	Start definition of associative array
`    enableHighAccuracy: true,`	Set request to try for high accuracy
`    timeout: 10000};`	Set timeout limit
`var addressref;`	Will hold reference to address div element
`var distanceref;`	Will hold reference to distance div element
`var headerref;`	Will hold reference to header div element
`var geocoder;`	Will hold geocoder object
`function init() {`	Header for **init** function
`addressref = document.getElementById("address");`	Set **addressref**
`headerref = document.getElementById("header");`	Set **headerref**
`distanceref = document.getElementById("distance");`	Set **distanceref**
`geocoder = new google.maps.Geocoder();`	Create and set **geocoder** to be Geocoder object
`if (navigator.geolocation) {`	Does browser recognize `navigator.geolocation`?

Code Line	Description
`navigator.geolocation.getCurrentPosition(handler, problemhandler, positionopts);`	If so, make the call with parameters as shown
`}`	Close clause
`else {`	Else
`if (document.getElementById("place")) {`	If there is a place with ID place
`document.getElementById("place").innerHTML = "I'm sorry but geolocation services are not supported by your browser";`	Set its contents to give message
`document.getElementById("place").style.color = "#FF0000";`	Turn contents red
`}`	Close clause
`}`	Close outer else clause
`}`	Close function
`var listener;`	Variable for listener (set but not used as variable)
`var map;`	Will be used to hold map
`var blatlng;`	Will hold the latitude/longitude object for the base
`var myOptions;`	Will hold the options used in bringing in a map
`function handler(position) {`	Header for handler function; if geolocation successful, it is invoked with the parameter position
`var mylat = position.coords.latitude;`	Set to the latitude
`var mylong = position.coords.longitude;`	Set to the longitude
`makemap(mylat,mylong);`	Invoke (my) makemap function
`document.coutput.lat.value = mylat;`	Display the latitude

Code Line	Description
`document.coutput.lon.value = mylong;`	Display the longitude
`document.coutput.acc.value = position.coords.accuracy;`	Display the accuracy
`reversegeo(blatlng);`	Invoke (my) function `reversegeo`
`}`	Close handler function
`function reversegeo(latlng) {`	Header for the `reversegeo` function
`geocoder.geocode({'latLng': latlng}, function(results, status) {`	Invoke the `geocode` method with a `latLng` object. The second parameter is an antonymous function. The function definition starts in this line and concludes 11 lines down, right before the closing bracket for the `reversegeo` function.
`if (status == google.maps.GeocoderStatus.OK) {`	If the status returned with a value equal to the `google.maps.GeocoderStatus.OK` value
`if (results[0]) {`	If `results[0]` exists
`addressref.innerHTML = results[0].formatted_address;`	Display this result
`} else {`	Otherwise
`alert("No results found");`	Issue alert message
`}`	Close clause
`}`	Close outer clause
`else {`	Else (the status was not OK)
`alert("Geocoder failed due to: " + status);`	Issue alert message
`}`	Close clause

Code Line	Description
`});`	Close function definition, close Geocode method call
`}`	Close **reversegeo** function
`function problemhandler(prob) {`	Header for **problemhandler** function; **prob** will have information on the failure
`switch(prob.code) {`	**switch** statement based on **prob.code**
`case 1:`	A code of 1 is returned if the user declines to share location information.
`document.getElementById("place").innerHTML = "User declined to share the location information.";`	Issue message
`break;`	Leave the switch
`case 2:`	A code of 2 is to be returned if errors are detected by the program performing the geocoding.
`document.getElementById("place").innerHTML = "Errors in getting base location.";`	Issue message
`break;`	Leave the switch
`case 3:`	A code of 3 is to be returned if the geocoding takes too long. You can specify a time limit in the original call to the geocode method.
`document.getElementById("place").innerHTML = "Timeout in getting base location.";`	Issue message
`}`	Close **switch** statement
`document.getElementById("header").innerHTML = "Base location needs to be set!";`	In all cases, set contents of header

Code Line	Description
`}`	Close `problemhandler` function
`var rxmarker = "rx1.png";`	Red *x*; used for the base
`var bxmarker = "bx1.png";`	Black *x*; used for clicks
`function makemap(mylat,mylong) {`	Header for `makemap` function
`    var marker;`	Will hold marker
`    blatlng = new google.maps.LatLng(mylat,mylong);`	Create a `LatLng` object and set the global variable `blatlng`
`    myOptions = {`	Start setup of the associated array for options for the map
`        zoom: 14,`	Set zoom to constant 14
`        center: blatlng,`	Set the center of the map to be `blatlng`
`        mapTypeId: google.maps.MapTypeId.ROADMAP`	Set the map type to be a `ROADMAP`. Other possibilities are `SATELLITE`, `TERRAIN` and `HYBRID`.
`    };`	Close array
`    map = new google.maps.Map(document.getElementById("place"), myOptions);`	Invoke the `Map` constructor method to bring in a map with the indicated options; set the `map` variable
`    marker = new google.maps.Marker({`	Create a marker
`        position: blatlng,`	Position `blatlng`
`        title: "center",`	Title `"center"` This is text that will appear when you use the mouse to move the cursor near the marker.
`        icon: rxmarker,`	Icon for marker set to be my custom `rxmarker`

Code Line	Description
`map: map });`	Marker is on map; close `Marker` method call
`listener = google.maps.event.addListener(map, 'click', function(event) {`	Set up event handling for clicking the map; function is defined here
`checkit(event.latLng);`	Function is the line `checkit(event.latLng)`
`});`	Close definition of function and call to `addListener`
`}`	Close `makemap`
`function checkit(clatlng) {`	Header for `checkit` function
`var distance = dist(clatlng,blatlng);`	Calculate distance from the position given by the input parameter to the base location held in `blatlng`
`distance = Math.floor((distance+.005)*100)/100;`	Round off the distance to two decimal places
`var distanceString = String(distance);`	Convert distance to a string
`marker = new google.maps.Marker({`	Create a marker
`position: clatlng,`	When the user clicks on the map . . .
`title: distanceString,`	. . . make the title the formatted distance
`icon: bxmarker,`	. . . mark with a black *x*
`map: map });`	. . . mark map; close the array, close the call to `Marker`
`reversegeo(clatlng);`	Invoke `reversegeo`
`distanceref.innerHTML = "You clicked "+distanceString+" km from base.";`	Display distance information

Code Line	Description
`}`	Close `checkit` function
`function dist(point1, point2) {`	Header for distance between two points
`var R = 6371; // km`	Factor for kilometers
`// var R =  3959; // miles`	Factor for miles; keep in code just in case
`var lat1 = point1.lat()*Math.PI/180;`	Convert to radians
`var lat2 = point2.lat()*Math.PI/180 ;`	Convert to radians
`var lon1 = point1.lng()*Math.PI/180;`	Convert to radians
`var lon2 = point2.lng()*Math.PI/180;`	Convert to radians
`var d = Math.acos(Math.sin(lat1)*Math.sin(lat2) + Math.cos(lat1)*Math.cos(lat2) * Math.cos(lon2-lon1)) * R;`	Calculation based on spherical law of cosines
`return d;`	Return distance
`}`	Close `dist` function
`</script>`	Closing script tag
`</head>`	Closing head tag
`<body onLoad="init();">`	Body tag, including setting up call to init();
`<header id="header">Base location (small red x) is your current geolocation.</header>`	Header element
`<div id="place" style="width:600px; height:400px"></div>`	Div with ID place where Google Maps will go
`<form name="coutput">`	Form tag
`Base Latitude: <input type="text" name="lat"> degrees. Longitude: <input type="text" name="lon"> degrees. Accuracy: <input type="text" name="acc"> meters.  `	Text and input elements (all used for output/display in this example)

Code Line	Description
`</form>`	Closing form tag
`Last address <div id="address"></div>`	Div for addresses
`Distance <div id="distance"></div>`	Div for distances
`</body>`	Closing body tag
`</html>`	Closing `html` tag

You can build on the basic geolocation program in many ways. For example, you can use the information along with the `dist` function in a way similar to what was demonstrated in the last chapter to do something based on how close the user was to any of a set of fixed locations. The e-mail geolocation project builds on the basic project in another way. It uses the information to send an e-mail to someone of the user's choice. An informal summary/outline of the e-mail geolocation application follows:

- `init`: For initialization, including invoking the call for geolocation, which is done asynchronously

- `handler` *and* `problemhandler`: For completing the geolocation

- `makemap`: For bringing in the Google Map

- `checkit`: For responding to clicks on the map and invoking `dist`

- `reversegeo`: For determining an address from a latitude/longitude value

- `sendemailp` *(a separate program to run on the server)*: For performing the sending of e-mail

Table 6-3 lists all the functions and describes how they are invoked and what functions they invoke. The structure that has served us well in other situations is somewhat lacking now. The `sendemailp.php` function is invoked through the `action` property setting in the second `<form>` tag in the body element:

```
<form name="msg" action="sendemailp.php" method="post">
```

Table 6-3. *Functions in the E-mail Geolocation Project (Same As the Basic Geolocation Project)*

Function	Invoked/Called By	Calls
init	Invoked by action of the onLoad attribute in the <body> tag	
handler	Invoked by action of the getCurrentPosition call in init	makemap, reversegeo
reversegeo	Invoked in handler	
problemhandler	Invoked by action of the getCurrentPosition call in init	
makemap	Invoked by the handler	
checkit	Invoked by action of addListener in makemap	dist
dist	Invoked by checkit	

Table 6-4 shows the complete code for geolocationkmemail.html. New code statements and changed code statements have comments.

Table 6-4. *Code for the E-mail Geolocation Application*

Code Line	Description
`<!DOCTYPE html>`	
`<html>`	
`<head>`	
`<title>Where am I?</title>`	
`<meta charset="UTF-8">`	
`<style>`	
`header {font-family:Georgia,"Times New Roman",serif;`	
`        font-size:20px;`	
`        display:block;`	
`}`	
`</style>`	

Code Line	Description
`<script type="text/javascript" charset="UTF-8" src="http://maps.google.com/maps/api/js?sensor=false"></script>`	
`<script type="text/javascript" charset="UTF-8">`	
`var positionopts;`	
`positionopts = {`	
`        enableHighAccuracy: true,`	
`        timeout: 10000} ;`	
`var headerref;`	
`var geocoder;`	
`function init() {`	
`  headerref = document.getElementById("header");`	
`  geocoder = new google.maps.Geocoder();`	
`  if (navigator.geolocation) {`	
`   navigator.geolocation.getCurrentPosition(handler, problemhandler, positionopts);`	
`  }`	
`else {`	
`  if (document.getElementById("place")) {`	
`    document.getElementById("place").innerHTML = "I'm sorry but geolocation services are not supported by your browser";`	
`    document.getElementById("place").style.color = "#FF0000";`	
`  }`	
`  }`	

Code Line	Description
`}`	
`var listener;`	
`var map;`	
`var blatlng;`	
`var myOptions;`	
`function handler(position) {`	
`var mylat = position.coords.latitude;`	
`var mylong = position.coords.longitude;`	
`var result;`	
`makemap(mylat,mylong);`	
`document.coutput.lat.value = mylat;`	
`document.coutput.lon.value = mylong;`	
`document.coutput.acc.value = position.coords.accuracy;`	
`reversegeo(blatlng);`	
`}`	
`function reversegeo(latlng) {`	
`geocoder.geocode({'latLng': latlng}, function(results, status) {`	
`if (status == google.maps.GeocoderStatus.OK) {`	
`if (results[0]) {`	
`document.msg.subject.value = results[0].formatted_address;`	Put value in the subject input element of the message form

Code Line	Description
`        } else {`	
`            alert("No results found in reverse geocoding.");`	
`        }`	
`    }`	
`    else {`	
`        alert("Geocoder failed due to: " + status);`	
`    }`	
`  });`	
`}`	
`function problemhandler(prob) {`	
`    switch(prob.code) {`	
`    case 1:`	
`        document.getElementById("place").innerHTML = "User declined to share the location information.";`	
`        break;`	
`    case 2:`	
`        document.getElementById("place").innerHTML = "Errors in getting base location.";`	
`        break;`	
`    case 3:`	
`        document.getElementById("place").innerHTML = "Timeout in getting base location.";`	
`    }`	

Code Line	Description
`document.getElementById("header").innerHTML = "Base location needs to be set!";`	
`}`	
`var xmarker = "x1.png";`	
`function makemap(mylat,mylong) {`	
`var marker;`	
`blatlng = new google.maps.LatLng(mylat,mylong);`	
`myOptions = {`	
`zoom: 14,`	
`center: blatlng,`	
`mapTypeId: google.maps.MapTypeId.ROADMAP`	
`};`	
`map = new google.maps.Map(document.getElementById("place"), myOptions);`	
`marker = new google.maps.Marker({`	
`position: blatlng,`	
`title: "center",`	
`icon: xmarker,`	
`map: map });`	
`listener = google.maps.event.addListener(map, 'click', function(event) {`	
`checkit(event.latLng);`	
`});`	

Code Line	Description
`}`	
`function checkit(clatlng) {`	
`    var distance = dist(clatlng,blatlng);`	
`    var result;`	
`    distance = Math.floor((distance+.005)*100)/100;`	
`    var distanceString = String(distance)+" km. away.";`	
`    var newcoords = String(clatlng.lat())+" lat. "+String(clatlng.lng())+" lng.";`	Used as part of message body
`    distanceString = newcoords+" "+distanceString;`	Used as part of message body
`    marker = new google.maps.Marker({`	Note that default icon is used
`        position: clatlng,`	
`        title: distanceString,`	
`        map: map });`	
`    document.msg.body.value = document.msg.body.value + " However, I really am at "+distanceString;`	Add to message body
`}`	
`function dist(point1, point2) {`	
`    var R = 6371; // km`	
`    // var R =  3959; // miles`	
`    var lat1 = point1.lat()*Math.PI/180;`	
`    var lat2 = point2.lat()*Math.PI/180 ;`	
`    var lon1 = point1.lng()*Math.PI/180;`	

Code Line	Description
`        var lon2 = point2.lng()*Math.PI/180;`	
`var d = Math.acos(Math.sin(lat1)*Math.sin(lat2) +` `Math.cos(lat1)*Math.cos(lat2) * Math.cos(lon2-lon1)) * R;`	
`    return d;`	
`  }`	
`</script>`	
`</head>`	
`<body onLoad="init();">`	
`<header id="header">Base location (small red x) is your current` `geolocation.</header>`	
`<div id="place" style="width:600px; height:350px"></div>`	
`<form name="coutput">`	
`Base Latitude: <input type="text" name="lat"> degrees. Longitude:` `<input type="text" name="lon"> degrees.`	
`Accuracy: <input type="text" name="acc"> meters.  `	
`</form>`	
`<form name="msg" action="sendemailp.php" method="post">`	Form tag with specification of the `action` attribute causing `sendemailp.php` to be invoked, and specification of the `method` attribute causing the call to be made by the POST method
`  <p>Your email (for reply)`	Label for the From input field
`    <input type="email" name="from" required/>`	This field is required and is of type `email`

Code Line	Description
`To email`	Label for the To input field
`<input type="email" name="to" required  />`	This field is required and is of type `email`
`</p>`	Force a line break
`Subject: <input type="text" name="subject" size="100" />`	Subject will be set by `reversegeo`
`<p>`	Line break
`Body of message (you may change it)  `	Label for body of message
`<TEXTAREA NAME="body" COLS=40 ROWS=5>`	Text area set up for input consisting of 5 rows and 40 columns,
`My geolocation is at the address given in the subject line.`	Initial text
`</TEXTAREA>`	Close `textarea` element
`</p>`	Line break
`<input type="submit" value="SEND" />`	Submit button
`</form>`	Closing form tag
`</body>`	Closing body tag
`</html>`	Closing `html` tag

The e-mail application requires a PHP script to do the actual work of sending the e-mail. My `sendemailp.php` program is shown in Table 6-5.

Table 6-5. *Code for the PHP Script for Sending E-mail*

Code Line	Description
`<?php`	Delimiter for PHP code
`$to = $_POST['to'];`	Set the variable $to to the value of the form input with name **to**
`$subject = $_POST['subject'];`	Set the variable $variable to the value of the form input with name **subject**
`$body = $_POST['body'];`	Set the variable $body to the value of the form input with the name **body**
`$headers = "From: " . $_POST['from'];`	Set the variable $headers to be a string starting with **From:** followed by the value of the form input with name **from**
`if (mail($to, $subject, $body,$headers)) {`	Invoke the **mail** function, if it works
`echo("Your message was sent");`	Output success message
`} else {`	Else
`echo("There was a problem:  the body is $body,  the to is $to,  subject is $subject,  headers is $headers.");`	Output longer message, with the contents of all the variables
`}`	Close clause
`?>`	End the PHP

You may find uses for sending e-mail for other applications besides ones using geolocation. You also can build on this application in other more substantial ways, such as including other information in the e-mail content.

If you have an application in which you do not want to depend on geolocation exclusively, you may consider using a form in which the user can type in an address. You can use geocoder.geocode with the address parameter to obtain the latitude/longitude and bring in a map using that value. Another alternative is to have a list of places such as I presented in Chapter 4.

Testing and Uploading the Application

You need to be online to test the first application since that is the only way to make contact with Google Maps, but the HTML file and the files for the marker icons (bx1.png and rx1.png) can be on your local computer. To test the e-mail application, you need to run the program from your server. That is, you need to upload all the files to the server. My files are `geolocationkmemail.html`, `rx1.png`, and `sendemailp.php`. Moreover, I'll repeat what I mentioned earlier: you need to check that the server allows PHP and allows PHP to send e-mail. To make this concrete, for example, my standard server at my college allows some use of PHP, but not e-mail. The local IT group set up a special server for my database course that does the job!

Summary

In this chapter, you continued using the Google Maps API. You learned how to use the following:

- Geolocation

- Google Maps API and geocoding for addresses

- A PHP script to do e-mail

In the next chapter, we leave geography for the smaller but still spatially fascinating world of paper folding. We will explore how to produce directions for an origami of a talking fish using JavaScript, HTML5 video, and the drawing of photographs on canvas.

CHAPTER 7

Origami Directions: Using Math-Based Line Drawings, Photographs, and Videos

In this chapter, you will learn the following:

- How to use mathematics to write JavaScript functions to produce precise line drawings

- A methodology for combining line drawings, photographs, and videos, along with text for sequential instructions

- A methodology that facilitates development by letting you proceed in steps, and even go back and insert or change previous work

Introduction

The project for this chapter is a sequential set of directions for folding an origami model, a talking fish. However, you may read it with any topic in mind in which you want to present to your viewer a sequence of diagrams, including the ability to move forward and back, and with the diagrams consisting of line drawings or images from files or video clips.

▧ **Note** Origami refers to the art of paper folding. It is commonly associated with Japan, but has roots in China and Spain as well. Traditional folds include the water bomb, the crane, and the flapping bird. Lillian Oppenheimer is credited with popularizing origami in the United States and started the organization that became the American national organization OrigamiUSA. She personally taught me the business card frog in 1972. An HTML5 program for the business card frog is included in the downloads for this chapter. Origami is a vibrant art form practiced around the world, as well as a focus of research in mathematics, engineering, and computational complexity.

Figure 7-1 shows the opening screen of the Talking Fish application, `origamifish.html`. The screen shows the standard conventions for origami diagrams, modified by me to include color. The standard origami paper, called kami, is white on one side and a nonwhite color on the other.

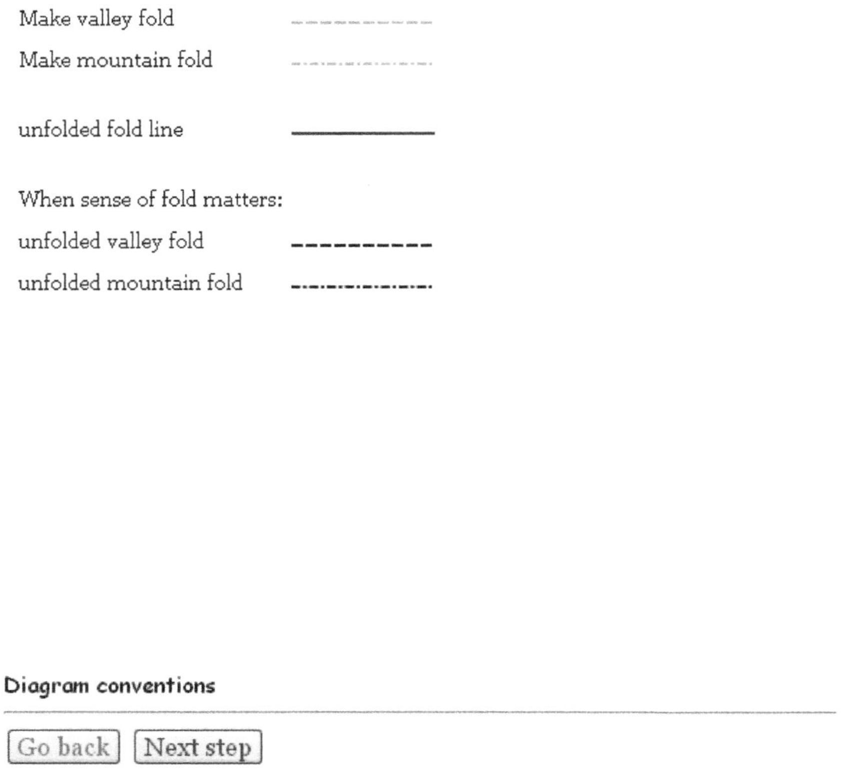

Make valley fold

Make mountain fold

unfolded fold line

When sense of fold matters:

unfolded valley fold

unfolded mountain fold

Diagram conventions

[Go back] [Next step]

Figure 7-1. *Opening screen*

▪ **Note**   I have reduced the set of origami moves. For example, I omitted the representation for a reverse fold, which is used to turn the lips inside out. These folds generally are preceded by what are termed preparation folds, which I describe for the talking fish.

The folder can click "Next step" (at this point in the sequence, "Go back" does nothing) to get to the first actual step of the instructions, shown in Figure 7-2. Of course, it is possible to add programming to remove the "Go back" button at the start and the "Next step" button at the end.

Make quarter turn.

[Go back] [Next step]

Figure 7-2. *First step, showing the square of paper. The instructions say to turn the paper.*

Skipping ahead, Figure 7-3 shows a later step in the folding. Notice that the colored side of the paper is showing. An unfolded fold line is indicated by the skinny vertical line, and the fold to be made next (folding down the corner) is shown by a colored diagonal of dashes in the upper-right corner.

Fold down the right corner to the fold marking a third.

[Go back] [Next step]

***Figure 7-3.** Folding a corner down to a fold line*

Later in the construction of the model, the folder must perform a sink fold. This is considered a difficult move. Figure 7-4 shows what is called the crease pattern prior to the sink: the folds are indicated as mountain folds or valley folds.

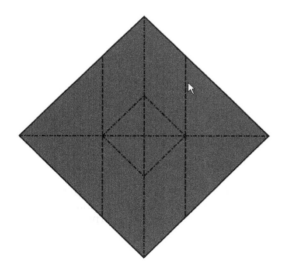

Push sides to sink middle square.

[Go back] [Next step]

***Figure 7-4.** Step with standard diagram for sink*

I decided to supplement the line drawing with a video clip showing the sink step. Figure 7-5 shows a frame from the video. I (the folder) have used the video controls to pause the action. The folder can replay the video clip and go back to the crease pattern repeated times.

Sink square, collapse model.

[Go back] [Next step]

Figure 7-5. Paused video showing sink step

Sinking is still a challenge, but viewing the video clip can help. The folder can re-play and pause the video clip. Figure 7-6 shows the next step after the sink. Going from line drawing to video clip to line drawing is easy for the user/folder, and it will turn out to be straightforward for the developer as well.

Now fold back the right flap to center valley fold. You are bisecting the indicated angle.

[Go back] [Next step]

Figure 7-6. *Step after sink (first video clip)*

The next step requires the folder to fold the triangular flap on the right backward, dividing the angle. Notice that the angle is indicated by an arc.

Moving on again in the folding, there is a step for which I decided that a photograph or two was the best way to convey what needs to be done. Figure 7-7 shows a picture of a model in process, viewed from above (looking into the mouth down the throat of the fish).

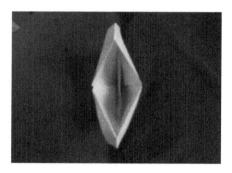

Stick your finger in its mouth and move the inner folded material to one side

[Go back] [Next step]

Figure 7-7. *Photograph showing fish throat*

Figure 7-8 shows the result of moving the folded material to one side, as instructed in the directions shown in Figure 7-7.

Throat fixed.

[Go back] [Next step]

Figure 7-8. *Photograph of the fish with the throat fixed*

The directions end with another video clip, this one showing the fish talking, performed by the folder gently pressing on the top and bottom. Figure 7-9 shows a frame in the video.

Talking fish.

[Go back] [Next step]

Figure 7-9. *Video showing talking fish*

Critical Requirements

There is a standard format for origami directions, commonly referred to as diagrams, and I built on that standard. In this approach, each step shows the next fold to be made using a set typography. The most basic folds either assume a valley shape when unfolded or a mountain shape, and this is indicated by dashed or dotted and dashed lines. Often, folds are unfolded in the process of making an origami model. Sometimes the places where there were folds are indicated by thin lines and sometimes they are indicated by dashes for valley folds and dots and dashes for mountain folds.

My aim was to produce line drawings, similar to those found in books, with calculations for the coordinate positions of the critical points and lines. I did not want to make drawings by hand and scan them, nor did I want to use a typical engineering CAD program. I did not want to measure and record lengths or angles, but have JavaScript do that task for me. This would work even for folds done "to taste," as the origami jargon goes, because I could determine the exact positions I chose to use. Using basic algebra, geometry, and trigonometry provides a way to achieve exact positions for the line drawings by calculating the coordinates of endpoints of lines.

Steps for origami typically come with text instructions. Also, arrows are sometimes used. I wanted to follow the standard while still taking advantage of the fact that these instructions would be delivered on a computer, with color and the opportunity for other media.

Thinking about the talking fish and some other folds, I decided to make use of photographs and videos for operations for which line drawings may not be good enough for you.

■ **Note** The challenge I set myself for the origami diagrams was to follow the standard but also take advantage of new technology of HTML5. This is typical when moving to a new medium and technology. You do not want to abandon a standard that your audience may feel is essential, but you also want to use what is available if it solves real problems.

A subtler requirement is that I wanted to test the application as I developed it. This meant a flexible but robust way to specify steps.

HTML5, CSS, JavaScript Features, and Mathematics

I will now describe the HTML5 features and the programming techniques used to address the requirements for the origami directions project. The best approach is to start with the overall mechanism for presenting steps, and then explain how I derived the first set of values for the positions. Then I'll explain the utility functions for drawing the valley, mountain, and arrows, and for calculating intersection points and proportions. Lastly, I will review briefly the display of images and the playing of video.

Overall Mechanism for Steps

The steps for the origami directions are specified by an array called steps. Each element of the array is itself a two-element array holding the name of a function and a piece of text that will appear on the screen. The final value of the steps array in origamifish.html is the following:

```
var steps= [
    [directions,"Diagram conventions"],
                [showkami,"Make quarter turn."],
    [diamond1,"Fold top point to bottom point."],
    [triangleM,"Divide line into thirds and make valley folds and unfold "],
    [thirds,"Fold in half to the left."],
    [rttriangle,"Fold down the right corner to the fold marking a third. "],
    [cornerdown,"Unfold everything."],
    [unfolded,"Prepare to sink middle square by reversing folds as indicated ..."],
    [changedfolds,"note middle square sides all valley folds, some other folds changed.↵
 Flip over."],
    [precollapse,"Push sides to sink middle square."],
    [playsink,"Sink square, collapse model."],
    [littleguy,"Now fold back the right flap to center valley fold. You are bisecting the↵
 indicated angle."],
```

```
[oneflapup,"Do the same thing to the flap on the left"],
[bothflapsup,"Make fins by wrapping top of right flap around 1 layer and left around↵
back layer"],
[finsp,"Now make lips...make preparation folds"],
[preparelips,"and turn lips inside out. Turn corners in..."],
[showcleftlip,"...making cleft lips."],
[lips,"Pick up fish and look down throat..."],
[showthroat1,"Stick your finger in its mouth and move the inner folded material to one↵
side"],
[showthroat2,"Throat fixed."],
[rotatefish,"Squeeze & release top and bottom to make fish's mouth close and open"],
[playtalk,"Talking fish."]
];
```

I did not come up with the steps array when I began building the application. Instead, I added to the steps array as I went along, including inserting new entries and changing the content and/or the names of the functions. I began with the following definition of the steps array:

```
var steps= [
    [showkami,"Make quarter turn"],
                [diamond,"Fold top point to bottom point."]
            ];
```

It took me some time to get into the rhythm of showing the last stage of folding, with the addition of markings for the next step. The end result is a presentation using a single HTML page that proceeds through 21 steps containing vector drawings, photographs, and video, following a similar format to a PowerPoint presentation—that is, with the ability to go forward or backward.

Going forward and backward are done by the functions donext and goback. But first I need to explain how the whole thing starts. As has been the case for all the projects so far, a function called init is invoked by the action of the onLoad attribute in the <body> tag. The code sets global variables and invokes the function for presenting the next step, donext. The init function is

```
function init() {
    canvas1 = document.getElementById("canvas");
    ctx = canvas1.getContext("2d");
    cwidth = canvas1.width;
    cheight = canvas1.height;
    ta = document.getElementById("directions");
    nextstep = 0;
    ctx.fillStyle = "white";
    ctx.lineWidth = origwidth;
    origstyle = ctx.strokeStyle;
    ctx.font = "15px Georgia, Times, serif";
    donext();
}
```

The variable nextstep is the pointer, so to speak, into the steps array. I start it off at zero.

The donext function has the task of presenting the next step in the progression of steps to produce the origami model. The function starts by checking if it is within range; that is, if it has been incremented to point beyond the end of the steps array, the value of nextstep is set to the last index. Next, the function pauses and removes from display the last video. It restores the canvas to its full height, which my code would have changed when playing a video clip. The function also sets the video variable to undefined, so the removal statements do not have to be executed again for that video. In all cases, donext clears the canvas and resets the `linewidth`. The `donext` function then presents the `nextstep` step. The display includes parts: a graphic part consisting of a line drawing, video or image and a text part consisting of the instructions. The `donext` function invokesg the drawing function indicated by he first (i.e., 0th) element of the inner array:

```
steps[nextstep][0]();
```

and displays the text, using the second (i.e., 1st) element of the inner array:

```
tx.innerHTML = steps[nextstep][1];
```

The last statement in the `donext` function is to increment the pointer. The whole `donext` function is

```
function donext() {
    if (nextstep>=steps.length) {
        nextstep=steps.length-1;
    }
    if (v) {
        v.pause();
        v.style.display = "none";
        v = undefined;
        canvas1.height = 480;
    }
    ctx.clearRect(0,0,cwidth,cheight);
    ctx.lineWidth = origwidth;
    steps[nextstep][0]();
    ta.innerHTML = steps[nextstep][1];
    nextstep++;
}
```

Coding the `goback` function took much longer in thinking time than its size would suggest. The `nextstep` variable holds the index for the next step. This means that going back requires the variable to be decremented by 2. A check must be made that the pointer is not too low—that is, less than zero. Lastly, the `goback` function invokes `donext` to display what has been set as `nextstep`. The code is

```
function goback() {
    nextstep = nextstep -2;
    if (nextstep<0) {
        nextstep = 0;
    }
    donext();
}
```

User Interface

The user, who I refer to as the folder, has two buttons, labeled "**Next step**" and "**Go back**." They are implemented using the HTML5 button element, and invoke the `goback` and `donext` functions, respectively. My choice of two different colors for the buttons—red for "**Go back**" and green for "Next step"—can be debated, as can the fact that the wording is not consistent. However, it does give me a chance to remind you of the significance of the word *Cascading* in the name *Cascading Style Sheets*. I use a directive in the style element in the head element and then I also use the following markup in the body element: The last style directive is what is controlling and gives the buttons the colors.

```
<hr/>
<button onClick="goback();" style="color: #F00">Go back </button>
<button onClick="donext();" style="color: #03F">Next step </button>
```

The color designations, each only three characters, are the equivalent of #FF0000 and #0033FF.

These two sections have described the basic mechanism for sequential directions. It assumes that each step is represented by a function and text. The next section will show how the coordinate values are set.

Coordinate Values

The line drawing is accomplished using HTML5 canvas functions and variables, mostly indicating x and y values. The variables appear in the code as **var** statements with initializations. I wrote these statements as I worked through making the model step by step, though in terms of JavaScript, they act as constants, and the values are set when the program is loaded. Figure 7-10 shows the third step of the sequence, with annotations for points a, b, c, and d.

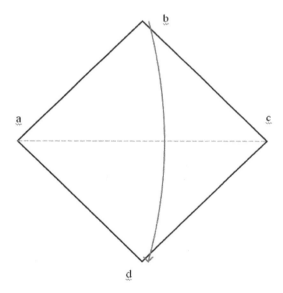

Figure 7-10. *Labels for corners*

How did I determine the coordinates for the four points? As a foundation, I specified the location of point a. I also specified that the width and height of the paper was four inches and the conversion from inches to pixels was 72. The variable declarations are

```
var kamiw = 4;
var kamih = 4;
var i2p = 72;
var ax = 10;
var ay = 220;
```

The variable names kamiw and kamih refer to the width and height of the standard square paper for origami. From now on, everything is calculated. The first value required is the size of the diagonal of the paper. For a square, using the Pythagorean theorem, the diagonal is the length of a side times the square root of 2. The following statement setting the variable diag multiples the side (kamiw) by the square root of 2 and by the factor indicating the inches-to-pixels conversion.

```
var diag = kamiw* Math.sqrt(2.0)*i2p;
```

Most other programming languages contain built-in code for many standard mathematical functions so programmers do not have to reinvent the wheel. In JavaScript, these generally are supplied as methods of the Math class. You can do online searches to determine the exact names and usage.

With this, the values for the positions b, c, and d are expressions using the existing values.

```
var bx = ax+ .5*diag;
var by = ay - .5*diag;
var cx = ax + diag;
var cy = ay;
var dx = bx;
var dy = ay + .5*diag;
```

I developed the expressions for the variables by making the model and determining how new positions were based on old ones. These variables are used by the functions specified in the steps array to draw lines indicating the edges of the model, fold lines, arrows, and angles. Some calculations used general mathematical formulas. The next two sections cover the utility functions: functions used by the step functions.

Utility Functions for Display

A valley fold is indicated by a line made up of dashes. A mountain fold is indicated by a line made up of dots and dashes. Either one can be the default color (black) or another color. I need to set up variables for the basics: dash length, dot length, the gap between two dashes, the gap between the dots, and the gap between the last dot and a dash. It is easiest to understand what is needed by looking at the functions first and then defining the necessary values. The valley function is defined as follows:

```
function valley(x1,y1,x2,y2,color) {
    var px=x2-x1;
    var py = y2-y1;
    var len = dist(x1,y1,x2,y2);
    var nd = Math.floor(len/(dashlen+dgap));
    var xs = px/nd;
    var ys = py/nd;
    if (color) ctx.strokeStyle = color;
    ctx.beginPath();
    for (var n=0;n<nd;n++) {
        ctx.moveTo(x1+n*xs,y1+n*ys);
        ctx.lineTo(x1+n*xs+dratio*xs,y1+n*ys+dratio*ys);
    }
    ctx.closePath();
    ctx.stroke();
    ctx.strokeStyle = origstyle;
}
```

The valley function determines how many dashes there will be. This is done by dividing the length of the valley line by the total length of a dash and the gap between dashes. If this is not a whole number, the last-and-partial-dash-gap combination is dropped. The Math.floor method accomplished this for us. Math.floor(4.3) returns 4.

The variables xs and ys are the increments in x and y, respectively. The color parameter may or may not be present. The if (color) statement changes the stroke color if the parameter is present. The heart of the function is the for loop that draws each dash.

The mountain function is similar, but more complicated because of the nature of the mountain fold typography: combinations of dashes followed by a gap equal to a dot, then a dot, and then another gap. The mountain function is as follows:

```
function mountain(x1,y1,x2,y2,color) {
    var px=x2-x1;
    var py = y2-y1;
    var len = dist(x1,y1,x2,y2);
    var nd = Math.floor(len/ddtotal);
    var xs = px/nd;
    var ys = py/nd;
    if (color) ctx.strokeStyle = color;
    ctx.beginPath();
    for (var n=0;n<nd;n++) {
        ctx.moveTo(x1+n*xs,y1+n*ys);
        ctx.lineTo(x1+n*xs+ddratio1*xs,y1+n*ys+ddratio1*ys);
        ctx.moveTo(x1+n*xs+ddratio2*xs,y1+n*ys+ddratio2*ys);
        ctx.lineTo(x1+n*xs+ddratio3*xs,y1+n*ys+ddratio3*ys);
    }
    ctx.closePath();
    ctx.stroke();
    ctx.strokeStyle = origstyle;
}
```

With the statements of the functions in mind, here is how I define the variables used by both functions:

```
var dashlen = 8;
var dgap = 2.0;
var ddashlen = 6.0;
var ddot = 2.0;
var dratio = dashlen/(dashlen+dgap);
var ddtotal = ddashlen+3*ddot;
var ddratio1 = ddashlen/ddtotal;
var ddratio2 = (ddashlen+ddot)/ddtotal;
var ddratio3 = (ddashlen+2*ddot)/ddtotal;
```

Lines are used to show the edges of the paper. I set the width for these lines to be 2. For places in which the paper has been folded and then unfolded, I use a skinnier line: line width set to 1. I wrote a function to make skinny lines:

```
function skinnyline(x1,y1,x2,y2) {
    ctx.lineWidth = 1;
    ctx.beginPath();
    ctx.moveTo(x1,y1);
    ctx.lineTo(x2,y2);
```

```
    ctx.closePath();
    ctx.stroke();
    ctx.lineWidth = origwidth;
}
```

At one point for the directions for the origami fish, I decided to use short, downward-pointing arrows. I wrote a general function for it, which you can study in the commented code in the "Building the Application and Making It Your Own" section. There were two places when I decided to show a long curved arrow, either horizontal or vertical. This turned out to be the longest function in the project, and I will not go into more detail here. You can study the function in the complete commented code listing. Fortify yourself with the drink of your choice. This is a complex function because of the many cases that need to be handled separately: a vertical arrow going up or down, or a horizontal arrow going left to right or right to left. The arrow is made as an arc of a circle whose center is calculated to be far away from the arc, and two little lines indicating the arrow head.

Utility Functions for Calculation

You have seen the first mathematical calculation required for this project in previous chapters. It's called dist, and it calculates the distance between two points:

```
function dist(x1,y1,x2,y2) {
    var x = x2-x1;
    var y = y2-y1;
    return Math.sqrt(x*x+y*y);
}
```

The next function to discuss is determining the intersection point between two lines. The intersection is a point that satisfies the equation for both lines. In the origami fish example, look at Figure 7-14. I (my program) will need to calculate the intersection of the line from k to n and the line from s to q. Look further along in this chapter to Figure 7-17. The xx point is the intersection. The code from the program is

```
var xxa = intersect(sx,sy,qx,qy,kx,ky,nx,ny);
var xxx = xxa[0];
var xxy = xxa[1];
```

Lines are defined by two points, and each point is defined by two numbers. This means that the intersect function has $2 \times 2 \times 2$ input parameters. My function is not general; it only works when the lines are not vertical and when there is indeed an intersection. This is acceptable for my use for the origami fish, but if you take this for another application, you may need to do more work.

Let's now focus on the mathematical representation of lines. There are different equations, but the one I use is called the *point slope* form. The slope of a line is the change in y divided by the change in x between any two points. Following convention, the slope is named m. The equation for a line with slope m going through the point (x1,y1) is

$$y - y1 = m * (x - x1)$$

Note that this line is mathematics, not JavaScript. Returning now to programming, I determined the slopes and equations for each of the lines passed to the intersect function.

The intersect function sets m12 to be the slope of the line going from (x1 y1) to (x2,y2), and m34 to be the slope of the line going from (x3,y3) to (x4,y4). The code essentially sets the two y values:

$$y = m12 * (x - x1) + y1 \text{ and } y = m34 * (x - x3) + y3$$

The next step is to set these two expressions equal to each other and solve for x. What this accomplishes is calculating a value for x that lies on both lines. With that value of x, I use one of the two equations to get the corresponding y. The pair x,y represents a point—in fact, the only point—that is on both lines. This is what is meant by *intersection*. I write the code for the function to return array [x,y]. Here is the complete code:

```
function intersect(x1,y1,x2,y2,x3,y3,x4,y4) {
    // only works on line segments that do intersect and are not
    // vertical
    var m12 = (y2-y1)/(x2-x1);
    var m34 = (y4-y3)/(x4-x3);
    var m = m34/m12;
    var x = (x1-y1/m12-m*x3+y3/m12)/(1-m);
    var y = m12*(x-x1)+y1;
    return ([x,y]);
}
```

At this point, you may have had a sudden drop in confidence that whatever you do remember from high school mathematics classes may not apply because the coordinate system for the screen is upside down. The vertical values increase moving down the screen. It turns out that these equations still work (although our interpretation may differ). For example, a line that starts at (0,0) and goes to (100,100) has a calculated slope of positive 1, even though we may think of it as sloping down. In the upside-down world, it has positive slope.

Another calculation required for the origami fish is what I have named *proportion*. This function takes five input parameters. (x1,y1) and (x2,y2) define a line segment. The fifth parameter is p, indicating proportion. The task of the function is to calculate the (x,y) position on the line segment that is p of the way from (x1,y1) to (x2,y2).

```
function proportion(x1,y1,x2,y2,p) {
    var xs = x2-x1;
    var ys = y2-y1;
    var x = x1+ p*xs;
    var y = y1 + p* ys;
    return ([x,y]);
}
```

This covers what I term the utility functions of the origami project. The three calculation functions would be applicable to other applications.

Step Line Drawing Functions

The functions for producing the diagrams for a step in the sequence use the path-drawing facilities of HTML5 and the variables, which have been set using the calculation utility functions or built-in Math methods. I won't cover all of them in this section, but will explain a couple. For example, the function triangleM (more on this function following) has the task of producing the diagram for the step shown in Figure 7-11.

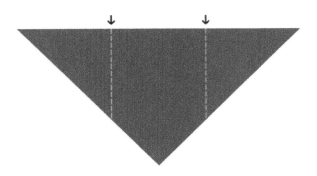

Divide line into thirds and make valley folds and unfold

[Go back] [Next step]

Figure 7-11. *Dividing-into-thirds step*

■ **Note** My instructions do not suggest ways to do this. A common way that folders do this is to make a guess for the point one-third of the way from one end—say, the left. Fold the right point to that point and make a tiny pinch. Then fold the left end to the pinch, and repeat until you don't see a change in the pinch marks. This method demonstrates some nice mathematics, namely limits. Whatever error you make in your initial guess will be reduced to one-quarter of its original size. If you keep doing this, you'll quickly get to something acceptable.

Figure 7-12 shows the picture annotated with labels for the critical points e, f, g, and h.

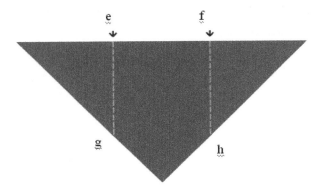

Figure 7-12. *Dividing a line into thirds and folding*

The variables defining the four points are

```
var e = proportion(ax,ay,cx,cy,.333333);
var ex = e[0];
var ey = e[1];
var f = proportion(ax,ay,cx,cy,.666666);
var fx = f[0];
var fy = f[1];
var g = proportion(ax,ay,dx,dy,.666666);
var gx = g[0];
var gy = g[1];
```

The function triangleM is defined as follows:

```
function triangleM() {
    triangle();
    shortdownarrow(ex,ey);
    shortdownarrow(fx,fy);
    valley(ex,ey,gx,gy,"orange");
    valley(fx,fy,hx,hy,"orange");
}
```

The function draws a triangle, and then draws two short downward arrows above e and f, and then draws two valley lines of color orange.

The triangle function is defined to be

```
function triangle() {
  ctx.fillStyle="teal";
  ctx.beginPath();
  ctx.moveTo(ax,ay);
  ctx.lineTo(cx,cy);
  ctx.lineTo(dx,dy);
  ctx.lineTo(ax,ay);
  ctx.closePath();
  ctx.fill();
  ctx.stroke();
}
```

The triangle function is not general, but draws this specific triangle. A general function would be

```
function generaltriangle(px,py, qx,qy, rx,ry, scolor, fcolor) {
  ctx.fillStyle=fcolor;
  ctx.strokeStyle = scolor;
  ctx.beginPath();
  ctx.moveTo(px,py);
  ctx.lineTo(qx,qy);
  ctx.lineTo(rx,ry);
  ctx.lineTo(px,py);
  ctx.closePath();
  ctx.fill();
  ctx.stroke();

}
```

Also, do not assume that I knew to write this function. I probably put this coding into the first function and then when I got to the next step of the model, realized that I needed a triangle again. I extracted the code I had written and renamed the first function `triangleM` (for "triangle marked"). I had the `triangleM` function and the `thirds` function each invoke the function named `triangle`.

Figure 7-13 shows a step in the model that I will illustrate with a function I named `littleguy`, because that is what it looks like to me.

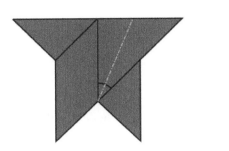

Now fold back the right flap to center valley fold. You are bisecting the indicated angle.

[Go back] [Next step]

Figure 7-13. *After sink, what I call littleguy*

Figure 7-14 shows the labeling of the critical points.

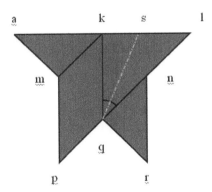

Figure 7-14. *Labeling of critical points for littleguy*

The definitions of the corresponding variables are

```
var kx = ax+diag/3;
var ky = ay;
var lx = kx + diag/3;
var ly = ay;
var mx = ax + diag/6;
var innersq = Math.sqrt(2)*diag/6;
var my = ay + innersq*Math.sin(Math.PI/4);
var nx = ax+diag/3+diag/6;
var ny = my;
var px = mx;
var py = dy;
var rx = nx;
var ry = py;
var qx = kx;
var qy = hy;
```

Notice that I don't try to be sparing with variables. Yes, rx is the same value as nx, but it is easier for me to think of them as distinct things.

The code for littleguy follows:

```
function littleguy() {
    ctx.fillStyle="teal";
    ctx.beginPath();
    ctx.moveTo(ax,ay);
    ctx.lineTo(kx,ky);
    ctx.lineTo(mx,my);
    ctx.lineTo(ax,ay);
    ctx.moveTo(kx,ky);
    ctx.lineTo(lx,ly);
    ctx.lineTo(px,py);
    ctx.lineTo(mx,my);
    ctx.lineTo(kx,ky);
    ctx.moveTo(nx,ny);
    ctx.lineTo(rx,ry);
    ctx.lineTo(qx,qy);
    ctx.lineTo(nx,ny);
    ctx.closePath();
    ctx.fill();
    ctx.stroke();
    skinnyline(qx,qy,kx,ky);
    ctx.beginPath();
    ctx.arc(qx,qy,30,-.5*Math.PI,-.25*Math.PI,false);
    ctx.stroke();
    mountain(qx,qy,sx,sy,"orange")
}
```

The description of the arc in degrees is that it goes from –90 degrees to –45 degrees. Note that zero degrees is horizontal and positive degrees go clockwise.

Figures 7-15, 7-16, 7-17, and 7-18 show the locations of the remaining critical positions for the model.

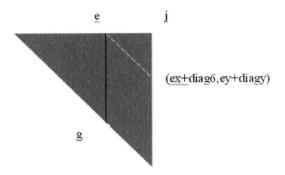

Figure 7-15. *Labeling at fold in half step*

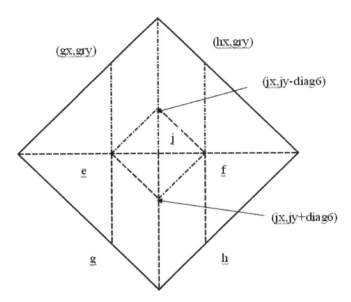

Figure 7-16. *Preparing to sink center*

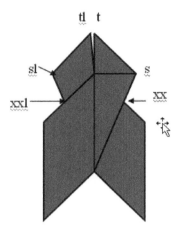

Figure 7-17. *After wraparound steps*

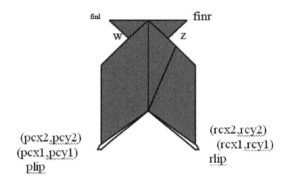

Figure 7-18. *After making lips*

Use the figures to help understand the code setting the values of variables. For example, as I mentioned in describing the `intersect` function, looking at 0s 7-14 and 7-17, you can see that the point xx, represented by xxx and xxy, is the intersection of the line from s to q and k to n.

One more of the step functions deserves explanation. The directions right before the end had the fish with the head pointed down the screen. I wanted to make the diagram right before the last video clip be oriented horizontally to match the video clip about to be displayed. This is accomplished using the canvas coordinate transformations of HTML5. The previous function is named `lips`. The `rotatefish` function saves the current, which is the original, coordinate system. It then translates to a point on the fish, invokes a rotation (90 degrees counterclockwise), and then undoes the translation. The `rotatefish` function then invokes the `lips` function, which draws the fish, but now oriented horizontally. Here is the code:

```
function rotatefish() {
   ctx.save();
   ctx.translate(kx,my);
   ctx.rotate(-Math.PI/2);
   ctx.translate(-kx,-my);
   lips();
   ctx.restore();
}
```

Displaying a Photograph

The steps that display a photograph in have the same structure as the ones producing a line drawing. For each image required for the application, I need to define an Image object and set the src property to the name of the image file. The following statements relate to the picture shown in Figure 7-7:

```
var throat1 = new Image();
throat1.src = "throat1.jpg";

function showthroat1() {
  ctx.drawImage(throat1,40,40);
}
```

The techniques shown in Chapter 5 to create a separate file defining the media and generating code (including HTML markup) automatically may be appropriate here. I wrote functions for each photograph and, as I explain in the next section, each video clip.

Presenting and Removing a Video

The origamifish.html file has video elements for each of the two video clips, one with the ID sink and the other with the ID talk. The style element has a directive for all videos to not display:

```
video {display: none;}
```

The functions playsink and playtalk each make the video display, set the current time to zero, play the video, and adjust the canvas height. The definition of playsink follows:

```
function playsink() {
   v = document.getElementById("sink");
   v.style.display="block";
   v.currentTime = 0;
   v.play();
   canvas1.height = 178;
}
```

With this discussion of the programming techniques and HTML5 features to use for the origami directions project, we are now ready to look at the application as a whole.

Building the Application and Making It Your Own

The quickest way to build on what you have learned in this chapter is to create directions for another craft project similar to paper folding in the presence of line drawings and the benefits of some photographs and video clips. You can build it step by step, creating the functions you need. It may turn out that some functions are what I call utility functions: functions used by other functions. You may also build up variables indicating positioning as you need them. An informal summary/outline of the origami fish application follows:

- `init` : for initialization
- `donext` and `goback` for moving forward and back through the steps
- Utility functions for drawing specific types of lines
- Utility functions for calculations
- Step functions (functions cited in the `steps` array)

Table 7-1 lists functions and groups of functions, and indicates how they are invoked and what functions they invoke.

Table 7-1. *Functions in the Origami Directions Project*

Function	Invoked/Called By	Calls
`init`	Invoked by action of the `onLoad` attribute in the `<body>` tag	`donext`
`donext`	Invoked by `init`, `goback`, and by the `onClick` attribute in a button tag	
`goback`	Invoked by the `onClick` attribute in a button tag	`donext`
Utility functions for drawing (`shortdownarrow`, `valley`, `mountain`, `skinnyline`, `curvedarrow`)	Invoked by the step functions	
Utility functions for calculations (`dist`, `intersect`, `proportion`)	Invoked mainly in `var` statements to set variables representing critical positions in the model	
Step functions	Invoked as elements in the `steps` array in `donext`. Some (`fins`, `triangle`, `diamond`, `rttriangle`, `diamondc`, and `lips`) are called by other step functions	Utility drawing functions, the other step functions indicated

Table 7-2 shows the code for the basic application, with comments for each line. Much of this code you have seen in previous chapters.

Table 7-2. *Insert Table Caption*

Code Line	Description
`<!DOCTYPE html>`	Header
`<html>`	html tag
`<head>`	Head tag
`<title>Origami fish</title>`	Complete title
`<style>`	Style tag
`button {font-size:large; font-family:Georgia, "Times New Roman", Times, serif;}`	Directive for formatting of buttons; note that color is specified for each button in the body element
`#directions {font-family:"Comic Sans MS", cursive;}`	Directive for formatting of all directions
`video {display:none; }`	Turn off display of all video elements until called on
`</style>`	Closing style tag
`<script>`	Starting script tag
`var ctx;`	Will hold canvas context for all drawing
`var cwidth;`	Width of canvas
`var cheight;`	Height of canvas
`var ta;`	Will hold element for text part of each step
`var kamiw = 4;`	Set width of paper
`var kamih = 4;`	Set height of paper
`var i2p = 72;`	Set inches to pixels

Code Line	Description
`var dashlen = 8;`	Set length of dash in valley fold
`var dgap = 2.0;`	Set gap between dashes
`var ddashlen = 6.0;`	Set dash length in mountain fold
`var ddot = 2.0;`	Set dot length in mountain fold
`var dratio = dashlen/(dashlen+dgap);`	Used for mountain line
`var ddtotal = ddashlen+3*ddot;`	Used for mountain line
`var ddratio1 = ddashlen/ddtotal;`	Used for mountain line
`var ddratio2 = (ddashlen+ddot)/ddtotal;`	Used for mountain line
`var ddratio3 = (ddashlen+2*ddot)/ddtotal;`	Used for mountain line; all values used for calculation of number of dashes and dots and start and extents of dashes and dots
`var kamix = 10;`	X position of paper in first step
`var kamiy = 10;`	Y position of paper in first step
`var nextstep;`	Pointer into `steps` array
`function dist(x1,y1,x2,y2) {`	Header for `dist` function
`    var x = x2-x1;`	Set difference in x
`    var y = y2-y1;`	Set difference in y
`    return Math.sqrt(x*x+y*y);`	Return square root of sum of squares
`}`	Close `dist` function
`function intersect(x1,y1,x2,y2,x3,y3,x4,y4) {`	Header for `intersect` function between two lines, indicated by 2 × 2 points
`    // only works on line segments that do intersection and`	Good comments to keep in code: assumes there is an intersection . . .

Code Line	Description
`// are not vertical`	. . . and assumes lines aren't vertical; if they were, the code would be dividing by zero, which would produce an error
`var m12 = (y2-y1)/(x2-x1);`	Compute slope
`var m34 = (y4-y3)/(x4-x3);`	Compute slope
`var m = m34/m12;`	Used in calculation
`var x = (x1-y1/m12-m*x3+y3/m12)/(1-m);`	Solve for x
`var y = m12*(x-x1)+y1;`	Solve for y
`return ([x,y]);`	Return pair
`}`	Close `intersect` function
`function init() {`	Header for `init` function
`canvas1 = document.getElementById("canvas");`	Set `canvas1`
`ctx = canvas1.getContext("2d");`	Set context
`cwidth = canvas1.width;`	Set `cwidth`
`cheight = canvas1.height;`	Set `cheight`
`ta = document.getElementById("directions");`	Set `ta` to hold the element for the text directions
`nextstep = 0;`	Initialize `nextstep`
`ctx.fillStyle = "white";`	Set fill style; will be used for erasing
`ctx.lineWidth = origwidth;`	Set line width (set earlier)
`origstyle = ctx.strokeStyle;`	Save stroke color
`ctx.font = "15px Georgia, Times, serif";`	Set font
`donext();`	Start with 0th step

Code Line	Description
`}`	Close `init` function
`function directions() {`	Header for directions, the first '"step" shown
`    ctx.fillStyle = "black";`	Change fill style, for use in text
`    ctx.font = "15px Georgia, Times, serif";`	Set font
`    ctx.fillText("Make valley fold", 10,20);`	Output explanation
`    valley(200,18,300,18,"orange");`	Make sample orange valley line
`    ctx.fillText("Make mountain fold",10,50);`	Output explanation
`    mountain(200,48,300,48,"orange");`	Make sample orange mountain line
`    ctx.fillText("unfolded fold line",10,100);`	Output explanation
`    skinnyline(200,98,300,98);`	Make sample skinny line for unfolded fold line
`    ctx.fillText("When sense of fold matters:",10,150);`	Output explanation
`    ctx.fillText("unfolded valley fold", 10,180);`	Continue
`    valley(200,178,300,178);`	Make sample old valley
`    ctx.fillText("unfolded mountain fold",10,210);`	Output explanation
`    mountain(200,208,300,208);`	Make sample old mountain
`    ctx.fillStyle = "white";`	Change fill style back
`}`	Close directions function
`function donext() {`	Header for **donext** function
`    if (nextstep>=steps.length) {`	Check if **nextstep** is too big
`        nextstep=steps.length-1;`	Reset
`    }`	Close clause

Code Line	Description
`if (v) {`	Check if **v** is set
`v.pause();`	Pause the video
`v.style.display = "none";`	Make it not display
`v = undefined;`	Set **v** to undefined
`canvas1.height = 480;`	Restore height
`}`	Close clause
`ctx.clearRect(0,0,cwidth,cheight);`	Clear canvas
`ctx.lineWidth = origwidth;`	Reset line width
`steps[nextstep][0]();`	Invoke the appropriate step function
`ta.innerHTML = steps[nextstep][1];`	Display the accompanying text
`nextstep++;`	Increment **nextstep**
`}`	Close **donext** function
`function goback() {`	Header for **goback**
`nextstep = nextstep -2;`	Decrement **nextstep** by 2 (because it is already 1 ahead)
`if (nextstep<0) {`	Check if **nextstep** is now too low
`nextstep = 0;`	Reset
`}`	Close clause
`donext();`	Invoke **donext**
`}`	Close **goback** function
`function shortdownarrow(x,y) {`	Header for short-downward-arrow function
`ctx.beginPath();`	Start path

Code Line	Description
`ctx.moveTo(x,y-20)`	Move to right above the (x,y) position
`ctx.lineTo(x,y-7);`	Draw line to just above the (x,y)
`ctx.moveTo(x-5,y-12);`	Move to the left and up
`ctx.lineTo(x,y-7);`	Draw diagonal line
`ctx.moveTo(x+5,y-12);`	Move to the right and up
`ctx.lineTo(x,y-7);`	Draw diagonal line
`ctx.closePath();`	Close path
`ctx.stroke();`	Draw the complete path: a short arrow
`}`	Close `shortdownarrow` function
`function proportion(x1,y1,x2,y2,p) {`	header for `proportion` function
`var xs = x2-x1;`	Set difference in x
`var ys = y2-y1;`	Set difference in y
`var x = x1+ p*xs;`	Calculate new x
`var y = y1 + p* ys;`	calculate new y
`return ([x,y]);`	Return pair
`}`	Close `proportion` function
`function skinnyline(x1,y1,x2,y2) {`	Header for `skinnyline` function
`ctx.lineWidth = 1;`	Set line width
`ctx.beginPath();`	Start path
`ctx.moveTo(x1,y1);`	Move to start
`ctx.lineTo(x2,y2);`	Line to finish

Code Line	Description
`ctx.closePath();`	Close path
`ctx.stroke();`	Make stroke
`ctx.lineWidth = origwidth;`	Reset line width
`}`	Close `skinnyline`
`var origstyle;`	Will hold original color
`var origwidth = 2;`	Set to line width for most lines
`function valley(x1,y1,x2,y2,color) {`	Header for `valley` function
`var px=x2-x1;`	Set difference in x
`var py = y2-y1;`	Set difference in y
`var len = dist(x1,y1,x2,y2);`	Determine length
`var nd = Math.floor(len/(dashlen+dgap));`	How many dashes and gaps
`var xs = px/nd;`	Call this the x factor
`var ys = py/nd;`	Call this the y factor
`if (color) ctx.strokeStyle = color;`	If the `color` parameter was given, set stroke color to this value
`ctx.beginPath();`	Begin path
`for (var n=0;n<nd;n++) {`	Loop for number of dashes
`ctx.moveTo(x1+n*xs,y1+n*ys);`	Move to next position
`ctx.lineTo(x1+n*xs+dratio*xs,y1+n*ys+dratio*ys);`	Draw dash
`}`	Close `for` loop
`ctx.closePath();`	Close path

Code Line	Description
`ctx.stroke();`	Draw the path
`ctx.strokeStyle = origstyle;`	Reset stroke style
`}`	Close **valley** function
`function mountain(x1,y1,x2,y2,color) {`	Header for mountain function
`var px=x2-x1;`	Set difference in x
`var py = y2-y1;`	Set difference in y
`var len = dist(x1,y1,x2,y2);`	Determine length
`var nd = Math.floor(len/ddtotal);`	Determine number of dash and dot combinations
`var xs = px/nd;`	Set x factor
`var ys = py/nd;`	Set y factor
`if (color) ctx.strokeStyle = color;`	If the **color** parameter was given, set stroke color to this value
`ctx.beginPath();`	Begin path
`for (var n=0;n<nd;n++) {`	Loop for number of combinations
`ctx.moveTo(x1+n*xs,y1+n*ys);`	Move to next one
`ctx.lineTo(x1+n*xs+ddratio1*xs,y1+n*ys+` `ddratio1*ys);`	Draw the dash
`ctx.moveTo(x1+n*xs+ddratio2*xs,y1+n*ys+` `ddratio2*ys);`	Move to start of dot
`ctx.lineTo(x1+n*xs+ddratio3*xs,y1+n*ys+` `ddratio3*ys);`	Draw the dot
`}`	Close loop
`ctx.closePath();`	Close path

Code Line	Description
`ctx.stroke();`	Draw the path
`ctx.strokeStyle = origstyle;`	Reset stroke style
`}`	Close mountain function
`function curvedarrow(x1,y1,x2,y2,px,py){`	Header for curvedarrow from (x1,y1) to (x2,y2) offset by (px,py)
`var arrowanglestart;`	Start Angle
`var arrowanglefinish;`	Finish angle
`var d = dist(x1,y1,x2,y2);`	Distance
`var rad=Math.sqrt(4.25*d*d);`	The value 4.25 arrived at by experimentation to get an attractive curve to the arrow
`var ctrx;`	X-coordinate of center of arc that is curved arrow
`var ctry;`	Y-coordinate
`var ex;`	For the two little lines that make up the head of the arrow
`var ey;`	For the two little lines that make up the head of the arrow
`var angdel = Math.atan2(d/2,2*d);`	Angle of the arc
`var fromhorizontal;`	Angle where arc starts
`ctx.strokeStyle = "red";`	Set color
`ctx.beginPath();`	Begin path
`if (y1==y2) {`	Horizontal arrow case
`arrowanglestart = 1.5*Math.PI-angdel;`	Set starting angle
`arrowanglefinish = 1.5*Math.PI+angdel;`	Set ending angle

Code Line	Description
`ctrx = .5*(x1+x2) +px;`	Calculate center x
`ctry = y1+2*d +py;`	Calculate center y
`if (x1<x2) {`	For arrows going left to right

`ctx.arc(ctrx,ctry,`
`rad,arrowanglestart,arrowanglefinish,`
`false);`
	Draw arc

`fromhorizontal=2*Math.PI-` `arrowanglefinish;`	Used in calculation
`ex = ctrx+rad*Math.cos(fromhorizontal);`	Set x increment
`ey = ctry - rad*Math.sin(fromhorizontal);`	Set y increment
`ctx.lineTo(ex-8,ey+8);`	Draw first little line
`ctx.moveTo(ex,ey);`	Move to other end
`ctx.lineTo(ex-8,ey-8);`	Draw line
`}`	Close arrows left to right
`else {`	Right to left
`ctx.arc(ctrx,ctry, rad,arrowanglefinish,arrowanglestart,` `true);`	Draw arc
`fromhorizontal=2*Math.PI- arrowanglestart;`	Calculate for the lines
`ex = ctrx+rad*Math.cos(fromhorizontal);`	Set x for little lines
`ey = ctry - rad*Math.sin(fromhorizontal);`	Set y for little lines
`ctx.lineTo(ex+8,ey+8);`	Draw first line
`ctx.moveTo(ex,ey);`	Move to end of other line
`ctx.lineTo(ex+8,ey-8);`	Draw line

Code Line	Description
`}`	End clause
`ctx.stroke();`	Do the drawing for either case
`}`	End horizontal case
`else if (x1==x2) {`	Vertical line
`arrowanglestart = -angdel;`	Set starting angle
`arrowanglefinish = angdel;`	Set finishing angle
`ctrx = x1-2*d+px;`	Calculate center x
`ctry = .5*(y1+y2) + py;`	Calculate center y
`if (y1<y2) {`	If downward arrow
`ctx.arc(ctrx,ctry,rad,arrowanglestart,` `    arrowanglefinish,false);`	Draw arc
`fromhorizontal=- arrowanglefinish;`	For calculation
`ex = ctrx+rad*Math.cos(fromhorizontal);`	Calculate x for little lines
`ey = ctry - rad*Math.sin(fromhorizontal);`	Calculate y for little lines
`ctx.lineTo(ex-8,ey-8);`	Draw first little line
`ctx.moveTo(ex,ey);`	Move to end
`ctx.lineTo(ex+8,ey-8);`	Draw second little line
`}`	End downward clause
`else {`	Upward clause

`ctx.arc(ctrx,ctry,`
`rad,arrowanglefinish,arrowanglestart,`
`    true);`
	Draw arc

`fromhorizontal=- arrowanglestart;`	For calculation

Code Line	Description
`ex = ctrx+rad*Math.cos(fromhorizontal);`	Calculate x for little lines
`ey = ctry - rad*Math.sin(fromhorizontal);`	Calculate y for little lines
`ctx.lineTo(ex-8,ey+8);`	Draw first little line
`ctx.moveTo(ex,ey);`	Move to end of second line
`ctx.lineTo(ex+8,ey+8);`	Draw little line
`}`	End clause
`ctx.stroke();`	Draw arc
`}`	Close vertical case
`    ctx.strokeStyle = "black";`	Reset color
`}`	
`// specific to fish`	What follows is specific to the fish model
`var steps= [`	Instruction steps: Function name and accompanying text
`    [directions,"Diagram conventions"],`	
`      [showkami,"Make quarter turn."],`	
`    [diamond1,"Fold top point to bottom point."],`	
`    [triangleM,"Divide line into thirds and make valley folds and unfold "],`	
`    [thirds,"Fold in half to the left."],`	
`    [rttriangle,"Fold down the right corner to the fold marking a third. "],`	
`    [cornerdown,"Unfold everything."],`	
`    [unfolded,"Prepare to sink middle square by reversing`	

Code Line	Description
folds as indicated ..."],	
[changedfolds,"note middle square sides all valley folds, some other folds changed. Flip over."],	
[precollapse,"Push sides to sink middle square."],	
[playsink,"Sink square, collapse model."],	
[littleguy,"Now fold back the right flap to center valley fold. You are bisecting the indicated angle."],	
[oneflapup,"Do the same thing to the flap on the left"],	
[bothflapsup,"Make fins by wrapping top of right flap around 1 layer and left around back layer"],	
[finsp,"Now make lips...make preparation folds"],	
[preparelips,"and turn lips inside out. Turn corners in..."],	
[showcleftlip,"...making cleft lips."],	
[lips,"Pick up fish and look down throat..."],	
[showthroat1,"Stick your finger in its mouth and move the inner folded material to one side"],	
[showthroat2,"Throat fixed."],	
[rotatefish,"Squeeze & release top and bottom to make fish's mouth close and open"],	
[playtalk,"Talking fish."]	
];	
var diag = kamiw* Math.sqrt(2.0)*i2p;	Length of diagonal
var ax = 10;	Set x for left corner

Code Line	Description
`var ay = 220;`	Set y for left corner
`var bx = ax+ .5*diag;`	Calculate b (top corner)
`var by = ay - .5*diag;`	
`var cx = ax + diag;`	Calculate c (right)
`var cy = ay;`	
`var dx = bx;`	Calculate d (bottom)
`var dy = ay + .5*diag;`	
`var e = proportion(ax,ay,cx,cy,.333333);`	See Figure 7-12 for e through h
`var ex = e[0];`	
`var ey = e[1];`	
`var f = proportion(ax,ay,cx,cy,.666666);`	
`var fx = f[0];`	
`var fy = f[1];`	
`var g = proportion(ax,ay,dx,dy,.666666);`	
`var gx = g[0];`	
`var gy = g[1];`	
`var h = proportion(cx,cy,dx,dy,.666666);`	
`var hx = h[0];`	
`var hy = h[1];`	
`var jx = ax + .5*diag;`	See Figures 7-15 and 7-16
`var jy = ay;`	
`var diag6 = diag/6;`	

Code Line	Description
`var gry = ay-(gy-ay);`	
`var kx = ax+diag/3;`	See Figure 7-14 for k through s
`var ky = ay;`	
`var lx = kx + diag/3;`	
`var ly = ay;`	
`var mx = ax + diag/6;`	
`var innersq = Math.sqrt(2)*diag/6;`	
`var my = ay + innersq*Math.sin(Math.PI/4);`	
`var nx = ax+diag/3+diag/6;`	
`var ny = my;`	
`var px = mx;`	
`var py = dy;`	
`var rx = nx;`	
`var ry = py;`	
`var qx = kx;`	
`var qy = hy;`	
`var dkq = qy-ky;`	
`var sx = kx +` `(dkq/Math.cos(Math.PI/8))*Math.sin(Math.PI/8);`	
`var sy = ay;`	
`var tx = kx;`	See Figure 7-17
`var ty = qy-dist(qx,qy,lx,ly);`	

Code Line	Description
`var xxa = intersect(sx,sy,qx,qy,kx,ky,nx,ny);`	
`var xxx = xxa[0];`	
`var xxy = xxa[1];`	
`var xxlx = kx-(xxx-kx);`	
`var xxly = xxy;`	
`var slx = kx- (sx-kx);`	
`var sly = sy;`	
`var tlx = tx-5;`	
`var tly = ty;`	
`var dkt=ky-ty;`	
`var finlx = kx-dkt;`	See Figure 7-18
`var finly = ky;`	
`var finrx = kx+dkt;`	
`var finry = ky;`	
`var w = Math.cos(Math.PI/4)*dkt;`	
`var wx = kx-.5*dkt;`	
`var wy = w*Math.sin(Math.PI/4)+ky;`	
`var zx = kx+.5*dkt;`	
`var zy = wy;`	
`var plipx = px;`	
`var plipy = py-10;`	
`var rlipx = rx;`	

Code Line	Description
`var rlipy = ry-10;`	
`var plipex = px - 10;`	
`var plipey = plipy;`	
`var rlipex = rx + 10;`	
`var rlipey = rlipy;`	
`var rclipcleft1 = proportion(rlipex,rlipey,rlipx,rlipy,.5);`	
`var pclipcleft1 = proportion(plipex,plipey,plipx,plipy,.5);`	
`var rclipcleft2 = proportion(rlipex,rlipey,qx,qy,.1);`	
`var pclipcleft2 = proportion(plipex,plipey,qx,qy,.1);`	
`var rcx1 = rclipcleft1[0];`	
`var rcy1 = rclipcleft1[1];`	
`var rcx2 = rclipcleft2[0];`	
`var rcy2 = rclipcleft2[1];`	
`var pcx1 = pclipcleft1[0];`	
`var pcy1 = pclipcleft1[1];`	
`var pcx2 = pclipcleft2[0];`	
`var pcy2 = pclipcleft2[1];`	
`var v;`	Will hold video element
`var throat1 = new Image();`	Define Image object
`throat1.src = "throat1.jpg";`	Set `src`
`var throat2 = new Image();`	Define Image object

Code Line	Description
`throat2.src = "throat2.jpg"`	Set `src`
`var cleft = new Image();`	Define Image object
`cleft.src="cleftlip.jpg";`	Set `src`
`function showcleftlip() {`	Header for `showcleftlip`
`    ctx.drawImage(cleft,40,40);`	Draw image
`}`	close `showcleftlip`
`function showthroat1() {`	Header for `showthroat1`
`  ctx.drawImage(throat1,40,40);`	Draw image
`}`	Close `showthroat1`
`function showthroat2() {`	Header for `showthroat2`
`  ctx.drawImage(throat2,40,40);`	Draw image
`}`	Close `showthroat2`
`function playtalk() {`	Header for `playtalk`
`    v = document.getElementById("talk");`	Set to the talk video
`    v.style.display="block";`	Make visible
`    v.currentTime = 0;`	Set at start
`    v.play();`	Play
`    canvas1.height = 126;`	Adjust for height of video
`}`	Close `playtalk`
`function playsink() {`	Header for `playsink`
`    v = document.getElementById("sink");`	Set to the sink video
`    v.style.display="block";`	Make visible

Code Line	Description
`v.currentTime = 0;`	Set at start
`v.play();`	Play
`canvas1.height = 178;`	Adjusts for height of video
`}`	Close `playsink`
`function lips() {`	Header for `lips`
`ctx.fillStyle = "teal";`	Set color
`ctx.beginPath();`	Begin path
`ctx.moveTo(finlx,finly);`	Move to left corner of left fin
`ctx.lineTo(kx,ky);`	Draw to center
`ctx.lineTo(wx,wy);`	Draw back and down
`ctx.lineTo(finlx,finly);`	Draw up to start (left corner, left fin)
`ctx.moveTo(finrx,finry);`	Move to right fin
`ctx.lineTo(kx,ky);`	Draw to center
`ctx.lineTo(zx,zy);`	Draw down and right
`ctx.lineTo(finrx,finry);`	Draw up to right corner, right fin
`ctx.moveTo(mx,my);`	Move to m
`ctx.lineTo(kx,ky);`	Draw to k
`ctx.lineTo(xxx,xxy);`	Draw to xx
`ctx.lineTo(qx,qy);`	Draw down, center to q
`ctx.lineTo(plipx,plipy);`	Draw down, right
`ctx.lineTo(mx,my);`	Draw straight up to m
`ctx.moveTo(xxx,xxy);`	Move to xx

Code Line	Description
`ctx.lineTo(nx,ny);`	Draw right and down
`ctx.lineTo(rlipx,rlipy);`	Draw down to rlip
`ctx.lineTo(qx,qy);`	Draw to center q
`ctx.lineTo(xxx,xxy);`	Draw back to xx
`ctx.closePath();`	Close path
`ctx.fill();`	Fill in shape
`ctx.stroke();`	Outline shape
`ctx.fillStyle="white";`	Set to white
`ctx.beginPath();`	Begin path
`ctx.moveTo(qx,qy);`	Start at lower center
`ctx.lineTo(pcx2,pcy2);`	Draw to left top of lip
`ctx.lineTo(pcx1,pcy1);`	Draw to left outer lip
`ctx.lineTo(plipx,plipy);`	Draw over right slightly to bottom-corner plip
`ctx.lineTo(qx,qy);`	Draw back to center
`ctx.lineTo(rcx2,rcy2);`	Draw to right top of lip
`ctx.lineTo(rcx1,rcy1);`	Draw to right outer lip
`ctx.lineTo(rlipx,rlipy);`	Draw to bottom-corner rlip
`ctx.lineTo(qx,qy);`	Draw back to center
`ctx.closePath();`	Close path
`ctx.fill();`	Fill in white shape (two parts)
`ctx.stroke();`	Outline shapes

Code Line	Description
`skinnyline(kx,ky,qx,qy);`	Draw vertical center line
`ctx.fillStyle="teal";`	Reset to color
`}`	Close lips
`function rotatefish() {`	Header for `rotatefish`
`ctx.save();`	Save current coordinate system
`ctx.translate(kx,my);`	Move to a center point
`ctx.rotate(-Math.PI/2);`	Rotate 90 degrees
`ctx.translate(-kx,-my);`	Undo translation
`lips();`	Draw lips (the model up to this point)
`ctx.restore();`	Restore old coordinate system
`}`	Close `rotatefish`
`function preparelips() {`	Header for `preparelips`
`ctx.fillStyle="teal";`	Set color
`fins();`	Draw fins
`valley(qx,qy,rlipx,rlipy);`	Mark valley line
`valley(qx,qy,plipx,plipy);`	Mark valley line
`}`	Close `preparelips`
`function finsp() {`	Header for `finsp`
`ctx.fillStyle="teal";`	Set color
`fins();`	Draw fins
`valley(qx,qy,rlipx,rlipy,"orange");`	Draw valley fold
`valley(qx,qy,plipx,plipy,"orange");`	Draw valley fold

Code Line	Description
`}`	Close `finsp`
`function fins() {`	Header for fins
`    ctx.beginPath();`	Begin path
`    ctx.moveTo(finlx,finly);`	Move to left fin
`    ctx.lineTo(kx,ky);`	Draw line to center
`    ctx.lineTo(wx,wy);`	Draw line left and down
`    ctx.lineTo(finlx,finly);`	Draw to left fin
`    ctx.moveTo(finrx,finry);`	Move to right fin
`    ctx.lineTo(kx,ky);`	Draw to center
`    ctx.lineTo(zx,zy);`	Draw right and down
`    ctx.lineTo(finrx,finry);`	Draw back to right fin
`    ctx.moveTo(mx,my);`	Move to m (left and down)
`    ctx.lineTo(kx,ky);`	Draw to center
`    ctx.lineTo(xxx,xxy);`	Draw to xx
`    ctx.lineTo(qx,qy);`	Draw down to q
`    ctx.lineTo(px,py);`	Draw over to p
`    ctx.lineTo(mx,my);`	Draw left to m
`    ctx.moveTo(xxx,xxy);`	Move to xx
`    ctx.lineTo(nx,ny);`	Draw right to n
`    ctx.lineTo(rx,ry);`	Draw down to r
`    ctx.lineTo(qx,qy);`	Draw up and left to center
`    ctx.lineTo(xxx,xxy);`	Draw to xx

Code Line	Description
`ctx.closePath();`	Close path
`ctx.fill();`	Fill in shape
`ctx.stroke();`	Draw outline
`skinnyline(kx,ky,qx,qy);`	Draw skinny line indicated center fold
`}`	Close fins
`function bothflapsup () {`	Header for `bothflapsup`
`ctx.fillStyle="teal";`	Set color
`ctx.beginPath();`	Begin path
`ctx.moveTo(slx,sly);`	Move to corner
`ctx.lineTo(tlx,tly);`	Draw line up to tip
`ctx.lineTo(kx,ky);`	Draw line to center
`ctx.lineTo(xxlx,xxly);`	Draw line left and down
`ctx.lineTo(slx,sly);`	Draw back to tip
`ctx.moveTo(mx,my);`	Move down (on the left)
`ctx.lineTo(kx,ky);`	Draw line to center
`ctx.lineTo(sx,sy);`	Draw to right side
`ctx.lineTo(qx,qy);`	Draw down, left
`ctx.lineTo(px,py);`	Draw to bottom, left tip
`ctx.lineTo(mx,my);`	Draw up
`ctx.moveTo(tx,ty);`	Draw up
`ctx.lineTo(sx,sy);`	Draw to right
`ctx.lineTo(kx,ky);`	Draw to center

Code Line	Description
`ctx.lineTo(tx,ty);`	Draw up
`ctx.moveTo(xxx,xxy);`	Draw to right
`ctx.lineTo(nx,ny);`	Draw to right
`ctx.lineTo(rx,ry);`	Draw down to tip
`ctx.lineTo(qx,qy);`	Draw to center
`ctx.lineTo(xxx,xxy);`	Draw back to right
`ctx.closePath();`	Close path
`ctx.fill();`	Fill in shape
`ctx.stroke();`	Outline shape
`skinnyline(kx,ky,qx,qy);`	Add line indicating fold
`}`	Close `bothflapsup`
`function oneflapup() {`	Header for `oneflapup`
`ctx.fillStyle="teal";`	Set color
`ctx.beginPath();`	Begin path
`ctx.moveTo(ax,ay);`	Move to left corner
`ctx.lineTo(kx,ky);`	Draw to middle
`ctx.lineTo(mx,my);`	Draw down and left
`ctx.lineTo(ax,ay);`	Draw back to left corner
`ctx.moveTo(kx,ky);`	Move to middle
`ctx.lineTo(sx,sy);`	Draw to right
`ctx.lineTo(qx,qy);`	Draw down, middle
`ctx.lineTo(px,py);`	Draw left, down

Code Line	Description
`ctx.lineTo(mx,my);`	Draw up
`ctx.lineTo(kx,ky);`	Draw (back to) middle top
`ctx.moveTo(xxx,xxy);`	Draw right, down
`ctx.lineTo(nx,ny);`	Draw down
`ctx.lineTo(rx,ry);`	Draw down to right tip
`ctx.lineTo(qx,qy);`	Draw to center
`ctx.lineTo(xxx,xxy);`	Draw right, up
`ctx.moveTo(kx,ky);`	Move to middle
`ctx.lineTo(tx,ty);`	Draw to top
`ctx.lineTo(sx,sy);`	Draw down, right
`ctx.lineTo(kx,ky);`	Draw (back to) top
`ctx.closePath();`	Close path
`ctx.fill();`	Fill in shape
`ctx.stroke();`	Outline shape
`skinnyline(qx,qy,kx,ky);`	Draw fold line
`}`	Close `oneflapup`
`function littleguy() {`	Header for `littleguy`
`ctx.fillStyle="teal";`	Set color
`ctx.beginPath();`	Begin path
`ctx.moveTo(ax,ay);`	Move to left corner
`ctx.lineTo(kx,ky);`	Draw to center
`ctx.lineTo(mx,my);`	Draw left, down

Code Line	Description
`ctx.lineTo(ax,ay);`	Draw back to corner
`ctx.moveTo(kx,ky);`	Move to center
`ctx.lineTo(lx,ly);`	Draw to right corner
`ctx.lineTo(px,py);`	Draw down and left
`ctx.lineTo(mx,my);`	Draw up
`ctx.lineTo(kx,ky);`	Draw back to center
`ctx.moveTo(nx,ny);`	Move right and down
`ctx.lineTo(rx,ry);`	Draw down
`ctx.lineTo(qx,qy);`	Draw to lower center
`ctx.lineTo(nx,ny);`	Draw back, right
`ctx.closePath();`	Close path
`ctx.fill();`	Fill in shape
`ctx.stroke();`	Outline shape
`skinnyline(qx,qy,kx,ky);`	Draw fold line
`ctx.beginPath();`	Begin path
`ctx.arc(qx,qy,30,-.5*Math.PI,` `-.25*Math.PI,false);`	Draw arc to represent angle
`ctx.stroke();`	Draw as stroke
`mountain(qx,qy,sx,sy,"orange")`	Indicate mountain fold
`}`	Close `littleguy`
`function unfolded() {`	Header for `unfolded`
`diamond();`	Draw diamond shape

Code Line	Description
`valley(ax,ay,cx,cy);`	Indicate valley across paper
`valley(ex,ey,gx,gy);`	Indicate valley, midway and down on left
`valley(fx,fy,hx,hy);`	Indicate valley, midway and down on right
`mountain(ex,ey,gx,gry);`	Indicate mountain, midway and up on left
`mountain(fx,fy,hx,gry);`	Indicate mountain, midway and up, right
`valley(jx,jy,dx,dy);`	Valley from inner diamond to bottom
`mountain(jx,jy,bx,by);`	Mountain from inner diamond to top
`valley(ex,ey,jx,jy+diag6);`	Valley left, upper side of inner diamond
`valley(jx,jy-diag6,fx,fy);`	Valley right, lower side of inner diamong
`mountain(ex,ey,jx,jy-diag6);`	Mountain, left, lower side of inner diamond
`mountain(jx,jy+diag6,fx,fy);`	Mountain, right, top side of inner diamond
`}`	Close unfolded
`function precollapse() {`	Header for precollapse
`diamondc();`	Colored diamond
`mountain(ax,ay,cx,cy);`	Mountain across paper
`valley(ex,ey,gx,gy);`	Valley center, down on left
`valley(fx,fy,hx,hy);`	Valley center, down on right
`valley(ex,ey,gx,gry);`	Valley center, up on left

Code Line	Description
`valley(fx,fy,hx,gry);`	Valley center, up on right
`valley(jx,jy-diag6,jx,jy+diag6);`	Valley in middle of paper, vertical
`mountain(jx,jy-diag6,bx,by);`	Mountain from inner diamond up
`mountain(jx,jy+diag6,dx,dy);`	Mountain from inner diamond down
`mountain(ex,ey,jx,jy+diag6);`	Mountain, top, left side of inner diamond
`mountain(jx,jy-diag6,fx,fy);`	Mountain, top, right side of inner diamond
`mountain(ex,ey,jx,jy-diag6);`	Mountain, top, left side of inner diamond
`mountain(jx,jy+diag6,fx,fy);`	Mountain, top, right side of inner diamond
`}`	Close `precollapse`
`function changedfolds() {`	Header for `changedfolds`; note that this is the same as unfolded, except for sense (mountain versus valley) of some folds
`diamond();`	Draw diamond
`valley(ax,ay,cx,cy);`	Valley across paper
`mountain(ex,ey,gx,gy);`	Mountain, middle of paper, down on left
`mountain(fx,fy,hx,hy);`	Mountain, middle, down on right
`mountain(ex,ey,gx,gry);`	Mountain, middle, up on left
`mountain(fx,fy,hx,gry);`	Mountain, middle, up on right
`mountain(jx,jy-diag6,jx,jy+diag6);`	Mountain, middl,e vertical
`valley(jx,jy-diag6,bx,by);`	valley, inner diamond up

Code Line	Description
`valley(jx,jy+diag6,dx,dy);`	valley, inner diamond down
`valley(ex,ey,jx,jy+diag6);`	Valley, top, left side of inner diamond
`valley(jx,jy-diag6,fx,fy);`	Valley, top, right side of inner diamond
`valley(ex,ey,jx,jy-diag6);`	Valley, bottom, left side of inner diamond
`valley(jx,jy+diag6,fx,fy);`	Valley, bottom, right side of inner diamond
`}`	Close `changefolds`
`function triangleM() {`	Header for `triangleM`
`triangle();`	Draw triangle
`shortdownarrow(ex,ey);`	Indicate with arrow, one-third point
`shortdownarrow(fx,fy);`	Indicate with arrow, two-thirds point
`valley(ex,ey,gx,gy,"orange");`	Next valley fold
`valley(fx,fy,hx,hy,"orange");`	Next valley fold
`}`	Close `triangleM`
`function thirds() {`	Header for `thirds`
`triangle();`	Draw triangle
`skinnyline(ex,ey,gx,gy);`	Indicate folded line
`skinnyline(fx,fy,hx,hy);`	Indicate folded line
`curvedarrow(cx,cy,ax,ay,0,-20);`	Draw curve right to left, offset vertically
`valley(jx,jy,dx,dy,"orange");`	Draw (next) valley line
`}`	Close `thirds`

Code Line	Description
`function cornerdown() {`	Header for `cornerdown`
`rttriangle();`	Draw right triangle
`ctx.clearRect(ex,ey, diag6+5,diag6);`	Erase rectangle covering corner
`ctx.beginPath();`	Begin path
`ctx.moveTo(ex,ey);`	Move to start
`ctx.lineTo(ex+diag6,ey+diag6);`	Draw right and down
`ctx.lineTo(ex,ey+diag6);`	Draw straight down
`ctx.lineTo(ex,ey);`	Draw back to start
`ctx.closePath();`	Close path
`ctx.fill();`	Fill in triangle shape
`ctx.stroke();`	Outline triangle shape
`}`	Close `cornerdown`
`function showkami() {`	Header for `showkami`
`ctx.strokeRect(kamix,kamiy,kamiw*i2p,kamih*i2p);`	Draw a rectangle
`}`	Close `showkami`
`function diamond1() {`	Header for `diamond1`
`diamond();`	Draw diamond
`valley(ax,ay,cx,cy,"orange");`	Add orange valley
`curvedarrow(bx,by,dx,dy,10,0);`	Add vertical curved arrow
`}`	Close `diamond1`
`function diamondc() {`	Header for `diamondc`
`ctx.beginPath();`	Begin path

Code Line	Description
`ctx.moveTo(ax,ay);`	Move to left corner
`ctx.lineTo(bx,by);`	Line up and right
`ctx.lineTo(cx,cy);`	Line down and right
`ctx.lineTo(dx,dy);`	Line down and to middle
`ctx.lineTo(ax,ay)`	Line to start
`ctx.closePath();`	Close path
`ctx.fillStyle="teal";`	Set color
`ctx.fill();`	Fill in diamond
`ctx.stroke();`	Draw outline
`}`	Close `diamondc`
`function diamond() {`	Header for `diamond`
`ctx.beginPath();`	Begin path
`ctx.moveTo(ax,ay);`	Move to left corner
`ctx.lineTo(bx,by);`	Draw line up and over
`ctx.lineTo(cx,cy);`	Draw line down and over
`ctx.lineTo(dx,dy);`	Draw line down to center
`ctx.lineTo(ax,ay)`	Draw back to start
`ctx.closePath();`	Close path
`ctx.stroke();`	Draw outline
`}`	Close `diamond`
`function triangle() {`	Header for `triangle` function
`ctx.fillStyle="teal";`	Set to color

Code Line	Description
`ctx.beginPath();`	Begin path
`ctx.moveTo(ax,ay);`	Move to left corner
`ctx.lineTo(cx,cy);`	Draw line across
`ctx.lineTo(dx,dy);`	Draw line down
`ctx.lineTo(ax,ay);`	Draw line back up
`ctx.closePath();`	Close path
`ctx.fill();`	Fill in shape
`}`	Close `triangle`
`function rttriangle() {`	Header for `rttriangle`
`ctx.fillStyle="teal";`	Set color
`ctx.beginPath();`	Begin path
`ctx.moveTo(ax,ay);`	Move to left corner
`ctx.lineTo(jx,jy);`	Draw line across to middle
`ctx.lineTo(dx,dy);`	Draw line down
`ctx.lineTo(ax,ay);`	Draw line back up
`ctx.closePath();`	Close path
`ctx.fill();`	Fill in right triangle
`valley(ex,ey,ex+diag6,ey+diag6,"orange");`	Draw diagonal valley
`skinnyline(ex,ey,gx,gy);`	
`}`	Close `rttriangle`
`</script>`	Closing script tag
`</head>`	Closing head tag

Code Line	Description
`<body onLoad="init();">`	Body, with call to `init`
`<video id="sink" loop="loop" preload="auto"` `controls="controls" width="400">`	Video tag
`<source src="sink.mp4video.mp4" type='video/mp4;` `codecs="avc1.42E01E, mp4a.40.2"'>`	mp4
`<source src="sink.theora.ogv" type='video/ogg;` `codecs="theora, vorbis"'>`	OGG
`<source src="sink.webmvp8.webm" type='video/webm;` `codec="vp8, vorbis"'>`	WEBM
`Your browser does not accept the video tag.`	Message for old browsers
`</video>`	Closing video tag
`<video id="talk" loop="loop" preload="auto"` `controls="controls">`	Video tag
`<source src="talk.mp4video.mp4" type='video/mp4;` `codecs="avc1.42E01E, mp4a.40.2"'>`	mp4
`<source src="talk.theora.ogv" type='video/ogg;` `codecs="theora, vorbis"'>`	OGG
`<source src="talk.webmvp8.webm" type='video/webm;` `codec="vp8, vorbis"'>`	WEBM
`Your browser does not accept the video tag.`	Message for old browsers
`</video>`	Closing video tag
`<canvas id="canvas" width="900" height="480">`	Set up canvas
`Your browser does not recognize the canvas element`	Message for old browsers
`</canvas>`	Closing canvas tag
` `	Break
`<div id="directions"> Press buttons to advance or go back` `</div>`	Place to put directions

Code Line	Description
`<hr/>`	Horizontal rule
`<button onClick="goback();" style="color: #F00">Go back </button>`	Set up "Go back" button
`<button onClick="donext();" style="color: #03F">Next step </button>`	Set up "Next step" button
`</body>`	Closing body tag
`</html>`	Closing `html` tag

You can apply this methodology directly to preparing directions for other origami models or similar construction projects. However, do think more broadly about other topics in which line drawings would benefit from mathematical calculations and for which line drawings and images and videos could be used together. You don't have to know everything at the start. Be prepared to work through the project a step at a time.

Testing and Uploading the Application

The `origamifish.html` application can be fully tested on your own computer, assuming you download the photographs and the video clips. If and when you upload it or your own application to a server, you'll need to upload the HTML file, all the image files, and all the video files. Remember, to have an application work on all browsers, you need multiple formats for each video.

Summary

In this chapter, you learned how to build a substantial application for presenting directions involving line drawings, photographs, and video clips. The programming techniques included the following:

- The use of mathematics (algebra, geometry, and trigonometry) to make precise drawings

- The use of an array holding text and function names corresponding to each step

- The integration of photographs and video clips through the use of functions

In the next chapter, we'll tackle another project integrating photographs and video clips: the construction of a jigsaw puzzle that turns into a video when the player puts the puzzle together.

CHAPTER 8

Jigsaw Video: Using the Mouse and Touch to Arrange Images

In this chapter, you will learn the following:

- How to set up mouse and touch events to build an application to work on a variety of devices

- Ways to break up a picture into pieces and determine the coordinates for those pieces to produce a jigsaw puzzle

- How to calculate horizontal and vertical coordinates and manipulate `left` and `top` style attributes to reposition elements on the screen

- About the concept of tolerance or margin so your player does not have to be perfect to solve the puzzle

- How to make the jigsaw turn into a running video

Introduction

The project for this chapter is a jigsaw puzzle that becomes a video when complete. It has been tested on Chrome, Firefox, Opera, and Safari on computers equipped with a mouse, and on the iPhone and iPad using finger touch. The jigsaw pieces are positioned randomly on the screen each time the program is loaded, or the button is clicked to restart the program. Figure 8-1 shows an opening screen when the program is run on a desktop computer running the Firefox browser.

In the tent

Do jigsaw again. Feedback: [_____]

Figure 8-1. Opening screen on computer

On a computer, the player uses the mouse to move and reposition pieces. Randomly positioned pieces may end up on top of each other. Figure 8-2 shows the jigsaw pieces spread out. I did this using the mouse. My example has six rectangular-shaped pieces.

In the tent

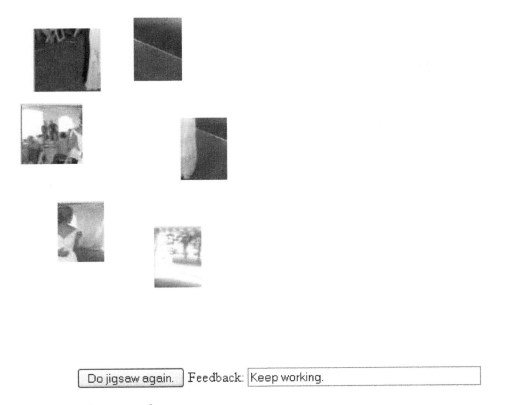

| Do jigsaw again. | Feedback: | Keep working. |

Figure 8-2. Pieces spread out

Figure 8-3 shows how I have made progress in putting the puzzle together. I can position the puzzle anywhere on the screen. Three pieces of the puzzle have been put together.

In the tent

Figure 8-3. Progress made on the puzzle

Notice that the box with the label Feedback says to keep working. Figure 8-4 shows the puzzle nearly complete.

In the tent

Do jigsaw again. Feedback: Keep working.

Figure 8-4. Just one piece left to fit into the jigsaw puzzle

The program allows for a margin of error, which I term the *tolerance*, when putting the pieces together. You can see by noticing the white border along the dance floor that the puzzle is not perfectly put together. When I move in the last piece, Figure 8-5 shows a screen capture shortly after my last move.

In the tent

Do jigsaw again.   Feedback: GOOD!

Figure 8-5. Pieces replaced by a video

Notice that the feedback now reads "GOOD!" A video has begun to play. The picture appears perfect. In fact, the six jigsaw pieces have been replaced by the video. Figure 8-6 shows the video with controls showing. The controls do not show automatically, but can be seen if the player puts the mouse on top of the lower part of the video. The video controls vary across the different browsers.

In the tent

Do jigsaw again. | Feedback: GOOD!

Figure 8-6. Video clip with controls

I decided to attempt the task of making the project work for an iPhone and iPad. This meant constructing a user interface that allows the player to use finger touches. To be more ambitious, I wanted to produce one program as a web site that would work for both mouse and touch. Figure 8-7 shows the opening screen on an iPhone.

Figure 8-7. Opening screen on an iPhone

Notice that you and the player cannot see the bottom part of the original screen with the "Do jigsaw again" button and the feedback. I decided to accept this in order to avoid squeezing the playing area or reducing the size of the pieces. Figure 8-8 shows the game in progress. The pieces have been moved using a finger on the screen.

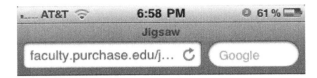

In the tent

Figure 8-8. Jigsaw game in progress on an iPhone

Figure 8-9 shows the screen immediately following successful completion of the puzzle.

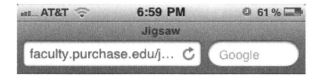

In the tent

Figure 8-9. *Video ready to play on an iPhone*

The iPhone operating system requires users to click the play button for all videos. This is considered a feature, not a bug, by the makers of the iPhone. Requiring a click does give the owner of the iPhone a chance to prevent downloading of a video, which takes time and battery power and may incur fees. For the jigsaw-to-video project, I would prefer it to be seamless, but I'll accept it as is. Figure 8-10 shows the video in play.

Figure 8-10. Video in play on an iPhone

With this introduction to what can be called the jigsaw-puzzle-with-video-reward project, we can go on to discuss the requirements for the project and the implementation.

Background and Critical Requirements

Three distinct circumstances inspired me to want to build this particular project. I had built jigsaw puzzles turning into videos in Adobe Flash for a Programming Games course that I taught, and many students were happy to use them as models for their own projects. When I was working on a US states educational game, which is the subject of the next chapter, I decided a jigsaw activity to put the states together was a good addition to other questions such as asking the player to identify a state by clicking on the state in a map of the whole USA. Lastly, I had a short video clip on my phone taken by the happy mother of the groom at her son's wedding. These circumstances were the motivation to create the jigsaw turning into video project.

The requirements for this project start with acquiring the images that will be the jigsaw pieces using as a base the first frame of a video clip. Next, since it will be necessary to determine if the jigsaw is complete—that is, if the pieces have been repositioned correctly—we must record the information showing the correct relative positions.

The main technical requirement is to build the user interface. The user interface consists of the mouse or finger touch actions, along with a button to do the jigsaw again and feedback provided in a text field.

The program presents the pieces randomly positioned on the screen. The player then moves the pieces either by using a mouse (mouse button down, move to drag the piece, and then mouse button up to release it) or a finger (touch down on the screen, move finger to drag, and then lift finger up). After each release of a piece, the program performs a calculation to see if the puzzle has been solved. This calculation must satisfy two requirements. The puzzle can be put together anywhere on the screen, and there needs to be a tolerance in the positioning of the pieces, since we can't require the positioning to be perfect (i.e., to the pixel).

When the puzzle is deemed complete, it turns into a video. More accurately, a video appears where the pieces were located on the screen.

HTML5, CSS, JavaScript, and Programming Features

The features used for the jigsaw video project are a mixture of HTML5 constructs and general programming techniques.

Acquiring the Images and Data for the Pieces

I will describe how I acquired the puzzle pieces for this project. What you do depends on the tools you have and what you feel comfortable using. The first task is to obtain the first frame of the video for use as the base of the jigsaw puzzle. I use SnagIt, a screen capture tool (www.techsmith.com/snagit/). You also can press the PC Print Screen key twice to capture the screen, or press Command+Shift+4 to get crosshairs on the Mac. In either case, you then bring the image into an image-editing package. However, if you are using video-editing software, it would make sense to use that. The next step is to perform the digital equivalent of cutting up the base picture with a jigsaw. I used Corel Paint Shop Pro and also Adobe Flash (more on that in the next chapter). You can use a standard rectangular selection tool, a freehand lasso, or a cropping tool. In Adobe Flash, you can draw lines to cut up the picture and select the pieces. An open source tool image editing is available at http://pixlr.com/.

While cutting up the individual pieces and saving each as its own image file, it is necessary to record the distances to the top-left corner of the piece from the top-left corner of the original picture. You need to cut up the puzzle to make the pieces and record how the pieces fit together. Figure 8-11 shows the location of one of the 6 jigsaw pieces, dan5.jpg, outlined on top of the base picture. I added the red border to this figure to show the individual piece.

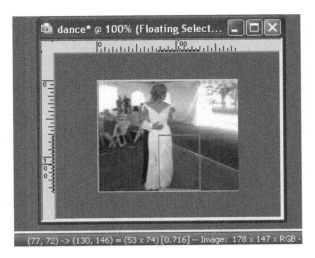

Figure 8-11. *Screenshot from Corel Paint Shop Pro*

At the bottom of Figure 8-11, the (77,72) indicates the location of the top-left corner of the picture relative to the original picture. I recorded these values for each individual jigsaw puzzle piece. These values are what are used to check if the player has put the pieces together. They could be used to present a complete jigsaw to the player. I did not think that was necessary in this case. You will see this operation in the next chapter. At this point in the development process, I can write the following lines of JavaScript code in my program:

```
var pieces = [
  "dan1.jpg","dan2.jpg","dan3.jpg","dan4.jpg","dan5.jpg","dan6.jpg"
  ];
var piecesx = [
0,71, 124,0,77,123  ];

var piecesy = [
 0,0,0,72,72,72
 ];
```

I refer to the `piecesx` and `piecesy` values as offsets (horizontal and vertical, respectively), for the pieces. Be aware that the array named `pieces` holds the names of the image files. The next section will describe the building of HTML elements for each piece. The array `pieceelements` will hold references to each element. To sum up, the application makes use of four arrays with information on the puzzle pieces.

Dynamically Created Elements

In Chapter 2, you read about the Family Collage project, in which images were repositioned on the canvas. I will take a somewhat different approach here. Each piece will be its own element, with the markup created dynamically. There is no canvas element. The markup is created in a function called `setupgame` invoked by the `init` function. The fact that I have three functions, `init`, `setupgame`, and `setupjigsaw`, is partially an artifact of the history of this project. I reused code created for the US states game, in which the jigsaw puzzle was just a part. However, breaking up a function into smaller pieces generally is a good thing to do. The init function does some work, calls setupgame, and also calls setupjigsaw. The setupjigsaw function is also invoked from endjigsaw. More generally, the way I wrote this application is not the only way it could be done. In some situations, here and in other chapters, I chose to write a function that is more general than needed, and in others I did not.

The setupgame function iterates over the data in three parallel arrays: pieces, which holds the image file names; piecesx, which holds the horizontal offset values; and piecesy, which holds the vertical offset values. New elements are created with the programmer-defined (my defined) type piece and positioned according to piecesx and piecesy values.

```
function setupgame() {
    var i;
    var x;
    var y;
    var uniqueid;
    var s;

    for(i=0;i<nums;i++) {

        uniqueid = "a"+String(i);
        s = document.createElement('piece');
         s.innerHTML = (
            "<img src='"+pieces[i]+"' id='"+uniqueid+"'/>");
        document.body.appendChild(s);
        thingelem = document.getElementById(uniqueid);
        x = piecesx[i] +100;
        y = piecesy[i] + 100;
        thingelem.style.top = String(y)+"px";
        thingelem.style.left = String(x)+"px";
        pieceelements.push(thingelem);

    }
    firstpkel = document.getElementById("a0");
    questionfel = document.getElementById("questionform");
    questionfel.style.left = "20px";
    questionfel.style.top = "400px";
    questionfel.feedback.value = "   ";

}
```

This code arranges the pieces so that they resemble the original picture, the first frame of the video clip. However, the setupjigsaw function is invoked right afterward so the player will not see the puzzle solution. After the for loop, another initialization is performed. The firstpkel variable points to the newly created element holding the first piece, the piece with ID a0. The assumption is that that piece is in the top-left corner, so when you create your puzzle, you are free to cut up the pieces any way you want. However, make sure the first one (zero index) is the top left, since this is the reference point the code uses to position the video clip. The calculation that positions the pieces correctly in relation to each other is independent of the special role of the first piece. The setupgame function also sets the positioning of the form element that holds the button and the feedback field.

Setting Up the Jigsaw Puzzle

The work of setting up the jigsaw puzzle starts with stopping the video and making it not display. This isn't necessary the very first time, but it is easier to have the code always perform these operations. The next task is to place the pieces randomly on the screen. The code does this using `Math.random` and `Math.floor`. You may want to experiment with other values for the constants 210 and 240 that I use. The `display` attribute is set to `inline` to make the pieces visible, but not with a line break, which would be the case if the code used `block`. When the circumstances occur to play the video, all the pieces are made invisible by setting the display to `none`, so this code is necessary.

```
function setupjigsaw() {
    v.pause();
    v.style.display = "none";
  doingjigsaw = true;
   pieceelements[choice].style.border="";
  var i;
  var x;
  var y;
  var thingelem;
    for (i=0;i<nums;i++) {
      x = 10+Math.floor(Math.random()*210);
      y = 50+Math.floor(Math.random()*240);
      thingelem = pieceelements[i];
      thingelem.style.top = String(y)+"px";
      thingelem.style.left = String(x)+"px";
      thingelem.style.display = "inline";
    }
        ...
}
```

> ▪ **Note** If you notice that a certain amount of complexity occurs in the coding to handle the issue of replaying the jigsaw game, this is typical. Restarting, reinitializing, and so on are more of a challenge than programming something to happen just once.

The next part of `setupjigsaw` involves setting up the event handling, which I will address in the next section.

Handling Mouse and Finger Touch Events

My approach was to implement the mouse events first and get those working. Then, when my ambitions rose to build an application for certain family members who use iPhones and iPads, I implemented the finger touch by making a touch event simulate a mouse event. For this reason, I will explain the mouse events first and then the touch events.

■ **Note** The event handling in this program does not make use of the new drag-and-drop features of HTML5. These features are intended for use when you need to write code that moves elements from one bin-like element into or onto another. The jigsaw project requires more precise positioning.

Using Mouse Events

The tasks for moving the jigsaw pieces are to

- recognize what piece, if any, is under the mouse cursor when the button has been pressed down;

- move the piece when the mouse moves, adjusting the location to make sure that the piece doesn't jump, but remains as if the cursor were attached to its original position, perhaps in the middle of the element; and

- release or drop the element when the player has released the mouse button.

You may recall similar operations in Chapter 2. This reasoning suggests that my code will set up at least three events, and this is what happens. The events are set for the document. The global variable d has been set to point to the HTML document:

```
var d = document;
```

In the setupjigsaw function, the following three statements set up the event handling for the three events:

```
d.onmousedown = startdragging;
d.onmousemove = moving;
d.onmouseup = release;
```

The task of startdragging is to determine what piece, if any, is under the cursor, since all the code knows, so to speak, at this point is that the mouse button is down somewhere on the document. To make this determination requires calculations based on information held by the event parameter to the function. The code uses conditional expressions (? and :) to define each of curX and curY one way if a global variable named ie is set to true; otherwise, it does something else. Yes, the ie stands for "Internet Explorer," but be aware that the application was not tested using Internet Explorer. I included this coding because it was present in multiple sources that I used for reference, and because I assume it will be necessary in future versions of Internet Explorer that do support all features of HTML5. The function starts

```
function startdragging(e)
{
    var o;
    var j;
    var i;
    curX = ie ? e.clientX+d.body.scrollLeft : e.pageX;
    curY = ie ? e.clientY+d.body.scrollTop  : e.pageY;
```

The code uses a for loop to check if the mouse is over each element of the pieceelements array. It breaks out of the loop as soon as the test returns true. This means that if one piece is on top of another, it is not necessarily the one on top, but the one first in the `pieceelements` array. This is probably an opportunity for improvement, to put it in a noncritical light.

```
for (i=0; i<nums;i++) {
    j = pieceelements[i];
    o = offset(j);
    if (curX >= o.x && curX <= o.x + j.width &&
        curY >= o.y && curY <= o.y + j.height)
      {
          break;
      }
}
```

At this point, the `for` loop either has terminated early or ends when the index variable `i` is equal to `nums`. This corresponds to it being determined whether the mouse is over one of the pieces or not. The code in `startdragging` also must determine where exactly the mouse cursor is in terms of the position of the piece. The variables `curX` and `curY`, which give the distances to where the mouse cursor is, and `o.x` and `o.y`, the values set by a function offset, are used to calculate `adjustX` and `adjustY`, the values used in a function `draw`. Look at Figure 8-12.

In the tent

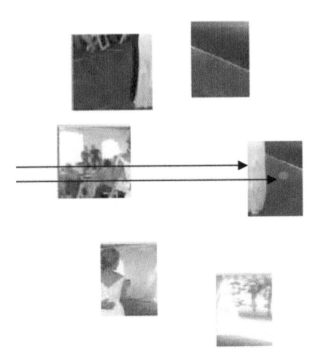

Figure 8-12. *The long, lower arrow represents curX; the short, upper arrow represents o.x.*

The dot in the piece at the right middle represents where the player has moved the mouse and pressed down on the button. (The dot does not appear during the game; I put it in the figure for reference.) The bottom arrow represents curX, the distance from the left side of the document to the mouse position. The top arrow represents o.x, the distance from the edge to this piece. The statement

```
adjustX = curX - o.x;
```

sets adjustX to be used when repositioning the piece to make it be dragged along by the movement of the mouse.

A global variable named mouseDown, initialized to be false, will be set to true in startdragging, checked in moving, and reset back to false in release. The rest of the startdragging function is

```
      if (i<nums) {
         movingobj = pieceelements[i];
         adjustX = curX -  o.x;
         adjustY = curY - o.y;
         mouseDown = true;
      }
};
```

Notice that nothing happens if the mouse is not over a piece when the player presses down on the mouse button.

The offset function is written to work when an element is a child of another element that may be a child of another element, and so on, and each element can be offset within its parent. The actual situation in this program is fairly simple: the piece elements are children of the body, which is zero offset from the document in each direction.

```
function offset(obj)
{
   var left = 0;
   var top  = 0;
   if (obj.offsetParent)
      do
      {
         left += obj.offsetLeft;
         top  += obj.offsetTop;
      } while (obj = obj.offsetParent);
   return {x: left, y: top};
}
```

Notice that the function returns a single element that is an associative array. Recall that associative arrays have named elements instead of indexed elements. The array has an x value set to the value left computed in the function, and a y value set to the value top computed in the function.

If the player uses the mouse to move the cursor on top of a puzzle piece and presses down, the global variable movingobj will point to the piece element and the global variable mouseDown will be true. The function moving is invoked when the event of the mouse moving occurs. The function is

```
function moving(e)
{
   if (!mouseDown) return;
   if (ie)
      draw(e.clientX+d.body.scrollLeft, e.clientY+d.body.scrollTop);
```

```
else
    draw(e.pageX, e.pageY);
}
```

The draw function does the work: repositioning the movingobj element:

```
function draw(x, y)
{
    var js = movingobj.style;
    js.left = (x - adjustX) + "px";
    js.top  = (y - adjustY) + "px";
}
```

The draw function does its work by changing the left and top attributes of the style of the movingobj. The moving function will be invoked by JavaScript over and over as long as the mouse is in motion.

The release function is invoked when the player releases the mouse button. It is just two statements:

```
function release(e){
    mouseDown = false;
    checkpositions();
}
```

Changing the variable mouseDown to false means that nothing will happen if and when the player moves the mouse until the player presses down on the mouse button again, invoking the startdragging function. This completes the mouse event handling. The checkpositions function is explained in the next section. However, there is one more thing to explain about mouse events before moving on to touch events. In the setupjigsaw function, I inserted code to create another object that has the effect of turning off the built-in drag-and-drop activities. The code creates a new element, gives it a name so it can be referenced in the style section, and appends it to the body. Without this extra element, the ghosts of the pieces are dragged, but they are not positioned where they are dropped.

```
var df = document.createElement('div');
df.id = "fullpage";
bodyel.appendChild(df);
```

In the style element, the created element with id "fullpage" is set to be aligned with the document and takes up all but the bottom 90 percent, leaving room for the button. The overflow: hidden directive hides the vertical scroll bar.

```
#fullpage
{
    display:block;
    position:absolute;
    top:0;
    left:0;
    width:100%;
    height:90%;
    overflow: hidden;
    z-index: 1;

}
```

Using Finger Touches

It is time to explain how touch events can be made to mimic mouse events. The basic touch events are defined as follows by the W3C (see www.w3.org/TR/2011/WD-touch-events-20110505):

- **touchstart**: This is triggered when a touch is initiated (mouse equivalent: mouseDown).

- **touchmove**: This is triggered when a touch moves (mouse equivalent: mouseMove).

- **touchend**: This is triggered when a touch ends (mouse equivalent: mouseUp). This one is a bit special on the iPhone; see following.

- **touchcancel**: A user agent must dispatch this event type to indicate when a touch point has been disrupted in an implementation-specific manner.

The setupjigsaw function establishes the event handler for four touch events to be a function I wrote called touchHandler:

```
d.addEventListener("touchstart", touchHandler, true);
d.addEventListener("touchmove", touchHandler, true);
d.addEventListener("touchend", touchHandler, true);
d.addEventListener("touchcancel", touchHandler, true);
```

The touchHandler function takes as a parameter a value set by JavaScript when the event occurs. Touches can involve more than one finger on the screen. You will be familiar with this if you use an iPhone and use a two-finger gesture to zoom in on the screen. For this application, my code only recognizes a single touch, as you can see in the code. If there is more than one touch, the function returns without doing anything. Note that even when touches is an array with just one member, you need to use the code touches[0] to get that one member.

If there is just one touch, the code creates a mouse event of the corresponding type. The touchcancel event does not have a corresponding type, and if that event happens, touchHandler returns without doing anything.

The initMouseEvent method essentially sends off a mouse event of the corresponding type at the location passed by the event parameter. There are several other parameters; the settings I indicate work for this application. The method is documented at https://developer.mozilla.org/en/DOM/event.initMouseEvent.

The code for touchHandler follows:

```
function touchHandler(event)
{
    var touches = event.changedTouches;
    if (touches.length>1) {
        return false;
    }
    var first = touches[0];
    var type = "";
        switch(event.type)
    {
        case "touchstart": type = "mousedown"; break;
        case "touchmove": type="mousemove"; break;
        case "touchend":  type="mouseup"; break;
        default: return;
    }
```

```
    var simulatedEvent = document.createEvent("MouseEvent");
        simulatedEvent.initMouseEvent(type, true, true, window, 1,
                            first.screenX, first.screenY,
                            first.clientX, first.clientY, false,
                            false, false, false, 0, null);
    first.target.dispatchEvent(simulatedEvent);
    event.preventDefault();
}
```

The last line of code is pretty important: the default action is prevented. One default action is scrolling the screen, and we don't want this to occur.

Calculating If the Puzzle Is Complete

Recall that I set the requirements for calculating if the puzzle is complete to be that the puzzle can be located anywhere on the screen and that the player does not have to be precise. Another more-or-less implicit requirement is that the checking be done automatically. After the player releases the mouse or lifts his or her finger, the release function invokes checkpositions. The checkpositions function is called after each move. Don't worry, JavaScript is doing the work, not you.

The checkpositions function computes the horizontal difference between the piecesx value and the style.left value of each piece element, and the vertical difference between the piecesy value and the style.top value of each piece element. The style.left and style.top values are character strings, not numbers, and include "px". The code needs to remove the "px", which stands for "pixels," and calculate the numeric value. The differences are stored in the arrays deltax and deltay.

The function calculates the average of these differences (one for x and one for y). If the puzzle were put together exactly according to the values in the piecesx and piecesy arrays, the differences would each be zero, and consequently, the averages for x and for y would each be 0. If the puzzle were put together such that the actual locations were each 100 pixels closer to the left side—that is, more left and 50 pixels further down the page, that is higher value y, then the averages would be 100 and 50. The puzzle would be put together perfectly, but at a location to the left and below the original location. The differences for x for all pieces would be 100 and the differences for y for all pieces would be 50. Each of the differences would have the same value as the corresponding (x or y) average.

The goal is to *not* require perfection. The tasks of the checkpositions function are to compute the differences in x and y, compute the two averages, and check if each of the differences is close enough to the average.

After computing the difference values, the function performs these tasks by iterating over each piece to compare it with the corresponding average. The check is done using absolute values, because our code doesn't care if a piece is a few pixels left or right or up or down. The criteria for being close enough is the value held in the variable tolerance. If the gap is bigger than tolerance for any piece, the puzzle is not considered complete. The critical if test is

```
if ((Math.abs(averagex - deltax[i])>tolerance) || (Math.abs(averagey-deltay[i])>tolerance)) {
        break;
    }
```

The doaverage function computes and returns the average value of numbers in an array. This is accomplished in the usual way. The variable sum is called an *accumulator*. It is initialized to zero. A for loop iterates over the elements in the array, adding each one to the variable sum.

```
function doaverage(arr) {
    var sum;
    var i;
    var n = arr.length;
    sum = 0;
    for(i=0;i<n;i++) {
        sum += arr[i];
    }
    return (sum/n);
}
```

The first part of checkpositions follows:

```
function checkpositions() {
    var i;
    var x;
    var y;
    var tolerance = 10;
    var deltax = [];
    var deltay = [];
    var delx;
    var dely;
    for (i=0;i<nums;i++) {
        x = pieceelements[i].style.left;
        y = pieceelements[i].style.top;
        x = x.substr(0,x.length-2);
        y = y.substr(0,y.length-2);
        x = Number(x);
        y = Number(y);
        delx = x - piecesx[i];
        dely = y - piecesy[i];
        deltax.push(delx);
        deltay.push(dely);
    }
    var averagex = doaverage(deltax);
    var averagey = doaverage(deltay);
    // check if any delta (x or y) is more than tolerance from average
    for (i=0;i<nums;i++) {
        if ((Math.abs(averagex - deltax[i])>tolerance) || (Math.abs(averagey-
deltay[i])>tolerance)) {
            break;
        }
    }
    if (i<nums) {
        questionfel.feedback.value = "Keep working.";
    }
```

I chose to display a message to the player giving feedback on the puzzle. The form element questionfel holds a reference to the form, and feedback is an input field.

I will describe what happens when the puzzle is deemed complete in the next section.

Preparing, Positioning, and Playing the Video and Making It Hidden or Visible

Preparing the video clip is the same as what you have seen for the other projects involving video. You need to create multiple encodings of the video. Also, as with the other projects, when we do not want the video to appear until a certain situation occurs, the style section contains the directive to make the video initially not visible, set it up to be positioned absolutely, and (when it is displayed) put it on top of everything else:

```
video {display:none; position:absolute; z-index: 100; }
```

Now we get to what happens in the checkpositions function when the puzzle is judged complete. The code writes "GOOD" in the feedback field, makes all the pieces not display, and starts the video. The video is positioned using the left and top values of firstpkel, set to the first piece. The currentTime of the video element is set to zero to play the video clip from the start. The play method is invoked. The code to write out "Good" and start the video is the last part of the checkpositions function. It is the else clause for the if statement checking on the differences of individual pieces from the average difference, and making use of the tolerance variable:

```
else {

        questionfel.feedback.value = "GOOD!";
        for (i=0;i<nums;i++) {
            pieceelements[i].style.display = "none";

        }
        v.style.left = firstpkel.style.left;
        v.style.top = firstpkel.style.top;
        v.style.display="block";
        v.currentTime = 0;
        v.play();
    }
}
```

You have seen several HTML5 features put to use, as well as programming tricks you can use in other applications. The next section will show you all the code for the project.

Building the Application and Making It Your Own

You can make these projects your own by using your own video clip. You also can make a jigsaw puzzle by itself, though you probably should wait to read the next chapter, which describes a more elaborate jigsaw puzzle and contains pointers on how to cut up more intricate shapes. This chapter also showed you how to feature touch events in your application. Here is an informal summary/outline of the jigsaw-to-video project:

- init: For initialization, including invoking calls to setupgame and setupjigsaw

- setupgame: For creating the pieces

- setupjigsaw: For randomly positioning the pieces and setting up event handling

- startdragging, moving, release, *and* touchhandler: For handling events

- checkpositions: For determining if the puzzle is complete
- offset: For calculating the position of pieces in motion
- draw: For actually doing the repositioning of pieces
- doaverage: For calculating the average of values in an array

Table 8-1 lists all the functions and indicates how they are invoked and what functions they invoke.

Table 8-1. *Functions in the Jigsaw-to-Video Project*

Function	Invoked/Called By	Calls
init	Invoked by action of the onLoad attribute in the <body> tag	setupgame, setupjigsaw
setupgame	Invoked by init	
setupjigsaw	Invoked by init and endjigsaw	
endjigsaw	Invoked by the onSubmit setting in the form in the body	setupjigsaw
checkpositions	Invoked by release	doaverage
doaverage	Invoked by checkpositions	
touchHandler	Invoked by event setting in setupjigsaw	
startdragging	Invoked by event setting in setupjigsaw and indirectly by touchHandler	offset
moving	Invoked by event setting in setupjigsaw and indirectly by touchHandler	draw
release	Invoked by event setting in setupjigsaw and indirectly by touchHandler	checkpositions
draw	Invoked by moving	
offset	Invoked by startdragging	

Table 8-2 shows the code for the basic application, with comments for each line. Much of this code you have seen in the previous chapters.

Table 8-2. *Complete Code for the Jigsaw-to-Video Project*

Code Line	Description
`<!DOCTYPE html>`	Header
`<html>`	html tag
`<head>`	Head tag
`<title>Jigsaw</title>`	Complete title element
`<meta name="viewport" content="width=device-width, user-scalable=yes, initial-scale=1.0, minimum-scale=1.0, maximum-scale=2.0" />`	Meta tag, necessary for iPhone to prevent browser from zooming into the page to compensate for a smaller screen
`<style>`	Style tag
`img {position:absolute; border:none; }`	Set positioning for all img elements to be absolute and remove borders.
`form {position: absolute; z-index: 10;}`	Set positioning for the form; place on top of `fullpage`
`body{ height:100%; margin: 30px; }`	Set body to take of the height of the screen, with the margin to be 30 pixels.
`video {display:none; position:absolute; z-index: 100; }`	Initial display setting for the video element is none, meaning not visible. Set; layer to be on top of everything else
`#fullpage`	Directive for the created page
`{display:block; position:absolute; top:0; left:0;`	Position absolutely
`width:100%;`	Take up whole width of screen
`height:90%;`	Take up most, but not all of height
`overflow: hidden;`	Stop display of vertical scroll
`z-index: 1;`	Position underneath
`}`	End directive

Code Line	Description
`</style>`	Closing style tag
`<script type="text/javascript">`	Script tag

`var pieces =`
`["dan1.jpg","dan2.jpg","dan3.jpg","dan4.jpg",`
`"dan5.jpg","dan6.jpg" ];`
	Hold names of image files for pieces

`var piecesx=[0,71, 124,0,77,123];`	Hold x offsets
`var piecesy = [0,0,0,72,72,72 ];`	Hold y offsets
`var v;`	Will hold video element
`var doingjigsaw = false;`	Set when doing jigsaw
`var firstpkel;`	Will hold first piece
`function init(){`	Header for `init` function
`v = document.getElementById("dance");`	Get reference to video
`   setupgame();`	Invoke `setupgame`
`   bodyel = document.getElementById("body");`	Get reference to body
`   formel =` `document.getElementById("questionform");`	Get reference to form
`   setupjigsaw();`	Invoke `setupjigsaw`
`}`	Close `init` function
`var bodyel;`	Will hold reference to body
`var formel;`	Will hold reference to form
`var nums = pieces.length;`	Number of pieces
`var pieceelements = [];`	Will hold list of piece elements
`var questionfel;`	Will hold reference to form

Code Line	Description
`function setupgame() {`	Header for `setupgame`
`var i;`	For indexing over pieces
`var x;`	For x value
`var y;`	For y value
`var uniqueid;`	Generated, unique ID for the puzzle pieces
`var s;`	Reference created element
`for(i=0;i<nums;i++) {`	Iterate over pieces
`uniqueid = "a"+String(i);`	Create a unique ID
`s = document.createElement('piece');`	Create an element
`s.innerHTML = (        "<img src='"+pieces[i]+"' id='"+uniqueid+"'/>");`	Set contents of element
`document.body.appendChild(s);`	Append to body
`thingelem = document.getElementById(uniqueid);`	Get reference to newly created image
`x = piecesx[i] +100;`	Set an x value
`y = piecesy[i] + 100;`	Set a y value
`thingelem.style.top = String(y)+"px";`	Use x to position the element
`thingelem.style.left = String(x)+"px";`	Use y to position the element
`pieceelements.push(thingelem);`	Add this element to `pieceelements`
`}`	Close `for` loop
`firstpkel = document.getElementById("a0");`	Save reference to first element (in upper-left corner) to use when positioning the video element

Code Line	Description
`questionfel = document.getElementById("questionform");`	Set reference to form
`questionfel.style.left = "20px";`	Position form horizontally
`questionfel.style.top = "400px";`	Position form vertically
`questionfel.feedback.value = "  ";`	Set feedback to zero
`}`	Close `setupgame` function
`function endjigsaw() {`	Header for `endjigsaw` function
`var df;`	For the `fullpage` element.
`if (doingjigsaw) {`	If doing jigsaw
`doingjigsaw = false;`	Set to `false`
`d.onmousedown = "";`	Remove event handling for `mousedown`
`d.onmousemove = "";`	Remove event handling for `mousemove`
`d.onmouseup = "";`	Remove event handling for `mouseup`
`df = document.getElementById("fullpage");`	Get reference
`bodyel.removeChild(df);`	Remove this element
`v.pause();`	Stop the video
`v.style.display = "none";`	Stop display of the video
`}`	Close clause
`setupjigsaw();`	Invoke `setupjigsaw`
`return false;`	Prevent page refresh
`}`	Close `endjigsaw` function
`function checkpositions() {`	Header for `checkpositions`

Code Line	Description
`var i;`	For indexing
`var x;`	For x value
`var y;`	For y value
`var tolerance = 10;`	Set tolerance for puzzle
`var deltax = [];`	Will hold all x differences
`var deltay = [];`	Will hold all y differences
`var delx;`	Used in calculation
`var dely;`	Used in calculation
`for (i=0;i<nums;i++) {`	Iterate over pieces
`x = pieceelements[i].style.left;`	Extract left attribute
`y = pieceelements[i].style.top;`	Extract top attribute
`x = x.substr(0,x.length-2);`	Remove px for pixels in `style.left`
`y = y.substr(0,y.length-2);`	Remove px for pixels in `style.top`
`x = Number(x);`	Convert to number
`y = Number(y);`	Convert to number
`delx = x - piecesx[i];`	Calculate difference from offset
`dely = y - piecesy[i];`	Calculate difference from offset
`deltax.push(delx);`	Add to `deltax` array
`deltay.push(dely);`	Add to `deltay` array
`}`	Close `for` loop
`var averagex = doaverage(deltax);`	compute average
`var averagey = doaverage(deltay);`	Compute average

311

Code Line	Description
`for (i=0;i<nums;i++) {`	Iterate over pieces (again)
`if ((Math.abs(averagex - deltax[i])>tolerance) || (Math.abs(averagey-deltay[i])>tolerance)) {`	Are any of the delta values too different from the average?
`break;`	If so, leave for loop
`}`	Close clause
`}`	Close for loop
`if (i<nums) {`	Did the for loop end early?
`questionfel.feedback.value = "Keep working.";`	Display need to keep working
`}`	Close clause
`else {`	Else (no premature break)
`questionfel.feedback.value="GOOD!";`	Display "GOOD"
`for (i=0;i<nums;i++) {`	Iterate over pieces
`pieceelements[i].style.display = "none";`	Make pieces not display
`}`	Close for loop
`v.style.left = firstpkel.style.left;`	Set video horitzontal (left) position to where `firstpkel` is.
`v.style.top = firstpkel.style.top;`	Set video vertical (top) position to where `firstpkel` is.
`v.style.display="block";`	Make video visible
`v.currentTime = 0;`	Set to start at beginning
`v.play();`	Play video
`}`	Close else clause

Code Line	Description
`}`	Close **checkpositions** function
`function doaverage(arr) {`	Header for **doaverage** function
`var sum;`	Will hold sum
`var i;`	For indexing
`var n = arr.length;`	The length of the array
`sum = 0;`	Initialize sum to zero
`for(i=0;i<n;i++) {`	**for** loop over array elements
`sum += arr[i];`	Add in the *i*th value
`}`	Close **for** loop
`return (sum/n);`	Return sum divided by n
`}`	Close **doaverage** function
`function setupjigsaw() {`	Header for **setupjigsaw** function
`v.pause();`	Stop video
`v.style.display = "none";`	Make video not display
`doingjigsaw = true;`	Set flag to **true**
`var i;`	For indexing
`var x;`	For x value
`var y;`	For y value
`var thingelem;`	For reference to piece element
`for (i=0;i<nums;i++) {`	Iterate over pieces
`x = 10+Math.floor(Math.random()*210);`	Calculate a random value for x
`y = 50+Math.floor(Math.random()*240);`	Calculate a random value for y

Code Line	Description
`thingelem = pieceelements[i];`	Extract *i*th element
`thingelem.style.top = String(y)+"px";`	Set its top attribute
`thingelem.style.left = String(x)+"px";`	Set its left attribute
`thingelem.style.display = "inline";`	Set display to visible (inline means no line breaks)
`}`	Close for loop
`d.onmousedown = startdragging;`	Set up event handling for mousedown
`d.onmousemove = moving;`	Set up event handling for mousemove
`d.onmouseup = release;`	Set up event handling for mouseup
`d.addEventListener("touchstart", touchHandler, true);`	Set up event handling for touchstart
`d.addEventListener("touchmove", touchHandler, true);`	Set up event handling for touchmove
`d.addEventListener("touchend", touchHandler, true);`	Set up event handling for touchend
`d.addEventListener("touchcancel", touchHandler, true);`	Set up event handling for touchcancel (to prevent default)
`var df = document.createElement('div');`	Create a new div
`df.id = "fullpage";`	Set ID
`bodyel.appendChild(df);`	Append to body
`questionfel.submitbut.value = "Do jigsaw again.";`	Display value for label
`questionfel.feedback.value = "  ";`	Erase feedback
`formel.style.zIndex = 100;`	Set form to be on top
`}`	Close setjigsaw function

Code Line	Description
`function touchHandler(event) {`	Header for `touchHandler`
`var touches = event.changedTouches;`	Extract all the touches
`if (touches.length>1) {`	If there is more than one
`return false; }`	Exit function
`var first = touches[0];`	Extract the first and only touch
`var type = "";`	Set type to empty string
`switch(event.type)    {`	Switch on the event type
`case "touchstart": type = "mousedown"; break;`	Set type
`case "touchmove":  type="mousemove"; break;`	Set type
`case "touchend":   type="mouseup"; break;`	Set type
`default: return;`	Exit function
`}`	Close switch
`var simulatedEvent = document.createEvent("MouseEvent");`	Create an event
`simulatedEvent.initMouseEvent(type, true, true, window, 1, first.screenX, first.screenY, first.clientX, first.clientY, false, false, false, false, 0, null);`	Call the `initMouseEvent` for the created event; pass the type; indicate bubble, cancellable, window, coordinates; note that the 0 stands for the standard (left) button
`first.target.dispatchEvent(simulatedEvent);`	Dispatch the created event
`event.preventDefault();`	Stop default action for the touch event
`}`	Close the `touchHandler` function
`var d = document;`	Point to the HTML document

315

Code Line	Description
`var ie= d.all;`	Flag for certain browsers, namely Internet Explorer
`var mouseDown = false;`	Initialize `mouseDown` to `false`
`var adjustX;`	For horizontal adjust value
`var adjustY;`	For vertical adjust value
`var movingobj;`	Will hold the moving element
`function release(e){`	Header for **release** function; the parameter is not used, but must be included
`    mouseDown = false;`	Set `mouseDown` back to `false`
`    checkpositions();`	Invoke checkpositions
`};`	Close release function
`function startdragging(e) {`	Header for **startdragging** function
`    var o;`	Will hold offsets
`    var j;`	Will hold the ith element
`    var i;`	For indexing
`    var curX = ie ? e.clientX+d.body.scrollLeft : e.pageX;`	Set x-coordinate from e, using conditional expression
`    var curY = ie ? e.clientY+d.body.scrollTop : e.pageY;`	Set y-coordinate from e, using conditional expression
`    for (i=0; i<nums;i++) {`	Iterate over pieces
`        j = pieceelements[i];`	Set j to be the ith piece element
`        o = offset(j);`	Calculate the offsets
`        if (curX >= o.x && curX <= o.x + j.width && curY >= o.y && curY <= o.y + j.height)`	Was mouse over this piece?

Code Line	Description
`{`	Start clause
`break;`	Leave **for** loop
`}`	Close clause
`}`	Close **for** loop
`if (i<nums) {`	Did **for** loop break early?
`movingobj = pieceelements[i];`	. . . set **movingobj**
`adjustX = curX - o.x;`	Calculate **adjustX**
`adjustY = curY - o.y;`	Calculate **adjustY**
`mouseDown = true;`	Set **mouseDown** to **true**
`}`	Close clause
`};`	Close **startdragging** function
`function moving(e) {`	Header for **moving** function
`if (!mouseDown) return;`	Return immediately if mouse button not down
`if (ie)`	Is **ie** set?
`draw(e.clientX+d.body.scrollLeft,` `e.clientY+d.body.scrollTop);`	Draw at this position
`else`	Else
`draw(e.pageX, e.pageY);`	Draw using these values
`};`	Close **moving** function
`function draw(x, y) {`	Header for **draw** function
`var js = movingobj.style;`	Set to style of moving object
`js.left = (x - adjustX) + "px";`	Set the left to the calculated value, concatenate the **px**

Code Line	Description
`js.top  = (y - adjustY) + "px";`	Set the top to the calculated value, concatenate the **px**
`}`	Close **draw** function
`function offset(obj) {`	Header for offset calculation
`    var left = 0;`	Set initial left
`    var top  = 0;`	Set initial top
`    if (obj.offsetParent)`	Check if there is any offset from parent
`        do{`	If so . . .
`        left += obj.offsetLeft;`	Add to the **left** value
`        top  += obj.offsetTop;`	Add to the **top** value
`        } while (obj = obj.offsetParent);`	Close the **do** clause; continue if this object has a parent
`    return {x: left, y: top};`	Return the calculated left and top as the x and y values of an associative array
`}`	Close **offset** function
`</script>`	Closing script tag
`</head>`	Closing head tag
`<body id="body" onLoad="init();">`	Body tag
`<h2>  In the tent</h2>`	Text on the screen
`<form id="questionform" name="questionform" onSubmit="return endjigsaw();" >`	Form tag
`<input name="submitbut" type="submit" value=" " size="30"/>`	Submit button
`Feedback: <input name="feedback" value="  " size="11" />`	Feedback label and field

Code Line	Description
`</form>`	Closing form tag
`<video id="dance" loop="loop" preload="auto" controls="controls" autoplay>`	Video tag
`<source src="dance.webm" type='video/webm; codec="vp8, vorbis"'>`	Source
`<source src="dance.mp4">`	Source
`<source src="dance.ogg" type='video/ogg; codecs="theora, vorbis"'>`	Source
`Your browser does not accept the video tag.`	Message for noncompliant browsers
`</video>`	Closing video tag
`</body>`	Closing body tag
`</html>`	Closing html tag

Testing and Uploading the Application

You can test the application on your local computer. When you upload it, you must upload the HTML file along with the video files and all the individual image files for the pieces. To test this on an iPad or iPhone, you need to upload the files to a server. The project is not an app—that is, a program to be downloaded to your iPad or iPhone—but a web site to be downloaded and run by a browser.

Summary

In this chapter, you learned how to build a jigsaw puzzle that turns into a video clip. The techniques included the following:

- Dynamically creating HTML markup to create elements
- Defining event handling for mouse events and touch events
- Changing the `style.left` and `style.top` attributes to reposition elements on the screen
- Placing the jigsaw pieces randomly on the screen

- Determining the coordinate values that indicated how the pieces fit together and using those values, along with a defined tolerance, to check if the jigsaw puzzle was put together adequately

- When appropriate, making the video appear and play

In the next chapter, we tackle another project that includes a jigsaw puzzle, along with other possible moves by the player. Because my jigsaw puzzle of the United States, and potentially yours, is challenging, I will explain a way to store the puzzle as a work-in-progress using the localStorage feature of HTML5.

CHAPTER 9

US States Game: Building a Multiactivity Game

In this chapter, you will learn the following:

- How to build a user interface for a game involving different types of player moves, including putting together a jigsaw puzzle

- How to use the mouse to reposition pieces

- How to acquire an image, break it up into pieces, and determine the coordinates for those pieces to produce a jigsaw puzzle

- How to encode and retrieve the current state of the jigsaw game

- How to use localStorage to store and retrieve the information, including using try and catch for situations when localStorage is not allowed

Introduction

The project for this chapter is an educational game in which the player/student clicks a state on a map of the United States in response to a text prompt, names a state that is indicated by a border by typing in the name, or puts the states that have been randomly positioned on the screen all together again. Figure 9-1 shows the opening screen.

Figure 9-1. *Opening screen of the US states game*

I followed the common practice and present a map with Alaska and Hawaii not in correct position nor proportionally sized. Note also that Rhode Island is bigger than it really is so there's enough room to click it. The game presents the player with different possibilities. Figure 9-2 shows the result of clicking the "Find the state" button.

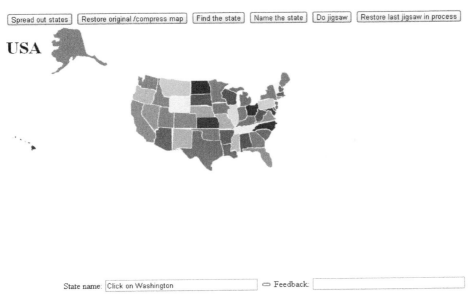

Figure 9-2. *The prompt is to find Washington.*

When I clicked Oregon, I saw what is shown in Figure 9-3.

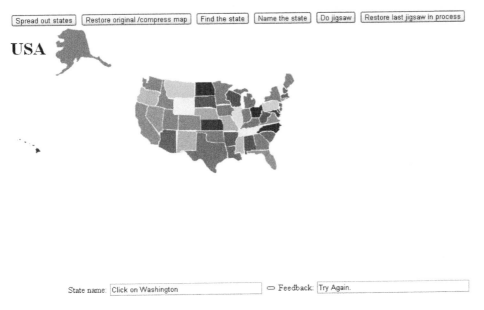

Figure 9-3. *Response to an incorrect choice*

When I clicked the correct choice, the application responded appropriately, as shown in Figure 9-4.

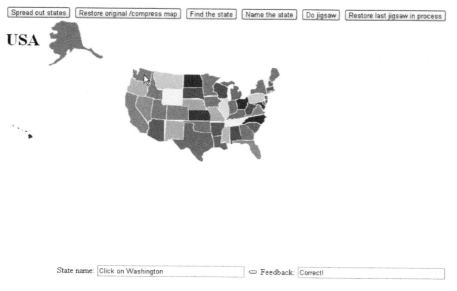

Figure 9-4. *Response to a correct answer*

I decided that it would be helpful to offer the player the option to spread out all the states. After clicking the button labeled "Spread out states," you see what is shown in Figure 9-5.

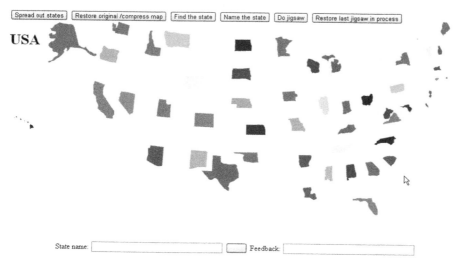

Figure 9-5. *The states spread out*

The player can use the "Restore original/compress map" button or keep playing with the states spread out. Clicking the "Name the state" button produces a prompt consisting of one randomly selected state surrounded by a border, as shown in Figure 9-6.

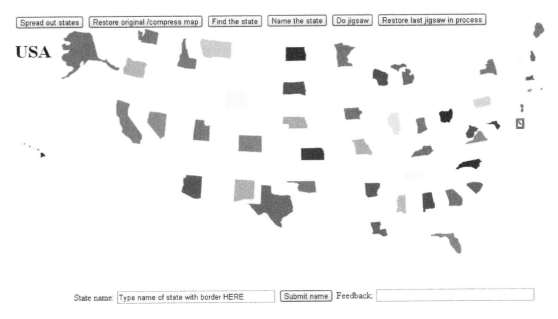

State name: [Type name of state with border HERE] [Submit name] Feedback: [   ]

Figure 9-6. *Border around the state to be named*

Notice the double-line border around Delaware, the very small state on the right-hand side (Atlantic coast) in the middle. This demonstrates a case in which the states being spread out would make a real difference for the player. Figure 9-7 shows the response to my typing in the correct answer.

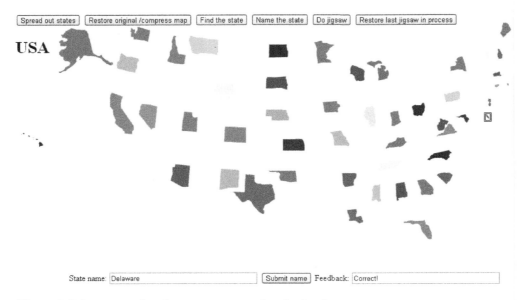

Figure 9-7. Response after the correct answer is submitted

The application also provides activity for the player in the form of a jigsaw puzzle. After clicking the "Do jigsaw" button, you will see something like Figure 9-8. I say "something like" because the states are arranged using pseudorandom processing, so they'll appear in different arrangements each time.

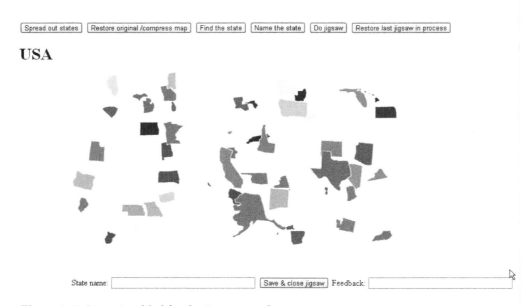

Figure 9-8. States jumbled for the jigsaw puzzle

The player can now use the mouse to drag and drop pieces in the same manner (and implemented the same way) as the jigsaw-to-video puzzle described in Chapter 8. Figure 9-9 shows my work in progress.

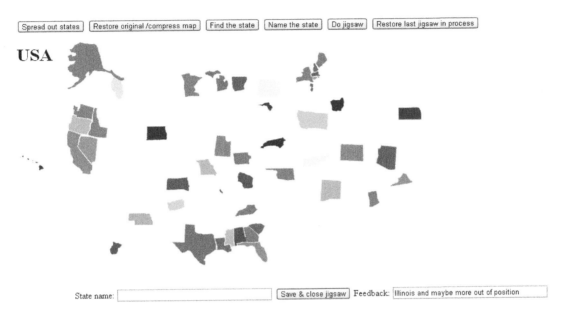

Figure 9-9. Jigsaw puzzle in progress

Observe that I have sorted out Alaska and Hawaii, five states in the West, seven states in the South, all of New England, and New York and New Jersey. The feedback says that Illinois and maybe more are out of position. The feedback could be improved, but it is not strictly programming that is the issue.

This was a challenging puzzle for me. In the interests of full disclosure, and also because it demonstrates a feature of the game, I clicked the "Save & close jigsaw" button, which allowed me to see the states all back in position. I then clicked "Restore last jigsaw in process" to get back to where I was. With this facility available to me, I was able to get to what is shown in Figure 9-10.

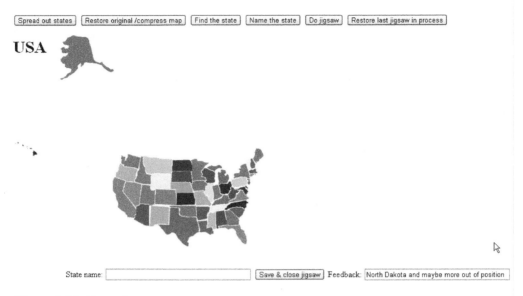

Figure 9-10. *Not quite correct*

The feedback indicates that something is wrong with North Dakota. After cheating—that is, clicking "Save & close jigsaw" and looking at the completed map—I realized that North Dakota and Kansas, two similar ectangular shapes, needed to be swapped. Figure 9-11 shows the correct arrangement.

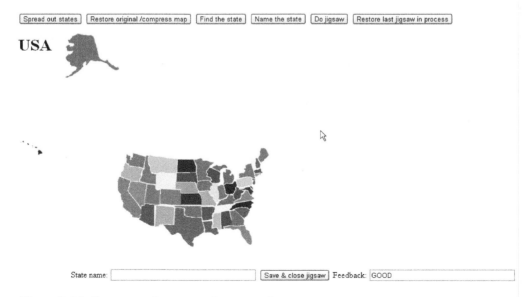

Figure 9-11. *Jigsaw puzzle put together correctly*

Notice that the positions of Alaska and Hawaii are not closely examined. The puzzle is deemed complete.

After this introduction showing the features of this educational game, I will describe the critical requirements for implementation.

Critical Requirements

The critical requirements for the educational game involve presenting the player with different types of activities. For the jigsaw puzzle activity, the application provides a save-and-restore feature. This feature can be used to take a look at the completed puzzle or to put the puzzle aside for a period of time and do something else. The task for the builder of the game is to provide the features of the user interface and ways for play to go from one type of activity to another.

The application requires the presentation of a complete map of the United States, with the individual states clickable. The first type of activity I described in the "Introduction" section was for the game to display the name of a state and prompt the player to click it. The application must be able to determine if the response was right or wrong and provide feedback.

The next type of activity I demonstrated is the opposite. A state on the map is marked in some way, and the player is prompted to type in the name. There are different ways to single out an individual state. I chose to put a border around the state to be named. The program must read in the player input and determine if the name was correct.

After implementing these two types of activities, it occurred to me that we have some very small states. I then decided to provide the spread-out feature and the capability of undoing it. This could be useful for other maps as well. I also modified the image representing tiny Rhode Island to be bigger.

Lastly, I decided to provide a way to see if people could put the states together. The application presents a jigsaw puzzle in which the states are randomly positioned on the screen, and the player uses the mouse to reposition them. It was at this point that I realized that I needed something different from the drag-and-drop-in-bins feature of HTML5. If you haven't already, you can now read Chapter 8 for how to implement a jigsaw puzzle. The US states game has two additional requirements: I need to build a way to enter jigsaw mode and exit it so that the buttons all work and so the player can click a state. I also need a way to save an incomplete puzzle. This wasn't necessary for the wedding dance featured in the jigsaw-to-video project in Chapter 8, but it is necessary for a jigsaw puzzle with 50 pieces. I also view this as an educational game, so it is appropriate to give players a chance to look at the completed map, and also to rest.

HTML5, CSS, JavaScript Features, Programming Techniques, and Image Processing

The features and techniques to implement the educational states game are, for the most part, things you have seen before. However, putting them together can be tricky, so there will be some redundancy between this chapter and the material in previous chapters.

Acquiring the Image Files for the Pieces and Determining Offsets

Image files for each of the 50 states are part of the downloads for this chapter. However, since you may want to make your own map puzzle, I will describe how to make the puzzle pieces and how to determine the information for checking positioning and for restoring the completed map.

The first tasks for making the individual pieces representing the states are to acquire a map of the United States (or the country or region you pick), and then produce an image file for each state. The web-based pixlr image-editing tool (http://pixlr.com/), Corel Paint Shop Pro, and other image-processing programs have a tool, usually called magic wand, for selecting areas of the same color. Figure 9-12 shows the pixlr toolbar with the magic wand tool selected.

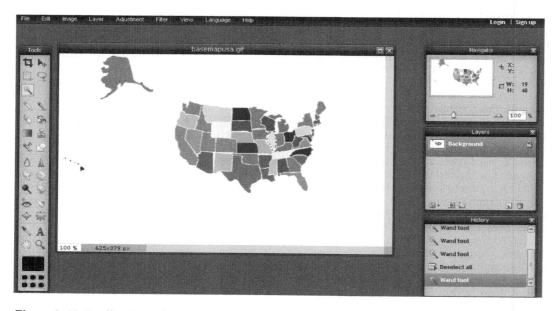

Figure 9-12. *Toolbar in pixlr*

On a map that uses a single color for each state (or country), the magic wand tool can select what is needed. The imprecise positioning and sizing of Alaska and Hawaii are appropriate trade-offs to make (and most US maps do this), but you may believe differently. Figure 9-13 shows the magic wand tool on top of Illinois.

Figure 9-13. *Map of the United States, with the magic wand on Illinois*

After clicking the light-green area representing Illinois, Illinois, and only Illinois, becomes selected, as shown in Figure 9-14. I will be copying and pasting this to save as its own image, but I need to describe something else first.

Figure 9-14. *State of Illinois selected*

The next step is to determine the relative position of each piece representing a state in terms of a base point. I demonstrated this in Chapter 8 for rectangular shapes. We have the same task here, but the shapes are, for the most part, not rectangles. One choice for a base location is the upper-right corner of the base map. Another is the origin of the base location. You will see that in Adobe Flash, this may not be the upper-left corner.

Consider the bounding box around each piece. You need to calculate the x distance and the y distance from the base location to the upper-left corner of the bounding box. The upper-left corner of the bounding box may not be on the state. Look at Illinois. The upper-left corner of its bounding box appears to be on the border of Iowa and Wisconsin. You will need to write down the information in order to incorporate the data into the program. I used Adobe Flash to do this, which I will describe. It is possible but somewhat more tedious to use pixlr. You need to determine the upper-left corner of the bounding box "by eye" and record the coordinates you see in the Navigator panel (see the upper right in Figure 9-12). Since pixlr is built on Flash, there may be a better way to do this than eyeballing and recording the mouse coordinates.

Back to using Flash, as I indicated, I used the magic wand selection tool to select each state. We'll continue with Illinois. I copied and then pasted the selection into a new symbol named Illinois. Figure 9-15 shows the state of Illinois as a symbol in the Flash development environment.

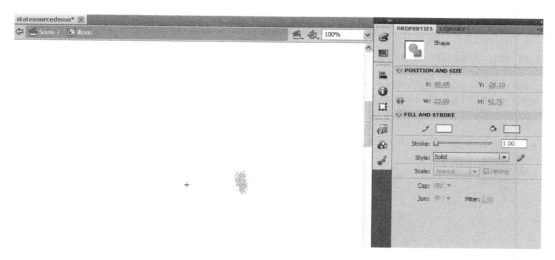

Figure 9-15. *Adobe Flash symbol for Illinois*

The crosshairs to the left of the green selected area are the base location. Flash has copied over the selected material with positioning corresponding to the origin of the original picture. The origin could be in the upper-left corner or anywhere else, but when I brought a map of the USA into Flash, the origin was closer to the center of the country. The critical factor is that it is the same point for each of the states. Now, notice in Figure 9-15 the x and y values: X: 88.65 and Y: –26.10. These are the numbers to record. They will serve as the offsets used to construct the map and to check if the jigsaw puzzle is complete.

The next step is to use Flash to produce a duplicate of each state symbol. Creating duplicate movie clip symbols is a feature of Flash. For example, I created a duplicate of Illinois, named it *illinoisclone*, selected it, and changed the X: and Y: values to 0 and 0. Figure 9-16 shows the results.

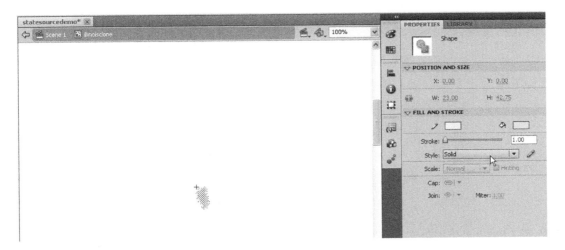

Figure 9-16. *Illinois moved to its new origin*

Notice that the crosshair (+) is now at the upper-left corner. For comparison, Figure 9-17 shows the original symbol for Hawaii and Figure 9-18 shows the adjusted image.

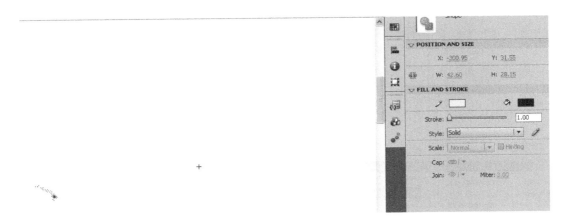

Figure 9-17. *Hawaii symbol*

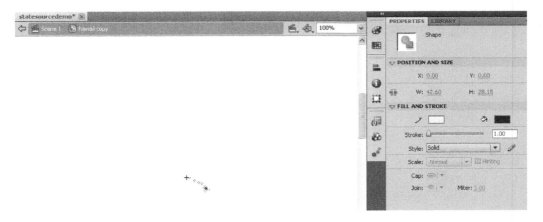

Figure 9-18. *Hawaii with adjusted origin*

If you decide to use Flash, you must use the File ➤ Export ➤ Export Image facility to produce an image file (see Figure 9-19).

Figure 9-19. *Exporting an image in Adobe Flash*

If you use another image-processing program, you save the images in the standard manner as GIFs or PNGs. You do want the images to have transparent backgrounds, so this may mean more work in an image-processing program to achieve this. The image elements in HTML are rectangular, so the transparency is crucial. The areas outside the actual state but within the bounding box must be transparent. I have included the facility of spreading out the pieces, but when the pieces aren't spread out, we want to keep the areas in the bounding box from blocking out other states.

I created arrays holding the names of the image files and the horizontal (x) and vertical (y) offset data. I also created an array listing the full names of the states. An alternative approach could be to systematically save the files with an underscore for any internal breaks—for example, North_Carolina.gif. I could write code to replace the underscore with a blank both for the game to display and for checking player's answers. However, I decided to produce the names directly. Having described the creation of the four parallel arrays holding everything the program needs for the states, it now is time to review how to create the elements.

Creating Elements Dynamically

Chapter 6 and Chapter 8 each involved generating HTML markup dynamically—that is, during runtime. The states game and other map games you may create will also feature this technique. The work is done in the function setupgame.

The code determines how many elements—that is, puzzle pieces, from the nums variable that has been set to be the length of the states array. If and when you build a puzzle with 10 countries, for example, nums will be set to 10. A for loop is used to construct an element for each state. Each element has a generated unique ID value. The attribute innerHTML of any element is set to be the markup. The code uses the information in the array variables states, statesx, and statesy. As was the case in the last chapter, the code converts numbers to character strings, and then concatenates the string "px" to make the values for setting the style.top and style.left attributes of the element. The code follows:

```
function setupgame() {
    var i;
    var x;
    var y;
    var uniqueid;
    var s;
    for(i=0;i<nums;i++) {
        uniqueid = "a"+String(i);
        s = document.createElement('state');
        s.innerHTML = (
                    "<img src='"+states[i]+"' id='"+uniqueid+"'/>");
        document.body.appendChild(s);
        thingelem = document.getElementById(uniqueid);
        x = statesx[i] +310;
        y = statesy[i] + 200;
        thingelem.style.top = String(y)+"px";
        thingelem.style.left = String(x)+"px";
        stateelements.push(thingelem);
    }
```

```
    questionfel = document.getElementById("questionform");
    questionfel.style.left = "100px";
    questionfel.style.top = "500px";
    questionfel.question.value = " ";
    questionfel.feedback.value = "   ";
}
```

The element is created of a custom defined type 'state'. Its innerHTML is set with the appropriate value. The positioning is done using the offset values in the statesx and statesy arrays (corresponding to the arrays I named piecesx and piecesy in Chapter 8). The second part of the setupgame function positions the form already present in the body element. The form will be used for the identifying and naming activities.

User Interface Overall

It is time to reveal the body element for the application since that will show the buttons for the various operations:

```
<body id="body" onLoad="init();">
<button onClick="spread();">Spread out states </button>
<button onClick="restore();">Restore original /compress map </button>
<button onClick="setupfindstate();">Find the state </button>
<button onClick="setupidentifystate();">Name the state</button>
<button onClick="setupjigsaw();">Do jigsaw</button>
<button onClick="restorepreviousjigsaw();">Restore last jigsaw in process </button>
<h1>USA</h1>
<form id="questionform" name="questionform" onSubmit="return checkname();">
State name: <input type="text" name="question" value="   " size="40"/>
<input name="submitbut" type="submit" value="      " size="30"/>
Feedback: <input type="text" name="feedback" value="   " size="40" />
</form>
</body>
```

The HTML markup produces the six buttons at the top of the screen (refer back to Figure 9-1). The buttons on top each invoke a function; more detail on each follows in the next few sections. The form at the bottom is used in distinct ways for each of the three different types of activity. This is a design decision; I am trying to be efficient with screen real estate, avoiding the clutter of multiple forms at the possible cost of confusion for the player.

User Interface for Asking the Player to Click a State

After the player clicks "Find the state," the application generates a question. Before choosing the state, the program removes any border that may exist around the last state chosen. This situation could arise if the player had just done the name a state activity. If this is the very first activity by the player, the code would not produce an error, but would merely set the border of the 0th state to empty, which is what it already was. It is a good habit to make the start of any activity do this type of housekeeping. It makes the application easier to change or upgrade in the future. Similarly, if the previous question also was an identifying question, the code would not produce an error. This transition from activity to activity must be attended to for the game to work smoothly. We do not want any state to have a border when the player has moved on to the next activity.

The `setupfindstate` function makes a random choice among the states. The global variable choice holds value made for the random choice. The function then sets up event handling for each of the elements corresponding to a state. The prompt for the player is placed in the question field of the form.

```
function setupfindstate(){
    var i;
    var thingelem;
    stateelements[choice].style.border="";
    choice = Math.floor(Math.random()*nums);
    for (i=0;i<nums;i++) {
     thingelem = stateelements[i];
     thingelem.addEventListener('click',pickstate,false);
    }
    var nameofstate = names[choice];
    questionfel.question.value = "Click on "+nameofstate;
    questionfel.feedback.value = "  ";
    questionfel.submitbut.value = "";
}
```

The appropriate player response for this activity is to click a state on the map. When the player clicks any state, JavaScript event handling is set up to invoke the `pickstate` function. The task of this function is to determine if the player's pick was the correct one. To do this, my code uses information in the event information passed to the function and the value in the global variable `choice` set by `setupfindstate`. The code for `pickstate` is

```
function pickstate(ev) {
    var picked = Number(ev.target.id.substr(1));
    if (picked == choice) {
    questionfel.feedback.value = "Correct!";
    }
    else {
       questionfel.feedback.value = "Try Again.";
    }
 }
```

Now I need to remind you of how I set the ID fields for each of the state elements. I used the index values 0 to 49 and added an *a* at the beginning. This addition of an *a* was not strictly necessary. I did it when I thought I may be creating other sets of elements. The `ev` parameter to `pickstate` has a target attribute referencing the target that received the click event. The ID of that target would be `a0`, or `a1`, or `a2`, and so forth. The `String` method `substr` extracts the substring of a string starting at the parameter, so `substr(1)` returns 0, 1, 2, and so on. My code turns the string into a number. It now can be compared to the value in the global variable `choice`.

You may decide to limit the number of tries a player can make and/or provide hints.

User Interface for Asking the Player to Name a State

After the player chooses to do the activity of naming a state, the `setupidentifystate` function is invoked. The task is to place a border around a state on the map and prompt the player to type in the name. For this operation, unlike the last one, my code puts in a value for the submit button. The function also removes the event handling for clicking a state.

```
function setupidentifystate(){
   stateelements[choice].style.border="";
      stateelements[choice].style.zIndex = "";
   choice = Math.floor(Math.random()*nums);
   stateelements[choice].style.border="double";
      stateelements[choice].style.zIndex = "20";
   questionfel.question.value = "Type name of state with border HERE";
   questionfel.submitbut.value = "Submit name";
   questionfel.feedback.value = "  ";
   var thingelem;
   for (i=0;i<nums;i++) {
    thingelem = stateelements[i];
    thingelem.removeEventListener('click',pickstate,false);
   }
}
```

The player's action is examined by the checkname function. This is already set up as the onsubmit attribute for the form. The function checkname actually does double-duty: if the current activity is doing the jigsaw, checkname ends that activity. Otherwise, checkname checks whether or not the player has typed in the correct name for the chosen state. The code in checkname follows:

```
function checkname() {
   if (doingjigsaw) {
      restore();
   }
   else {
   var correctname = names[choice];
   var guessedname = document.questionform.question.value;

   if (guessedname==correctname) {
      questionfel.feedback.value = "Correct!";
   }
   else {
      questionfel.feedback.value = "Try again.";

   }
   return false;
   }
}
```

Notice that again I do not limit the number of tries, nor do I give any hint or tolerance for misspelling.

Spreading Out the Pieces

The task of spreading out the states while maintaining their positional relationships is straightforward, though I did some experimentation with the constants to get the effect I wanted. The idea is to use the offset values in a systematic way. The offsets represent distances from a point roughly in the center of the map. My code stretches those offset values for all the states except Alaska and Hawaii. I have positioned Alaska and Hawaii to be the last two states. The code follows:

```
function spread() {
    var i;
    var x;
    var y;
    var thingelem;
    for (i=0;i<nums-2;i++) {   // don't move alaska or hawaii

        x = 2.70*statesx[i] +410;
        y = 2.70*statesy[i] + 250;
        thingelem = stateelements[i];
        thingelem.style.top = String(y)+"px";
        thingelem.style.left = String(x)+"px";
    }
}
```

Restoring the states is simply a matter of repositioning them at the values indicated in the statesx and statesy arrays. The restore function will be explained following, in the "Saving and Recreating the State of the Jigsaw Game and Restoring the Original Map" section.

Setting Up the Jigsaw Puzzle

Setting up the jigsaw activity involves randomly positioning the states on the screen and setting up the event handling for the mouse operations. It also means turning off the default drag-and-drop event handling and also turning off the buttons at the top of the screen. The submit button on the question form at the bottom of the screen will be left operational, and this button will perform the operation of saving the state of the jigsaw puzzle, as described in the next section. The only way to stop the jigsaw activity, restore the map, and return to the other activities is to click the button.

The newly created div with ID fullpage, created to prevent the drag-and-drop default action, is set up in the style section to not cover the bottom of the screen. The CSS is

```
#fullpage
{
    display:block;
    position:absolute;
    top:0;
    left:0;
    width:100%;
    height:90%;
    overflow: hidden;
    z-index: 1;
}
```

Recall that in CSS, the layering is done with the attribute z-index. In JavaScript, the attribute is zIndex. The setupjigsaw function follows:

```
function setupjigsaw() {
    doingjigsaw = true;
     stateelements[choice].style.border="";
    var i;
    var x;
    var y;
    var thingelem;
```

```
    for (i=0;i<nums;i++) {
      x = 100+Math.floor(Math.random()*600);
      y = 100+Math.floor(Math.random()*320);
      thingelem = stateelements[i];
      thingelem.style.top = String(y)+"px";
      thingelem.style.left = String(x)+"px";
      thingelem.removeEventListener('click',pickstate,false);
    }
  d.onmousedown = startdragging;
  d.onmousemove = moving;
  d.onmouseup = release;
  var df = document.createElement('div');
  df.id = "fullpage";
  bodyel.appendChild(df);
   questionfel.question.value = "";
   questionfel.submitbut.value = "Save & close jigsaw";
   questionfel.feedback.value = "  ";
   questionfel.style.zIndex = 100;
}
```

The player does the jigsaw puzzle by using the mouse to reposition the pieces. Please go back to Chapter 8 for the full details. The check for completeness is done each time the player lets up on the mouse button. The release function invokes the function I named checkpositions. The checkpositions puzzle computes the average difference in x and the average difference in y of the actual positions of the pieces to the offsets stored in the statesx and statesy arrays. The code then checks if any difference is more than the tolerance amount from the corresponding average. The function stops iterating over the pieces as soon as one is found to be out of place. For the very simple six-piece jigsaw puzzle in Chapter 8, my feedback to the player when this occurs is simply to display "Keep working." For the US states game, I wanted to do something more. What I decided to do was to report the first state in which either the x or the y difference was greater than the average. When most of the pieces are not in place, this information is not especially helpful, so this is an opportunity for improvement.

Saving and Recreating the State of the Jigsaw Game and Restoring the Original Map

As I noted previously, the only way to end the jigsaw activity is to click the submit button on the form. If the global variable doingjigsaw is true, then the restore function is invoked. The restore function will turn off the event handling for the mouse and remove the fullpage div. I realized that I could not complete the jigsaw puzzle in a single session and without cheating—that is, looking at the completed puzzle. I am getting better at it, however. This is what motivated me to implement a save-and-restore feature.

The next task is to encode the state of the jigsaw puzzle. The issue of defining application states depends, naturally enough, on the application. For the jigsaw puzzle, what needs to be stored are the style.top and style.left attributes of each of the elements. The goal is to have one character string hold all the information. What I do first is combine style.top and style.left into one string by using & to concatenate them. I then put each of these strings into an array using the following line:

```
xydata.push(thingelem.style.top+"&"+thingelem.style.left);
```

When all 50 strings have been placed in the array, my code uses the `join` method to combine everything in one big array, with the delimiter of my choice (;) separating them. This is the string that is stored using localStorage.

In HTML5, localStorage is a variation on cookies. Values are stored on the player's (client) computer as name/value pairs. A localStorage item is associated with the browser. The state of the jigsaw puzzle stored when using Firefox will not be available when using Chrome. For the name of the localStorage item, I use the name `jigsaw`, and for the value, the result of the `join` operation.

The localStorage facility may not work. For example, the player may have used the browser settings to prevent any use of localStorage or other, similar features. A localStorage item is associated with a specific web domain. Chrome allows setting and retrieving from a program on the local computer, but Firefox throws an error for retrieving data. My code uses `try` and `catch` to present an alert statement if there are problems. Figure 9-20 shows the result of trying to restore a jigsaw puzzle saved using Firefox when using a file on the local computer.

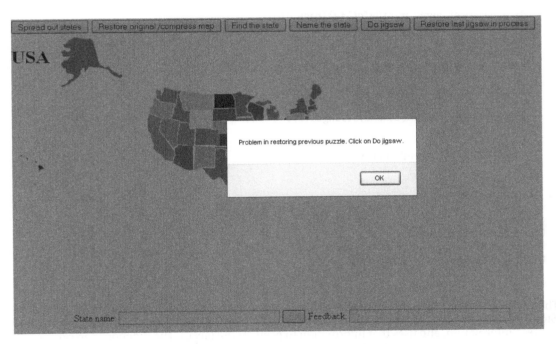

Figure 9-20. *Alert shown when trying to use localStorage locally with Firefox*

I repeat: this does not happen with Chrome, nor does it happen when the application is downloaded from a server when using Firefox.

There are two distinct functions: `restore` and `restorepreviousjigsaw`. Remember that the `restore` function does double-duty: it restores the original map after the pieces are spread out *and* it restores the original map after the player has done the jigsaw activity.

```
function restore() {
   var i;
   var x;
   var y;
   var thingelem;
   var df;
   var lsname = "jigsaw";
   var xydata = [];
   var stringdata;
   if (doingjigsaw) {
      doingjigsaw = false;
       d.onmousedown = "";
         d.onmousemove = "";
         d.onmouseup = "";
         df = document.getElementById("fullpage");
      bodyel.removeChild(df);
      for (i=0;i<nums;i++) {
          thingelem = stateelements[i];
          xydata.push(thingelem.style.top+"&"+thingelem.style.left);
      }
      stringdata = xydata.join(";");
      try {
         localStorage.setItem(lsname,stringdata);
       }
      catch(e) {
         alert("data not saved, error given: "+e);
      }
   }
   for (i=0;i<nums;i++) {
      x = statesx[i] +310;
      y = statesy[i] + 200;
      thingelem = stateelements[i];
      thingelem.style.top = String(y)+"px";
      thingelem.style.left = String(x)+"px";
   }
}
```

The restorepreviousjigsaw function attempts to read in the data stored as one long string in localStorage under the name jigsaw; decodes the string to be an array of 50 strings, each one holding the top and left information; and uses that information to position the pieces. The function then sets up event handling for the mouse events and sets up the fullpage div. Finally, the function sets the label of the submit button to indicate that this button saves and closes the puzzle. The code follows:

```
function restorepreviousjigsaw() {
   var i;
   var lsname = "jigsaw";
   var xydata;
   var stringdata;
   var ss;    // will hold combined top and left for a state
   var ssarray;
   var thingelem;
   try {
```

```
stringdata = localStorage.getItem(lsname);
xydata = stringdata.split(";");
for (i=0;i<nums;i++) {
  ss = xydata[i];
  ssarray = ss.split("&");
  thingelem = stateelements[i];
  thingelem.style.top = ssarray[0];
  thingelem.style.left = ssarray[1];
}

doingjigsaw = true;
stateelements[choice].style.border="";
d.onmousedown = startdragging;
                d.onmousemove = moving;
                d.onmouseup = release;
                 var df = document.createElement('div');
                df.id = "fullpage";
                bodyel.appendChild(df);
questionfel.question.value = "";
questionfel.submitbut.value = "Save & close jigsaw";
questionfel.feedback.value = "   ";
questionfel.style.zIndex = 100;
}
catch(e) {
    alert("Problem in restoring previous puzzle. Click on Do jigsaw.");}
}
```

Building the Application and Making It Your Own

You can make the project your own by refining and building on the states application, perhaps giving hints or keeping score, or using the application as a model for a different part of the world. For a different map, do pay attention to the special handling I use for Alaska and Hawaii. You probably will want to remove the nums-2 where it occurs. You can add another parallel array with the names of the capitals and make naming the capital and identifying a state with an indicated capital additional activities. You also can use this as a model for identifying parts of any diagram or picture (e.g., parts of the body). Notice that each activity has a function for setting up and a function for checking the response.

You can use what is described in Chapter 8 to make this project work with finger touches. The US states seemed too much for an iPhone, but it may work for an iPad. You can use the methods shown in Chapter 5 to extract the content to an external file. If you're feeling really brave, you may also want to experiment with using SVG (scalable vector graphics) to create a vector version of the map.

The application demonstrated individual features that you can use for other projects. An informal outline/summary of the functions in the states game follows:

- init is for initialization, including invoking setupgame.

- setupgame builds the state elements and positions the form.

- setupfindstate sets up the clicking state function and pickstate checks the player's response.

- setupidentifystate sets up the typing in the name, and checkname checks the response.

- setupjigsaw sets up the jigsaw puzzle. The functions startdragging, moving, and release, along with offset and draw, handle the player actions with regard to using the mouse to move pieces. The checkpositions function, along with doaverage, checks if the puzzle is complete.

- spread spreads out the pieces and restore restores the pieces to the original map locations. The restore function also saves the state of the jigsaw puzzle using localStorage.

- restorepreviousjigsaw extracts the information from localStorage to set up the puzzle as it was left.

More formally, Table 9-1 lists all the functions, and indicates how they are invoked and what functions they invoke. Notice that several functions are invoked as a result of the function being specified as a method of an object type.

Table 9-1. *Functions in the US States Game Project*

Function	Invoked/Called By	Calls
init	Invoked by action of the onLoad attribute in the <body> tag	setupgame
setupgame	Invoked by init	
pickstate	Invoked by addEventListener call in setupfindstate	
spread	Invoked by button	
restore	Invoked by button and checkname	
restorepreviousjigsaw	Invoked by button	
setupfindstate	Invoked by button	
setupidentifystate	Invoked by button	
checkname	Invoked as action of onSubmit in the form	restore
checkpositions	Invoked by release of mouse (mouseup event).	doaverage
doaverage	Invoked by checkpositions	
setupjigsaw	Invoked by button	

Function	Invoked/Called By	Calls
release	Invoked by setting up events in restorepreviousjigsaw and setupjigsaw	checkpositions
startdragging	Invoked by setting up events in restorepreviousjigsaw and setupjigsaw	offset
moving	Invoked by setting up events in restorepreviousjigsaw and setupjigsaw	draw
draw	Invoked by moving the mouse (mousemove event)	
offset	Invoked by startdragging	

Table 9-2 shows the code for the basic application, with comments for each line.

Table 9-2. Complete Code for the US States Game Project

Code Line	Description
`<!DOCTYPE html>`	Doctype header
`<html>`	html tag
`<head>`	Head tag
`    <title>USA States game</title>`	Complete title
`<style>`	Style tag
`img {position:absolute; }`	All image elements positioned absolutely
`form {position: absolute; z-index: 10;}`	Form positioned absolutely
`body{ height:100%; margin: 0; }`	Body styled to take up whole height
`#fullpage`	Style directive for the created div
`{ display:block; position:absolute; top:0; left:0; width:100%; height:90%; overflow: hidden; z-index: 1; }`	Take up whole width and nearly whole height; layer underneath
`</style>`	Closing style tag

Code Line	Description
`<script type="text/javascript">`	Script tag
`var names = [`	Names of the states; one of many parallel arrays with information on states; order and grouping here not important but order must be the same and Alaska and Hawaii last
`"Illinois","Iowa","Missouri","Oregon","Michigan",`	
`"Indiana","Vermont","New Hampshire","Maine","South Dakota","North Dakota",`	
`"Ohio","Wisconsin","Kentucky","Tennessee",`	
`"North Carolina","South Carolina","Georgia","Alabama","Mississippi",`	
`"Virginia","West Virginia","Maryland","Delaware","Pennsylvania","New Jersey","New York",`	
`"Rhode Island","Connecticut","Massachusetts","Louisiana","Arkansas","Minnesota",`	
`"Florida","Kansas",`	
`"Arizona","California","Colorado","Idaho","Montana","Nebraska",`	
`"Nevada","New Mexico","Texas","Oklahoma","Utah","Washington","Wyoming","Hawaii","Alaska"`	
`]`	End of names array
`var states = [`	Array for addresses of image files
`"illinois.gif",`	
`"iowa.gif",`	

Code Line	Description
"missouri.gif",	
"oregon.gif",	
"michigan.gif",	
"indiana.gif", "vermont.gif","newhampshire.gif","maine.gif","sou thdakota.gif","northdakota.gif",	
"ohio.gif","wisconsin.gif","kentucky.gif","tennes see.gif",	
"northcarolina.gif","southcarolina.gif","georgia. gif","alabama.gif","mississippi.gif",	
"virginia.gif","westvirginia.gif","maryland.gif", "delaware.gif",	
"pennsylvania.gif","newjersey.gif","newyork.gif",	
"rhodeislandbig.gif","connecticut.gif","massachus etts.gif","louisiana.gif","arkansas.gif","minneso ta.gif",	
"florida.gif","kansas.gif",	
"arizona.gif","california.gif","colorado.gif","id aho.gif","montana.gif","nebraska.gif",	
"nevada.gif","newmexico.gif","texas.gif","oklahom a.gif","utah.gif","washington.gif","wyoming.gif", "hawaii.gif","alaska.gif"	
];	End of address-of-image-files array
var statesx = [	Array of horizontal (x) offsets

Code Line	Description
88.65,60.15,65.40,	
-81.70,90.40,	
107.40,171.95,181.00,183.00,21.10,22.60,	
121.70,78.90,103.65,99.40,	
132.20,138.95,125.45,110.45,93.90,	
138.95,138.95,151.65,171.95,144.20,174.20,147.95,	
187.75,179.35,177.60,77.40,73.65,54.15,	
115.70,32.35,	
-44.95,-86.85,-8.15,-47.20,-32.15,21.10,	
-66.70,-11.15,-4.40,22.60, -36.70,-72.50,-15.65,-300.95,-230.30	
];	End of statesx array
var statesy = [	Array of vertical (y) offsets
-26.10,-29.85,-8.45,	
-64.75,-59.05,	
-22.70,-66.00,-67.30,-85.65,-47.15,-70.30,	
-27.90,-55.30,-3.60,12.90,	
5.20,21.45,26.40,27.90,29.65,	
-13.20,-17.10,-19.85,-20.85,-36.40,-31.35,-61.30,	
-41.85,-41.85,-50.85,47.10,21.15,-72.70,	
55.45,-2.85,	

Code Line	Description
`15.15,-35.75,-11.85,-76.70,-76.30,-23.85,`	
`-27.60,18.15,22.65,19.65,-22.35,-83.45,-` `41.75,31.55,-171.30`	
`];`	End of **statesy** array
`var doingjigsaw = false;`	Flag indicating if doing **jigsaw**
`function init(){`	Header for **init** function
`    setupgame();`	Invoke **setupgame**
`    bodyel = document.getElementById("body");`	Set reference to use to add **fullpage** div
`    questionfel =` `document.getElementById("questionform");`	Set reference to form
`}`	Close **init** function
`var bodyel;`	Used to hold reference to body
`var nums = states.length;`	Number of states
`var stateelements = [];`	Will hold the dynamically created elements
`var questionfel;`	Used to hold reference to form
`function setupgame() {`	Header for **setupgame** function
`    var i;`	For indexing
`    var x;`	For x value
`    var y;`	For y value
`    var uniqueid;`	For the unique ID created for each element
`    var s;`	Hold each newly created element
`    for(i=0;i<nums;i++) {`	Iterate over the states
`        uniqueid = "a"+String(i);`	Define an ID

Code Line	Description
`s = document.createElement('state');`	Create element

`s.innerHTML = (`
`"<img src='"+states[i]+`
`"' id='"+uniqueid+"'/>");`
	Set the HTML markup contents of the newly created element to be an image with the attributes as indicated

`    document.body.appendChild(s);`	Append to body
`thingelem = document.getElementById(uniqueid);`	Get the reference
`    x = statesx[i] +310;`	Calculate horizontal coordinate
`    y = statesy[i] + 200;`	Calculate vertical coordinate
`thingelem.style.top = String(y)+"px";`	Set `style.top` to be x
`thingelem.style.left= String(x)+"px";`	Set `style.left` to be y
`stateelements.push(thingelem);`	Add to `stateelements` array
`  }`	Close `for` loop
`questionfel.style.left = "100px";`	Position form horizontally
`questionfel.style.top = "500px";`	Position form vertically
`questionfel.question.value = " ";`	Clear out question field
`questionfel.feedback.value = "  ";`	Clear out feedback field
`}`	Close `setupgame` function
` function pickstate(ev) {`	Header for `pickstate` function
`var picked = Number(ev.target.id.substr(1));`	Extract and calculate index for the state the player picked
`  if (picked == choice) {`	Compare to choice
`questionfel.feedback.value = "Correct!";`	Display feedback as correct
`  }`	Close clause

Code Line	Description
else {	Else
questionfel.feedback.value = "Try Again.";	Display feedback to try again
}	Close clause
}	Close `pickstate` function
function spread() {	Header for `spread` function
var i;	For indexing
var x;	For x value
var y;	For y value
var thingelem;	For element
for (i=0;i<nums-2;i++) {	Iterate over 48 states
x = 2.70*statesx[i] +410;	Stretch out x and add constant
y = 2.70*statesy[i] + 250;	Stretch out y and add constant
thingelem = stateelements[i];	Get *i*th element
thingelem.style.top = String(y)+"px";	Set `style.top`
thingelem.style.left= String(x)+"px";	Set `style.left`
}	Close `for` loop
}	Close `spread` function
function restore() {	Header for restore function
var i;	For indexing
var x;	For x
var y;	For y
var thingelem;	For element reference

Code Line	Description
`var df;`	Used to remove fullpage
`var lsname = "jigsaw";`	Name for localStorage
`var xydata = [];`	Used for saving
`var stringdata;`	Used for saving
`if (doingjigsaw) {`	Check if **doingjigsaw** is true
`doingjigsaw = false;`	Set to **false**
`d.onmousedown = "";`	Remove event handling
`d.onmousemove = "";`	Remove event handling
`d.onmouseup = "";`	Remove event handling
`df=` `document.getElementById("fullpage");`	Get reference
`bodyel.removeChild(df);`	Remove **df**
`for (i=0;i<nums;i++) {`	Iterate over states
`thingelem = stateelements[i];`	Get reference to *i*th state element
`xydata.push(thingelem.style.top+"&"+thingelem.style.left);`	Create a string that combines top and left settings and add this to the **xydata** array
`}`	Close **for** loop
`stringdata = xydata.join(";");`	Generate a string from the array
`try {`	Try (since there may be problems with localStorage)
`localStorage.setItem(lsname,stringdata);`	Set localStorage item
`}`	end **try** clause
`catch(e) {`	**catch** clause

Code Line	Description
`alert("data not saved, error given: "+e);`	Error message
`}`	Close `catch` clause
`}`	Close if `doingjigsaw`
`for (i=0;i<nums;i++) {`	Iterate over states
`x = statesx[i] +310;`	Set x to be original x-coordinate
`y = statesy[i] + 200;`	Set y to be original y-coordinate
`thingelem = stateelements[i];`	Get reference to *i*th state
`thingelem.style.top = String(y)+"px";`	Set `style.top`
`thingelem.style.left= String(x)+"px";`	Set `style.left`
`}`	Close `for` loop
`}`	Close restore function
`function restorepreviousjigsaw() {`	Header for `restorepreviousjigsaw` function
`var i;`	For indexing
`var lsname = "jigsaw";`	Name used for localStorage
`var xydata;`	Will be used in extracting the data
`var stringdata;`	Will be used in extracting the data
`var ss;`	Will hold combined top and left for a state
`var ssarray;`	Will be used in extracting the data
`var thingelem;`	Reference of *i*th state element
`try {`	Try
`stringdata = localStorage.getItem(lsname);`	Fetch the data saved in localStorage under the name "jigsaw"

Code Line	Description
`xydata = stringdata.split(";");`	Generate an array from `stringdata`
`for (i=0;i<nums;i++) {`	Iterate over states
`ss = xydata[i];`	Extract the *i*th element of `xydata`
`ssarray = ss.split("&");`	Split this string to get two values
`thingelem = stateelements[i];`	Get the *i*th element
`thingelem.style.top = ssarray[0];`	Set `style.top` to be the 0th item
`thingelem.style.left = ssarray[1];`	Set `style.left` to be the 1st item
`}`	Close `for` loop
`doingjigsaw = true;`	set for doing the jigsaw
`stateelements[choice].style.border="";`	Remove any border
`d.onmousedown = startdragging;`	Set up event handling
`d.onmousemove = moving;`	Set up event handling
`d.onmouseup = release;`	Set up event handling
`var df = document.createElement('div');`	Create a div
`df.id = "fullpage";`	Give it an ID of `fullpage`
`bodyel.appendChild(df);`	Append to body
`questionfel.question.value = "";`	Clear out question field
`questionfel.submitbut.value = "Save & close jigsaw";`	Set label of the submit button
`questionfel.feedback.value = "  ";`	Clear out feedback field
`questionfel.style.zIndex = 100;`	Set form to be on top
`}`	Close `try` clause

Code Line	Description
`catch(e) {`	Catch
`    alert("Problem in restoring previous puzzle. Click on Do jigsaw.");}`	Display alert box
`}`	Close restorepreviousjigsaw function
`var choice = 0;`	Global variable holding right answer
`function setupfindstate(){`	Header for setupfindstate function
`    var i;`	For indexing
`    var thingelem;`	Reference to element
`    stateelements[choice].style.border="";`	Remove border of last choice, if there was one
`    choice = Math.floor(Math.random()*nums);`	Make a random choice for the question
`    for (i=0;i<nums;i++) {`	Iterate over the states
`      thingelem = stateelements[i];`	Set reference to *i*th element
`thingelem.addEventListener('click',pickstate,false);`	Set up event handling for this element
`    }`	Close for loop
`var nameofstate = names[choice];`	Use choice as index to names array
`    questionfel.question.value = "Click on "+nameofstate;`	Set the prompt
`    questionfel.feedback.value = "   ";`	Clear out feedback
`    questionfel.submitbut.value = "";`	Submit button not used for this task
`}`	Close setupfindstate function
`function setupidentifystate(){`	Header for setupidentifystate function
`stateelements[choice].style.border="";`	Remove previous border

Code Line	Description
`stateelements[choice].style.zIndex="";`	Put this state underneath what will be the next choice
`choice = Math.floor(Math.random()*nums);`	Make random choice
`stateelements[choice].style.border="double";`	Set border around the choice state
`stateelements[choice].style.zIndex="20"`	Make this element on top of others, so border will be on top
`questionfel.question.value = "Type name of state with border HERE";`	Set up prompt indicating where to type in answer
`questionfel.submitbut.value = "Submit name";`	Set up label for button
`questionfel.feedback.value = " ";`	Clear feedback field
`var thingelem;`	Used for holding references to elements
`for (i=0;i<nums;i++) {`	Iterate over states
`thingelem = stateelements[i];`	Set to be ith element
`thingelem.removeEventListener('click',pickstate,false);`	Remove event handling
`}`	Close for loop
`}`	Close setupidentifystate function
`function checkname() {`	Header for checkname function
`if (doingjigsaw) {`	If player was doing jigsaw, then . . .
`restore();`	. . . invoke restore
`}`	End clause
`else {`	Otherwise
`var correctname = names[choice];`	This is the correct name

Code Line	Description
`var guessedname = document.questionform.question.value;`	This was what the player typed in
`if (guessedname==correctname) {`	Was the player correct?
`questionfel.feedback.value = "Correct!";`	Display feedback
`}`	End clause
`else {`	Else
`questionfel.feedback.value = "Try again.";`	Display feedback
`}`	End clause
`return false;`	Return `false` to prevent refresh (may not be necessary)
`}`	End if-not-jigsaw clause
`}`	Close `checkname` function
`function checkpositions() {`	Header for `checkpositions` function
`var i;`	Indexing
`var x;`	For x
`var y;`	For y
`var tolerance = 20;`	Margin allowed for positioning
`var deltax = [];`	Will hold the x differences
`var deltay = [];`	Will hold the y differences
`var delx;`	Used in computation
`var dely;`	Used in computation
`for (i=0;i<nums-2;i++) {`	Iterate over first 48 states; doesn't check Alaska or Hawaii
`x = stateelements[i].style.left;`	X is this state's left

Code Line	Description
`y = stateelements[i].style.top;`	Y is this state's top
`x = x.substr(0,x.length-2);`	Remove px
`y = y.substr(0,y.length-2);`	Remove px
`x = Number(x);`	Convert to number
`y = Number(y);`	Convert to number
`delx = x - statesx[i];`	Calculate difference with the x offset
`dely = y - statesy[i];`	Calculate difference with the y offset
`deltax.push(delx);`	Add to `deltax` array
`deltay.push(dely);`	Add to `deltay` array
`}`	Close `for` loop
`var averagex = doaverage(deltax);`	Calculate average of all x differences
`var averagey = doaverage(deltay);`	Calculate average of all y differences
`for (i=0;i<nums;i++) {`	Iterate
`if ((Math.abs(averagex - deltax[i])>tolerance) || (Math.abs(averagey-deltay[i])>tolerance)) {`	Check if x difference or y difference is bigger than tolerance from the respective average
`break;`	If so, leave loop
`}`	Close clause
`}`	Close `for` loop
`if (i<nums) {`	Did the loop break prematurely?
`questionfel.feedback.value = names[i]+" and maybe more out of position";`	Set feedback to display the state that was found to be out of position
`}`	Close clause

Code Line	Description
else {	Else loop did not end prematurely; could put in check on Hawaii and Alaska here
questionfel.feedback.value = "GOOD";	Display feedback
}	Close clause
}	Close checkpositions function
function doaverage(arr) {	Header for doaverage function; parameter is an array
var sum;	Used as accumulator in computation
var i;	For indexing
var n = arr.length;	Length of array
sum = 0;	Initialize to zero
for(i=0;i<n;i++) {	Iterate over elements
sum += arr[i];	Add in the ith value
}	Close for loop
return (sum/n);	Return sum divided by number n
}	Close doaverage function
function setupjigsaw() {	Header for setupjigsaw function
doingjigsaw = true;	Set flag to true
stateelements[choice].style.border="";	Remove any previous border
var i;	For indexing
var x;	For x values
var y;	For y values
var thingelem;	Reference state element

Code Line	Description
`for (i=0;i<nums;i++) {`	Iterate over states
`x = 100+Math.floor(Math.random()*600);`	Choose random value for x
`y = 100+Math.floor(Math.random()*320);`	Choose random value for y
`thingelem = stateelements[i];`	Set *i*th element
`thingelem.style.top = String(y)+"px";`	Position for top
`thingelem.style.left =String(x)+"px";`	Position for left
`thingelem.removeEventListener('click',pickstate,f` `alse);`	Remove event handling
`}`	Close **for** loop
`d.onmousedown = startdragging;`	Set up event handling
`d.onmousemove = moving;`	Set up event handling
`d.onmouseup = release;`	Set up event handling
`var df = document.createElement('div');`	Create div
`df.id = "fullpage";`	Give it the ID
`bodyel.appendChild(df);`	Add to body
`questionfel.question.value = "";`	Clear out question field
`questionfel.submitbut.value = "Save & close` `jigsaw";`	Change the label on the submit button
`questionfel.feedback.value = "  ";`	Clear out feedback field
`questionfel.style.zIndex = 100;`	Set form on top
`}`	Close **setupjigsaw** function
`var d = document;`	Holds document

Code Line	Description
`var ie= d.all;`	The Internet Explorer check; note that application has not been checked for latest Internet Explorer version
`var mouseDown = false;`	Initialize flag to `false`
`var curX;`	Current x
`var curY;`	Current y
`var adjustX;`	Used for dragging
`var adjustY;`	Used for dragging
`var movingobj;`	The object being dragged
`function release(e){`	Header for release function
`    mouseDown = false;`	Set flag back to `false`
`    checkpositions();`	Invoke check for puzzle being done
`};`	Close -release function
`function startdragging(e) {`	Header for `startdragging` function
`    var o;`	Used to calculate offset
`    var j;`	Used to hold reference to element
`    var i;`	For indexing
`    curX = ie ? e.clientX+d.body.scrollLeft : e.pageX;`	Compute location of cursor in x
`    curY = ie ? e.clientY+d.body.scrollTop : e.pageY;`	Compute location of cursor in y
`    for (i=0; i<nums;i++) {`	Iterate over states
`        j = stateelements[i];`	Get the *i*th element
`        o = offset(j);`	Determine offset

Code Line	Description
`if (curX >= o.x && curX <= o.x + j.width && curY >= o.y && curY <= o.y + j.height)`	Check if mouse over the *i*th element
`{ break; }`	If so, leave for loop
`}`	End of clause
`if (i<nums) {`	Was for loop exited prematurely?
`movingobj = stateelements[i];`	Set up the *i*th as the moving object
`adjustX = curX- o.x;`	Amount in x piece is offset from mouse cursor
`adjustY = curY- o.y;`	Amount in y piece is offset from mouse cursor
`mouseDown = true;`	Set flag to true: object in motion
`}`	Close clause for mouse over an object
`}`	Close startdragging function
`function moving(e) {`	Header for moving function
`if (!mouseDown) return;`	If no object is being moved, return
`if (ie)`	Check if IE flag set
`draw(e.clientX+d.body.scrollLeft, e.clientY+d.body.scrollTop);`	Draw using these values
`else`	Else
`draw(e.pageX, e.pageY);`	Draw using these values
`}`	Close moving function
`function draw(x, y) {`	Header for draw function; this moves/drags the state
`var js = movingobj.style;`	Extract point to the style
`js.left = (x - adjustX) + "px";`	Change the style to new x (left) value
`js.top  = (y - adjustY) + "px";`	Change the style to new y (top) value

Code Line	Description
`}`	Close `draw` function
`function offset(obj) {`	Header for `offset` function; adds in all offsets of `obj` from ancestors
`    var left = 0;`	Initialize left
`    var top  = 0;`	Initialize top
`    if (obj.offsetParent)`	Is there a parent?
`        do {`	Then
`        left += obj.offsetLeft;`	Increment left
`        top  += obj.offsetTop;`	Increment top
`        } while (obj = obj.offsetParent);`	Keep going if there is a parent
`    return {x: left, y: top};`	Return array with the left and top values
`}`	Close `offset` function
`</script>`	Closing script tag
`</head>`	Closing head tag
`<body id="body" onLoad="init();">`	Body tag, with `onLoad` set to `init()`;
`<button onClick="spread();">Spread out states </button>`	Button to spread out states
`<button onClick="restore();">Restore original /compress map </button>`	Button to restore original map
`<button onClick="setupfindstate();">Find the state </button>`	Button to start `Find the state` task
`<button onClick="setupidentifystate();">Name the state</button>`	Button to start `Name the state` task
`<button onClick="setupjigsaw();">Do jigsaw</button>`	Button to start jigsaw

Code Line	Description
`<button onClick="restorepreviousjigsaw();">Restore last jigsaw in process </button>`	Button to restore saved jigsaw
`<h1>USA</h1>`	heading on screen for the USA puzzle
`<form id="questionform" name="questionform" onSubmit="return checkname();">`	Form tag, with onSubmit set to checkname call
`State name: <input type="text" name="question" value="    " size="40"/>`	Label and place for state name
`<input name="submitbut" type="submit" value=" " size="30"/>`	Submit button, value now empty
`Feedback: <input type="text" name="feedback" value="    " size="40" />`	Label and place for feedback
`</form>`	Closing form tag
`</body>`	Closing body tag
`</html>`	Closing html tag

Testing and Uploading the Application

The project can be tested locally (on your home computer) using Chrome. However, to test the localStorage facility for saving the current state of the puzzle, you need to upload the application for it to work using Firefox (and perhaps other browsers). This application requires the 50 files representing the states, so be sure and upload them as well (or whatever files correspond to the parts of the map for your application).

Summary

In this chapter, you learned how to build an educational game that featured different types of questions for the player. The HTML5 features and programming techniques included the following:

- Building a user interface involving text or visual prompts. Player responses included clicking elements on the screen and typing in text. After entering jigsaw mode, player actions were dragging and repositioning elements on the screen.

- How to encode and decode information using split and join methods.

- How to save and restore works-in-progress, including use of the `try...catch` construct.

- Reuse of techniques explained in the last chapter:

  - Creating HTML markup dynamically to create the piece elements on the screen

  - Placing the jigsaw pieces randomly on the screen

  - Determining the coordinate values that indicated how the pieces fit together, and using those values, along with a defined tolerance, to check if the puzzle was put together properly

  - Manipulating the positioning of the piece elements to spread out the pieces and restore them to their original locations

In Chapter 10, the final chapter, we'll explore the use of a MySQL database together with PHP, first introduced in Chapter 6.

Web Site Database: Using PHP and MySQL

In this chapter, you will do the following:

- Receive an introduction to databases and Structured Query Language (SQL)

- Learn how to create tables in a MySQL database

- Learn how to use PHP to insert, update, delete, and select records in tables in a database

- Explore the differences between client-side and server-side processing

- Learn techniques to build a basic user login system, including use of localStorage and the Secure Hash Algorithm for one-way encryption

Introduction

The project for this chapter is a database of information on web sites. Registered users—we'll call them finders—may add sites to the database, the site information consisting of the address (URL), along with a name, category, and description contributed by the finder. Finders are registered with IDs and passwords, presumably by a system administrator. A registered finder can change his or her password. Anyone can view the whole list of sites, or, by clicking a drop-down list generated dynamically to be a list of unique categories in the database, view the sites in a selected category. Finders can delete sites from the list.

■ **Note** I recognize that this is not as exciting as bouncing videos, talking fish, geographic portals to media, and jigsaw puzzles turning into video clips. Moreover, the application is just a little more than what is available to you through bookmarks on any browser. However, this application does serve as a good introduction to databases and the interactions of HTML5, JavaScript, PHP, and SQL—most notably form input validation. When you have a database to build, what you have learned in this chapter will get you started.

A characteristic of database applications such as this one, which is implemented using HTML5 with JavaScript, PHP, and MySQL, is that they consist of many separate programs. The programs, called *scripts*, are generally fairly short. This is different from the projects described in previous chapters. The list of scripts and their relationships will be given in the "Building the Application and Making It Your Own" section. Here I will show the application in use.

I start the presentation of the database application by showing the script to register a user/finder. This step may not be available to everyone. Figure 10-1 shows the opening screen.

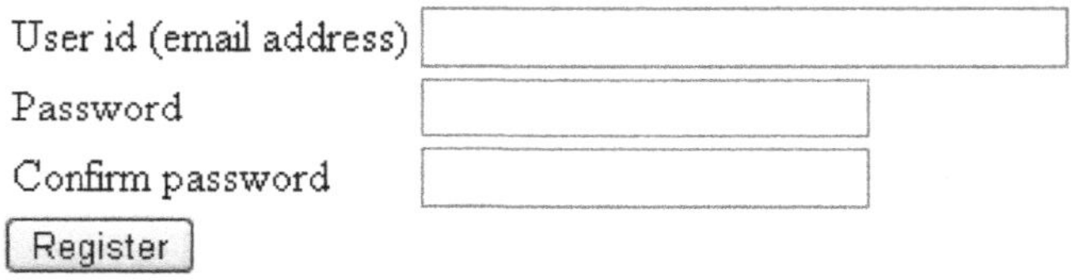

Figure 10-1. *Opening screen for registering finders (register.html)*

Figure 10-2 shows what I entered. (I often use Larry, Curly, and Moe, or Harpo, Groucho, Zeppo, and Chico, and I use very simple passwords.)

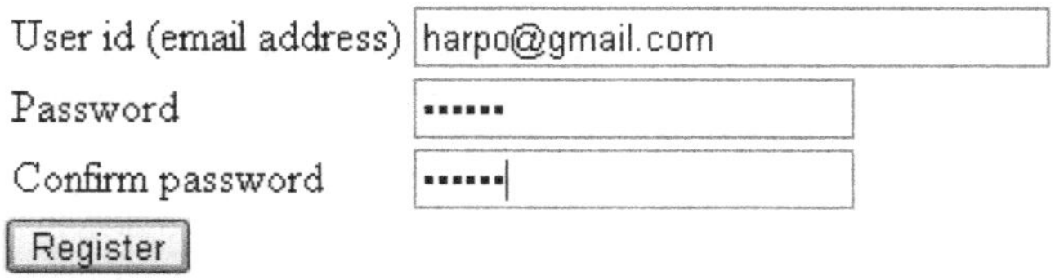

Figure 10-2. *Data entered for a new finder (register.html)*

Assuming the passwords match, the script replaces both fields with the encoded password and invokes another script. Figure 10-3 shows the results.

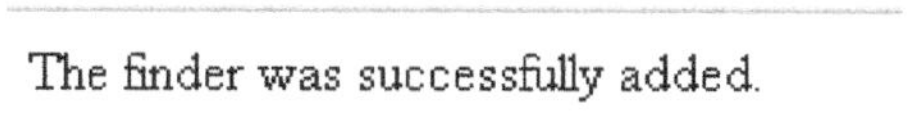

The finder was successfully added.

Figure 10-3. Successful addition of finder (completereg.php)

A characteristic of a database project is that attention needs to be paid to what can go wrong. For example, what if the person registering a new finder neglected to enter an e-mail address for the user ID? Figure 10-4 shows the response.

Figure 10-4. Response when ID wasn't an e-mail address (register.html)

Another error on the part of the person entering the data can be an incorrect password or the failure to correctly confirm a password. Figure 10-5 shows the response for this type of user error.

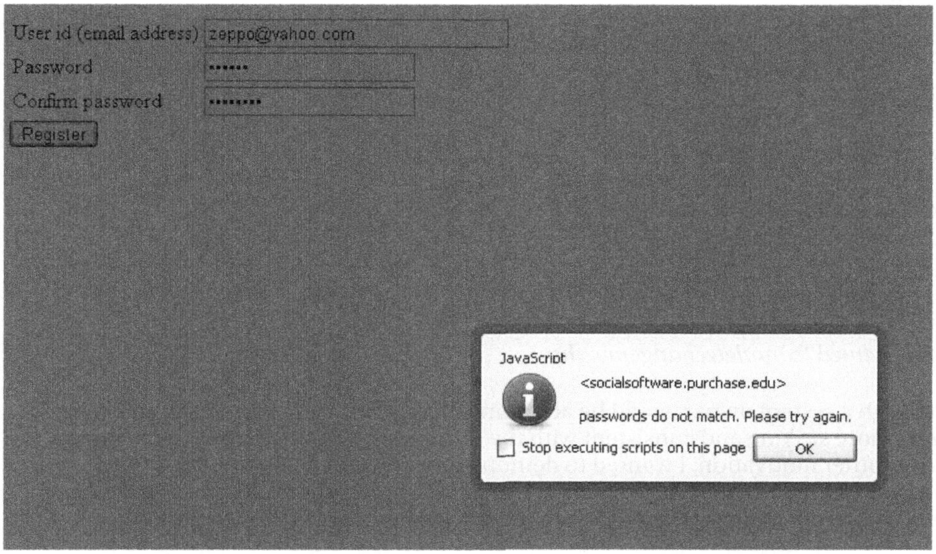

Figure 10-5. Passwords not matching (register.html)

These two types of user error are handled by different mechanisms. I will demonstrate a partial solution later.

Finders may change their passwords using the changepassword.html script. Figure 10-6 shows the opening screen.

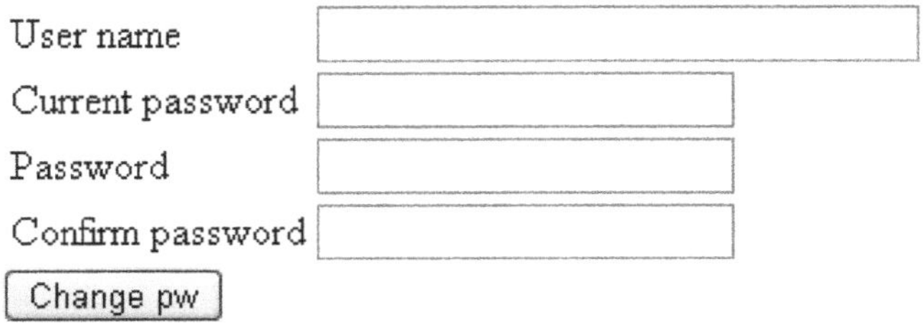

User name _____

Current password _____

Password _____

Confirm password _____

[Change pw]

Figure 10-6. Opening screen for changing password (changepassword.html)

Figure 10-7 shows data entered. The finder must know the current password, presumably given out by the system owner, to use the formal term.

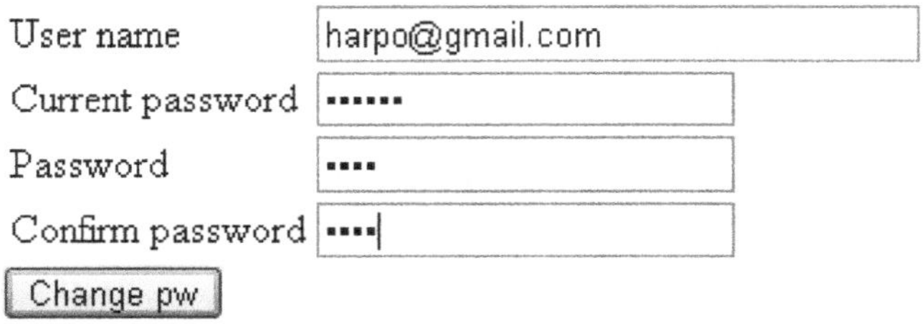

User name | harpo@gmail.com

Current password | •••••••

Password | ••••

Confirm password | ••••|

[Change pw]

Figure 10-7. Data entered (changepassword.html)

Figure 10-8 shows the result.

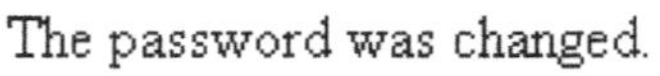

The password was changed.

Figure 10-8. Change accepted (completechangepw.php)

I decided that though a system owner would be accepting of the error response shown in Figure 10-5, I wanted something more striking and consistent with the other responses for finders—that is, end-users. Actually, I had another motivation: I wanted to demonstrate that you could use all the new features of HTML5 in your scripts that invoke PHP scripts or are composed by PHP code. Figure 10-9 shows the results of trying to change the password, but not entering the same password twice.

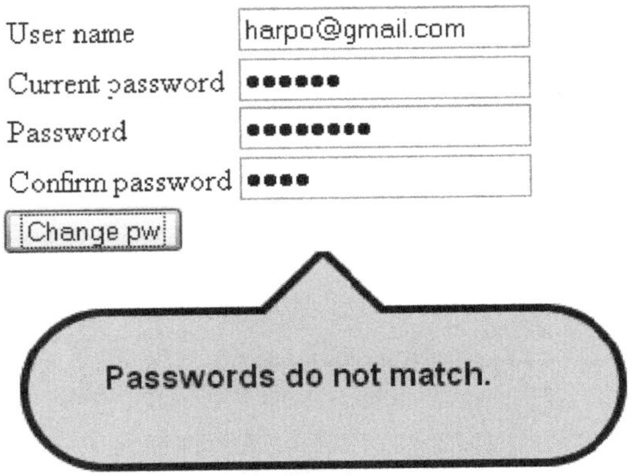

Figure 10-9. Response to bad input for changing password

I probably could have made this better—for example, by moving the "Passwords do not match" bubble closer to the input fields. One approach to doing this would be to use techniques such as shown in Chapter 4 for changing the zIndex of the canvas. Another possibility would be to reposition elements on the document. My main goal was to include the use of new HTML5 features in HTML files invoking PHP scripts.

Moving on, Figure 10-10 shows the opening screen for adding sites to the database.

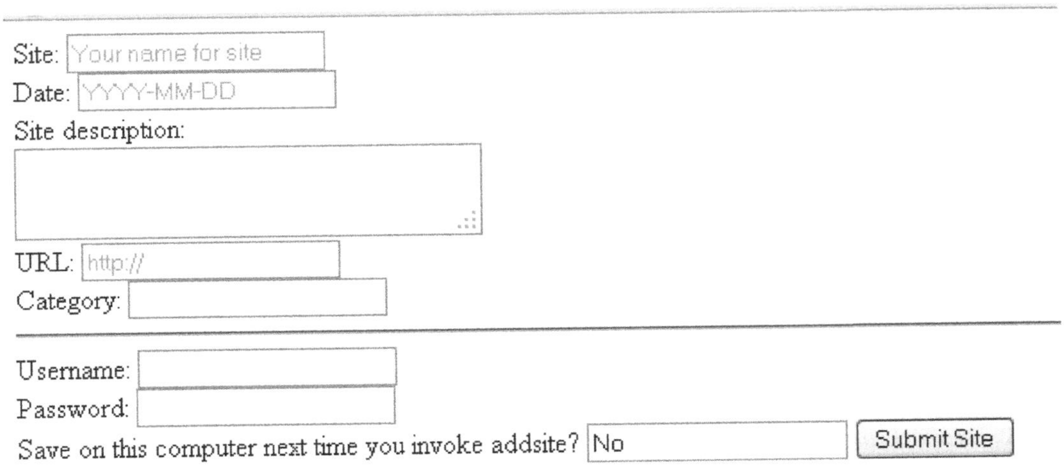

Figure 10-10. Opening screen for addsite.html

Notice the faint text, termed *placeholder text*, suggesting what needs to go in the input fields. Notice also that the finder must enter a username and password. The chance to save this information is offered, with the default being No. The finder must do something to save the information on the local computer. Figure 10-11 shows the data entered by the finder.

371

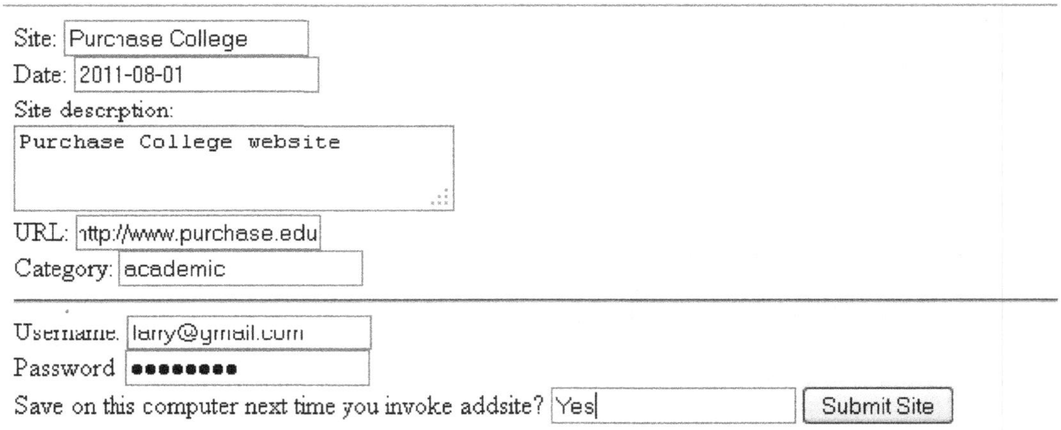

Site: Purchase College
Date: 2011-08-01
Site description:
Purchase College website
URL: http://www.purchase.edu
Category: academic

Username: larry@gmail.com
Password: ●●●●●●●●
Save on this computer next time you invoke addsite? Yes   Submit Site

Figure 10-11. *Form filled in for adding a site (addsite.html)*

If the operation is successful, the finder is informed, and another similar form is presented, as shown in Figure 10-12.

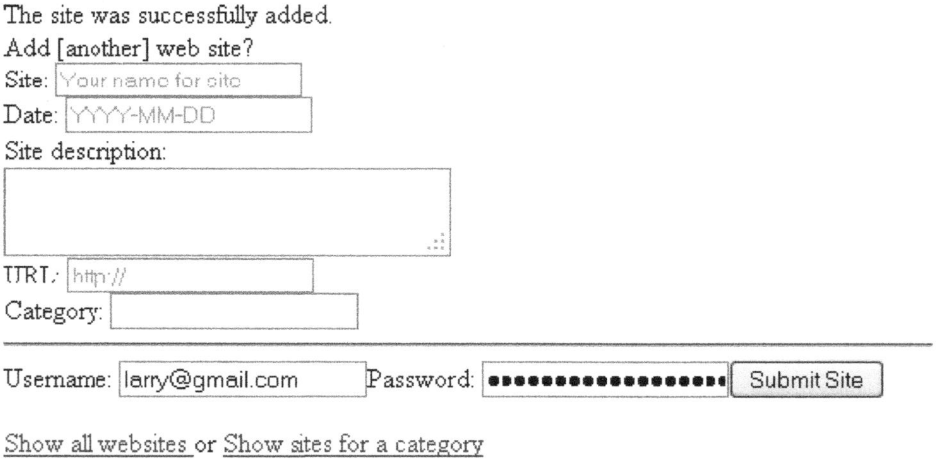

The site was successfully added.
Add [another] web site?
Site: Your name for site
Date: YYYY-MM-DD
Site description:

URL: http://
Category:

Username: larry@gmail.com   Password: ●●●●●●●●●●●●●●●●●●   Submit Site

Show all websites or Show sites for a category

Figure 10-12. *Feedback and chance to add another site or see sites (addsite.php)*

Notice that the password input field now has a long entry. This is the actual size of the encoded form of the password. Notice also that the finder is presented with the choices of seeing all web sites in the database, seeing all web sites in a category, or adding another site. If the finder clicks the first link, or goes directly to showsites.html, the current contents of the database are displayed, as shown in Figure 10-13.

Title	URL	Date	Description	Category	Finder
Purchase College	http://www.purchase.edu	2011-08-01	Purchase College website	academic	larry@gmail.com
Daily Kos	http://dailykos.com	2011-07-31	progressive blogs	political	moe@yahoo.com
Google	http://google.com	2011-07-30	search site	media	larry@gmail.com
Jeanine at Purchase	http://faculty.purchase.edu/jeanine.meyer	2011-07-28	JM's academic info	academic	moe@yahoo.com
Bogus	http://bogus.com	2011-07-20	another fake	fake	larry@gmail.com
Nate Silver	http://fivethirtyeight.com	2008-01-01	political polling	politics	larry@gmail.com

Figure 10-13. *Display of all sites (showsites.php)*

If you clicked the "Show sites for a category" link or went directly to the `showsitesbycategory1.php` script, you would see something like what is shown in Figure 10-14.

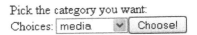

Figure 10-14. *Screen for picking a category*

Clicking the downward arrow causes a drop-down menu to appear holding the list of all categories currently in the database. Figure 10-15 shows what this looked like when I did it.

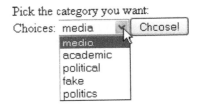

Figure 10-15. *Drop-down menu (showsitesbycategory1.php)*

In fact, I didn't select "media," but instead chose "academic." Figure 10-16 shows the results.

Sites in academic category

Title	URL	Date	Description	Finder
Purchase College	http://www.purchase.edu	2011-08-01	Purchase College website	larry@gmail.com
Jeanine at Purchase	http://faculty.purchase.edu/jeanine.meyer	2011-07-28	JM's academic info	moe@yahoo.com

Figure 10-16. *Sites marked as "academic" (showsitesbycategory2.php)*

By the way, anyone can go to `showsites.php` or `showsitesbycategory1.php` and see what is in the database. It is also possible for anyone to invoke `removesites.php`. However, actually removing any sites requires a username and password. An opening screen is shown in Figure 10-17.

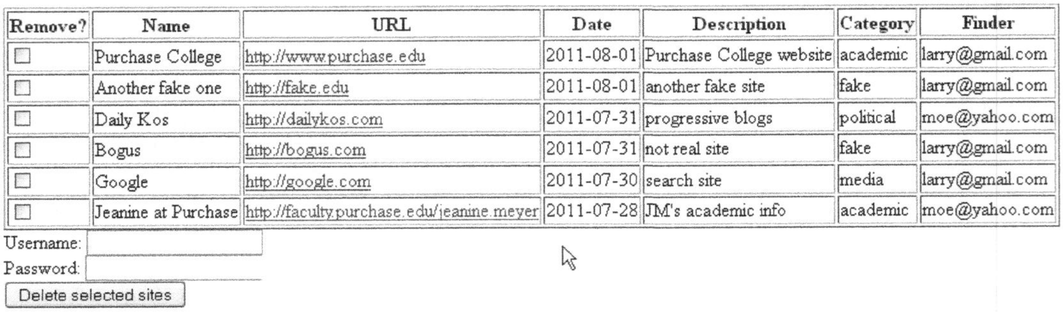

Remove?	Name	URL	Date	Description	Category	Finder
☐	Purchase College	http://www.purchase.edu	2011-08-01	Purchase College website	academic	larry@gmail.com
☐	Another fake one	http://fake.edu	2011-08-01	another fake site	fake	larry@gmail.com
☐	Daily Kos	http://dailykos.com	2011-07-31	progressive blogs	political	moe@yahoo.com
☐	Bogus	http://bogus.com	2011-07-31	not real site	fake	larry@gmail.com
☐	Google	http://google.com	2011-07-30	search site	media	larry@gmail.com
☐	Jeanine at Purchase	http://faculty.purchase.edu/jeanine.meyer	2011-07-28	JM's academic info	academic	moe@yahoo.com

Username:
Password:

Delete selected sites

Figure 10-17. *Chance to delete (remove) sites (removesites.php)*

Note that any registered finder can delete any site. This may be something you want to change. Figure 10-18 shows how the screen would appear if someone clicked on two sites but neglected to log in.

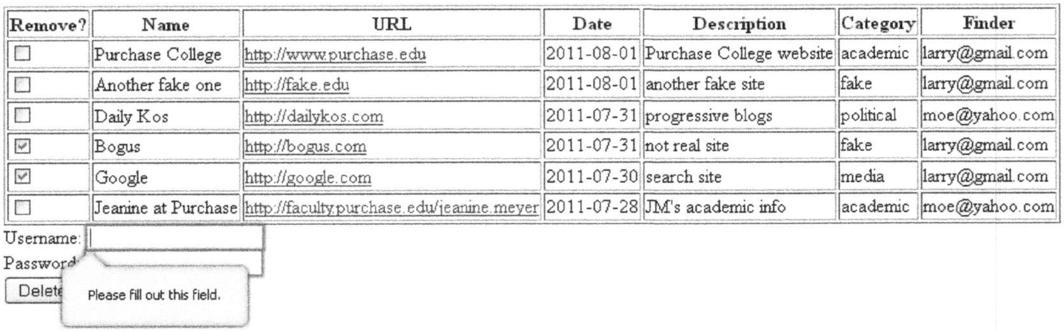

Remove?	Name	URL	Date	Description	Category	Finder
☐	Purchase College	http://www.purchase.edu	2011-08-01	Purchase College website	academic	larry@gmail.com
☐	Another fake one	http://fake.edu	2011-08-01	another fake site	fake	larry@gmail.com
☐	Daily Kos	http://dailykos.com	2011-07-31	progressive blogs	political	moe@yahoo.com
☑	Bogus	http://bogus.com	2011-07-31	not real site	fake	larry@gmail.com
☑	Google	http://google.com	2011-07-30	search site	media	larry@gmail.com
☐	Jeanine at Purchase	http://faculty.purchase.edu/jeanine.meyer	2011-07-28	JM's academic info	academic	moe@yahoo.com

Username:
Password:

Delete

Please fill out this field.

Figure 10-18. *Reminder that user ID and password are required (removesites.php)*

If the username and password are not valid, the application responds with feedback, as shown in Figure 10-19.

Problem with username and/or password.

Figure 10-19. *The username and password must be correct (completeremovesites.php).*

If the log-on information is valid, the sites are removed from the database and feedback is given, as shown in Figure 10-20.

The 2 selected sites were deleted.

Figure 10-20. Successful removal of two sites (completeremovesites.php)

Recall that I specified that I wanted the username and password saved on my local computer when visiting the `addsite` script using the Firefox browser (see Figure 10-11). At some point, I closed Firefox. When I returned to this program again using the Firefox browser, I was shown the screen in Figure 10-21. The saving and retrieving is browser-specific. Notice also that the answer to the question has been changed to Yes. The opt-in choice has been changed to an opt-out choice. If I change the Yes back to a No, the information will be erased from local storage.

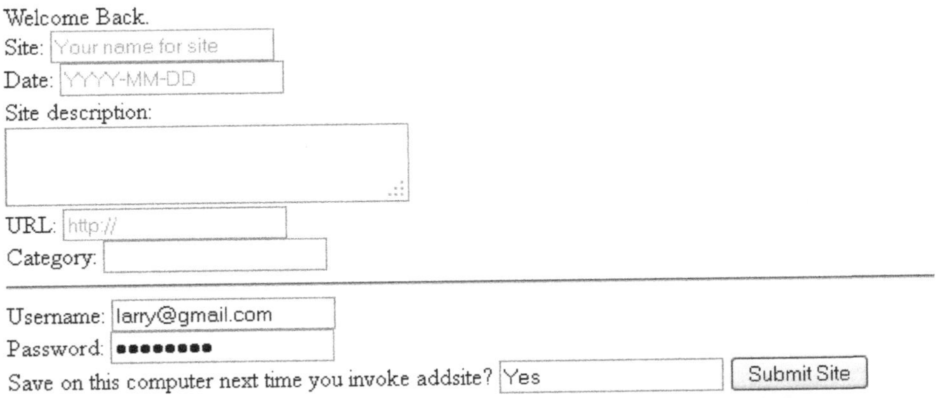

Welcome Back.
Site: [Your name for site]
Date: [YYYY-MM-DD]
Site description:
[   ]

URL: [http://]
Category: [   ]

Username: [larry@gmail.com]
Password: [●●●●●●●●]
Save on this computer next time you invoke addsite? [Yes]   [Submit Site]

Figure 10-21. Returning to addsite.html, with stored login info retrieved

The browsers handle input fields specified as dates differently. You can see in Figure 10-22 the opening screen for `addsite.html` in Opera.

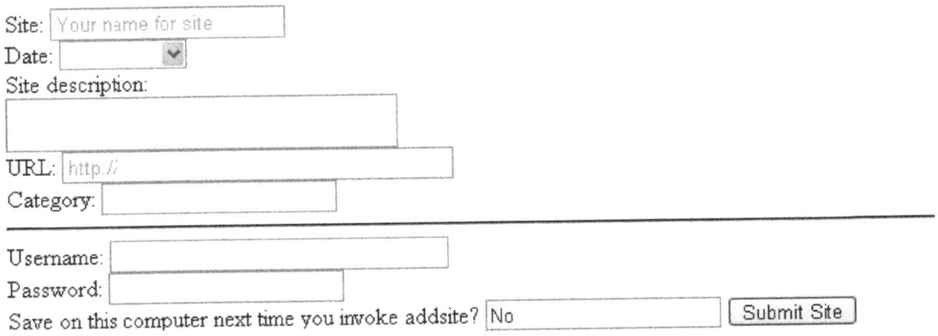

Site: [Your name for site]
Date: [▾]
Site description:
[   ]

URL: [http://]
Category: [   ]

Username: [   ]
Password: [   ]
Save on this computer next time you invoke addsite? [No]   [Submit Site]

Figure 10-22. Opening screen in Opera (addsite.html)

When I click the downward arrow in the input field next to Date:, I see what is shown in Figure 10-23.

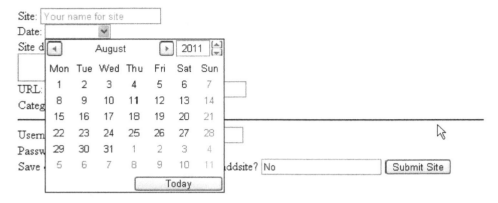

Figure 10-23. *Opera browser with date-picker calendar page (addsite.html)*

This completes the overview/introduction to the database application. In the next section, I will describe critical features required to produce the application, and in the following section, I will describe the different features of HTML5, MySQL, and PHP, along with programming techniques that satisfy the requirements.

Critical Requirements

The requirements for this project are, at the most fundamental, a way for people to save and share data. The data must persist—that is, last longer than the browser session of any individual user (i.e., finder or viewer). The project includes a user ID/password system to provide a basic level of security for the application. The security protection includes use of the Secure Hash Algorithm, a type of one-way encryption, for the passwords. This means that the passwords are stored in an encoded form in the database so that someone looking at the records in the database would not be easily able to determine the original password.

The project also provides a way for finders to set up persistent information for themselves, allowing them to conveniently save login information on their own computers. Yes, this is a trade-off of convenience vs. security.

The information on the sites includes web addresses, and the user ID is assumed to be an e-mail address. The HTML5 standard includes a specification that input fields of certain types be validated. In contrast, I pose the requirement that finders can enter any text as a category, and the program generates a menu of categories.

The database operations include adding, changing, deleting, and querying information. The changing (termed *updating*), deleting, and querying involve logical expressions.

SQL, PHP, HTML5, and JavaScript Features

I will start the explanation of the technical features to support the database project with a general introduction to databases, and then describe other programming techniques and HTML5, JavaScript, SQL, and PHP constructs. Keep in mind that you can see how these language features and programming techniques are used in context in the "Building the Application and Making It Your Own" section.

Relational Databases

The term *database* is typically reserved for what are called relational databases. Relational databases are organized into tables, which in turn consist of records, which contain fields. The fields can hold data in many different data types, including several distinct types for numbers, characters strings, date, date/time, and so on. When designing a production database, the choices of data types have significant effects on size and performance. One of the fields in the database may be marked as being a *primary key*. This means that it is unique among the values held in this field for the table. The database management system (DBMS), for example, MySQL, constructs other tables to speed up access.

A record in a table may contain one or more fields other than the primary key field that hold the primary key for another record, generally in another table. For example, a database for a store can contain tables for sales, products, and customers. The record for a simple sale typically contains a field that points into the product table and another field that points into the customer table. Another standard example is courses at a college. A record representing a course named "HTML5 Projects" can contain a field that points to another course record representing "Introduction to HTML," indicating a prerequisite for the course. Some courses have prerequisites and some do not.

The project for this chapter uses two tables: the `sitesfinders` table and the `finders` table. The `sitesfinders` table has the following fields:

- `sid`: Primary key
- `stitle`: Name of site
- `sdate`: Date of insertion
- `sdescription`: Description of site
- `scat`: Category of site
- `surl`: Web address
- `finderid`: ID for the finder who submitted this site

The `finders` table has the following fields:

- `finderid`: Primary key
- `username`: User ID for this finder (specified as an e-mail address)
- `epw`: Encoded password

There is a relationship between the two tables represented by the `finderid` field in the `sitesfinders` table. Each record for a site indicates which finder added the site to the database. Figure 10-24 shows a schematic representing the information, in the style of an entity relationship diagram (ERD).

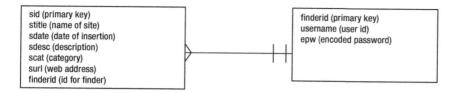

Figure 10-24. *Diagram for the database*

The so-called crow's feet markings on the line connecting the two rectangles indicate the possible number of records involved. Each record of a site refers to exactly one record in the **finders** table. The two short vertical lines indicate at most one and at least one. Putting it another way, each site refers to exactly one finder. In contrast, a finder can be referenced in any number of site records. There are other formats for ERDs and there are more complex relationships.

MySQL (**www.mysql.com/**) is an open source DBMS that supports relational databases. There are many others, including commercial products such as Oracle and DB2. The different database products compete on factors such as performance, ease of development and management tools, factors that can be critical for large, busy databases. The good news, and it is very good news and uncommon in technology, is how much the products have in common, including the table/record/field structure, the primary key concept, and SQL (to be described in the next section). The PHP language, also open source, has many commands defined for use specifically with MySQL, but it can be used for other DBMSs.

Just as I cautioned you in Chapter 6 to confirm that your server permits the use of PHP for sending e-mail, you will need to confirm that your server provides access to MySQL. Specifically, I will assume that you have a database assigned to you, a user ID for the database—which may or may not be the same as the user ID for uploading files to your server space—and a password to be used for accessing the database. Lastly, you need permissions to use each of the SQL commands discussed in the next section. Artful use of permissions is an appropriate tool for use in production systems. I (or rather the user ID I obtained from my local IT organization) had permission to do all operations except drop the whole database.

For this application, I followed the standard practice of putting the database information in one script and including that script in all the other scripts that access the database. Here is a censored version of my **opendbo.php** file. I have substituted blanks in the assignment statement for **$host**, **$user**, **$password**, and **$DBname** where I had information for my database:

```
?php
global $DBname, $link;
$host = '          ';
$user="        ";
$password="         ";
$DBname="          ";
$link=mysql_connect($host,$user,$password);
mysql_select_db($DBname,$link);
?>
```

Recall from Chapter 6 that variables in PHP start with dollar signs. Again, you will need to determine the values for **$host**, **$user**, **$password**, and **$DBname** based on discussions with your Internet service provider.

In **createresearchtables.php**, **addsite.php**, and the other PHP files, I use the statement

```
require("opendbo.php");
```

to bring in this code to establish the connection to MySQL and to select my assigned database.

SQL

SQL is a language just for database operations. Many online sources exist for SQL. Each statement, termed a *query*, invokes what would be considered a program. I introduce SQL by explaining the statements used in this project. The SQL queries will be constructed by PHP code and sent to the database as described following in the "Middleware: PHP" section. However, do keep in mind that SQL works for other database products.

■ **Note** Databases, and SQL in particular, comprise a much larger topic that what I aim to cover in this chapter. There are other SQL statements and there also are variations of the statements I will describe. The site www.mysql.com/ provides considerable information, including tools for database management such as MySQLWorkbench.

SQL has statements for creating tables and for dropping—that is, *removing*—tables. A common practice to prevent errors is to drop a table with a given name before creating it. An example of such a statement is

```
DROP TABLE sitesfinders
```

The DROP statement is pretty powerful, since it deletes the table and all the information in it.

I use the convention of capital letters for SQL terms and lowercase for names specific to my application. Before writing the CREATE TABLE statement, I need to determine what the fields will be—that is, the names of the fields and the data types and other specifications. For the table I named sitesfinders, the field information is

```
sid INT UNSIGNED NOT NULL AUTO_INCREMENT PRIMARY KEY,
stitle char(50),
sdate DATE,
surl char(100),
sdescription TEXT,
scategory char(30),
finderid INT
```

I spread this out on several lines for ease of reading. Let's start with the first field, named sid. It is set to be an unsigned integer. It cannot be null. The field will be designated as AUTO_INCREMENT. This means that MySQL will assign the values. This field is designated as the primary key. The values will be unique because MySQL will assign them. This is the common practice for fields that have no intrinsic unique identifiers, like Social Security numbers or ISBNs for books. Moving on, stitle, surl, and scategory are each set to hold character strings, with the amount of characters specified in parentheses. There are alternatives to the char data type, including TEXT, used for sdescription. Generally, there is a trade-off of space vs. time. A data type such as VARCHAR will take less space but require marginally more processing. The fid field is a simple integer. My PHP coding will ensure that each of these fields are specified each time a record is inserted, so I did not make the NON NULL designation. The complete SQL statement would be

```
CREATE TABLE sitesfinders (sid INT UNSIGNED NOT NULL AUTO_INCREMENT PRIMARY KEY, stitle
char(50), sdate DATE, surl char(100), sdescription TEXT, scategory char(30), finderid INT)
```

The statement for the `finders` table is similar:

```
CREATE TABLE finders (finderid INT UNSIGNED NOT NULL AUTO_INCREMENT PRIMARY KEY, username
char(50), epw char(64)
```

I may have been able to make the username a primary key, but I decided to let MySQL do the work.

Having created tables, now I'll go on to describe how to insert records. The format of the `INSERT` statement that I use for this project inserts a new record by listing all the values in the order in which they were defined in the `CREATE` statement. An example using constants, which do *not* appear in any of my code, would be:

```
INSERT INTO sitesfinders VALUES ('0','apress','2011-08-01','http://apress.com','my
publisher','media','1');
```

Two things must be explained for this totally artificial example. The `0` is a placeholder for the primary key field that MySQL assigns. The title, date, URL, description, and category are simply for illustration. The `1` at the end would point to the record in the `finders` table with primary key 1.

SQL provides a way to change one or more fields in a record or more than one record. This will be demonstrated in the change-password script. For now, consider this example:

```
UPDATE sitesfinders SET stitle = 'friends of ED' WHERE stitle = 'apress'
```

If there were multiple records with the `stitle` field set to `apress`, they would all be changed.

Notice that the equal sign is used in two different ways in the `INSERT` statement. The first equal is an assignment. The second one is a comparison test. There are no instances of `==` in SQL, unlike JavaScript and many other programming languages.

The powerhouse statement of SQL is the `SELECT` statement. This statement extracts what is termed a *recordset* from the tables. The statement

```
SELECT * FROM sitesfinders
```

extracts the entire table. The * indicates all the fields.

The next example of a `SELECT` statement is used to prepare the drop-down menu in the script for showing sites in a category.

```
SELECT DISTINCT scategory FROM sitesfinders
```

An artificial example of `SELECT` would be

```
SELECT stitle, surl FROM sitefinders WHERE scategory = 'media'
```

This statement produces a recordset with each row having two elements, the `stitle` and the `surl` fields from the records in which the `scategory` field was equal to `media`.

The real power of `SELECT` is demonstrated in statements involving what are termed *joins*. The web sites project makes use of two tables connected by the fact that the records in one table point to records in another. When displaying the information, I don't want to show the `finderid` fields. That is not meaningful information to anyone. I want to show the usernames that the finders actually entered. Look back at Figure 10-13, for example. That information is only in the `finders` table, not the `sitesfinders` table. Consider that in production applications, we want such information in one place so it can be changed easily. The `SELECT` statement used for the `showsites.php` script is

```
SELECT * FROM sitesfinders as s JOIN finders as f WHERE s.finderid = f.finderid ORDER BY sdate
DESC
```

The statement takes the two tables and joins them together when the WHERE condition is met. The s and the f are used to express the condition. The ORDER BY does what it sounds like with the DESC, indicating the most recent occurs first. The statement produces a table looking pretty much like Figure 10-13, but with each row having four additional fields: the sid holding the primary key for each record in sitesfinders; the finderid for the record; the same value finderid for the finders record; and the epw record, a very long string (explained following in the "Hash Function" section) representing the encoding of the finder password.

The DELETE statement does what it sounds like, and should be used cautiously. For the remove-sites operation, my PHP code constructs a character string with a list of all the primary keys for the sites to be removed. Here is an artificial example that would delete the records with keys 1 and 2:

```
DELETE FROM sitesfinders WHERE sid IN (1, 2)
```

I have given you a brief introduction to SQL. In the sections that follow, you will read about the creation of SQL queries from form input passed by the HTML scripts and about how the recordsets produced by SELECT queries are used to compose HTML pages.

Local Storage

You have read about a more complex use of HTML5 localStorage in Chapter 9. Recall that localStorage saves key/value pairs. What is saved is a character string that's under a given name and associated with the name of the server domain. The localStorage values are associated with a browser. For the US states project, the location (x- and y-coordinates) of each of the 50 states needed to be combined and encoded to produce one character string. For this application, my JavaScript code saves two small items: a username and a password. I had to think about if and when I wanted the code to save something, and how to communicate the options to the user. The localStorage methods are straightforward. An input field named saveok holds either No or something else. Anything else is considered a request to save the information. In the code that follows, references also are made to the un and the pw1 input fields:

```
if (document.f.saveok.value!="No") {
      try {
            localStorage.setItem("researchun",document.f.un.value);
            localStorage.setItem("researchpw",pw1);
      }
      catch(e) {
            alert("error on local storage "+e);
            }
      }
      else {  //no saving, remove anything saved
      try {
            localStorage.removeItem("researchun");
            localStorage.removeItem("researchpw");
      }
      catch(e) {
            //alert("error on local storage "+e);
            }
      }
```

The first alert("error on local storage "+e) statement would let someone know who had requested that local storage be used that there was a problem. I commented out the second alert since this was in response to a user saying that nothing was to be saved.

Hash Function

A password that is stored as is in a database could be read by anyone with access to the database, and a password sent through the Internet could be read by anyone with the ability to spy on the packets being sent over the communication lines. An approach to avoid these problems is to store not the password itself but an encoded version of it. The encoded version is sometimes called the *digest*. The encoding can be done using any of a number of algorithms, or one-way encryption functions. These algorithms have the property that their inverse function is not known. The SHA256 algorithm is such an algorithm. You may download a copy of this program from `www.webtoolkit.info/javascript-sha256.html`. The authors are given as Angel Marin and Paul Johnston.

When finders type in their passwords, my `encode` function immediately applies the `sha256` function. The result of this function is what is sent to the database when the finders are first registered or when passwords are changed. All comparisons are done between encoded versions—the digests—not the original passwords. This means, as was stated earlier, that even if someone knows the encoded version that resides in the database, the would-be intruder would not know enough to type in the original.

■ **Note** Security, including the treatment of passwords, is a large issue. Some people argue against client-side encoding. If and when you build a production system, you do need to evaluate your security arrangements.

Client Side vs. Server Side for Input Validation

As a reminder, the client computer is the one generally right in front of you, on which you run a browser program such as Firefox. Server computers are the ones holding the files that are downloaded by your browser. These files include HTML documents, image files, video files, and audio files. The previous section brought up the issue of encoding of the passwords using JavaScript in an HTML document to be run by the browser on the client computer. Another critical activity for database applications is validation of input. Many modern browsers check if an e-mail address entered into an input field of type `email` does indeed obey the formatting rules for e-mail. Look back at Chapter 6 for examples. The same thing is true for URLs. You also can use special CSS identifiers to reformat invalid input. The advantage of the browser doing this is that browser code generally is much faster than code we write in JavaScript. However, as I seem to be saying many times in the chapter, if and when you build a production system, you may choose not to depend on the HTML5 validation, but perform your own. By the way, MySQL also performs checks on the data used in `INSERT` or `UPDATE` statements. You can use the results of the MySQL query to determine if there were problems with the data.

Assuming there is validation to be done, the next issue is when and where to do it. I will describe the role of PHP as being in the middle, between code running on the browser and SQL running on the MySQL DBMS. The input validation to check if a username/password combination is valid—that is, belonging to a registered finder—must be done using the database, and so is done on the server.

After this philosophical discussion on input validation, here is how we code the mechanics. A `form` tag may have an `action` attribute and an `onsubmit` attribute. The `addsite.html` script contains the following `form` tag:

```
<form name="f" action="addsite.php"  onSubmit="return encode();"  method="post">
```

The HTML5 user validation takes place before the `encode` function is invoked. The `encode` function, defined in the `script` element of this document, runs on the client machine. The `addsite.php` script, a separate script, performs the server-side operations. If the `encode` function issues a return of `false`, then action does *not* proceed to `addsite.php`. If the `encode` function issues a return of `true`, then `action` does proceed. For the `addsite` task, the client operations include checking if the input has been submitted and is of the specified type. For the `register.html` script, a check is made that a password and a confirming password are identical. The server-side operations include checking if this is a registered finder—that is, if the username and password are in the database. The `addsite.php` script goes on to make the addition to the database.

Middleware: PHP

The PHP language performs the function of working between the browser and the database, hence the term *middleware*. A PHP script is often invoked as a result of the setting of the `action` attribute in a `form` tag. The PHP code extracts the form input, which I describe in detail next. Often, the PHP script uses the information to create an SQL query, which it passes on using special commands to MySQL. In many cases, the PHP script takes the results returned by MySQL and uses these to build a new HTML document. The PHP script runs on a server, *not* directly on the client computer (or more accurately, not interpreted by a browser on the client computer). The term *three-tier model* or *architecture* is used to describe the situation:

- A user interface operates on the client computer.

- Middleware expresses business rules operating on the server.

- Data or information logic operates on the DBMS.

The user interface (aka presentation layer) typically is programmed using HTML, CSS, and JavaScript, though there are other possibilities, such as Adobe Flash ActionScript, Java, and Processing. An alternative to PHP for middleware is ASP.NET. Lastly, as I have stated, there are other DBMSs, though the use of SQL is standard. The three-tier model is a simplification. Today's production systems may involve more layers.

Figure 10-25 shows some typical interactions.

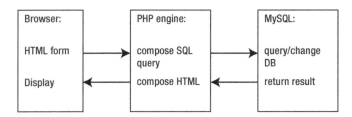

Figure 10-25. *Three-tier interactions*

The interactions shown in Figure 10-25 could represent what happens in the `addsite.html` and `addsite.php` scripts, or the `changepassword.html` and `completechangepassword.php` scripts, or the `register.html` and `completereg.php` scripts. In each of these cases, a pair of programs, one HTML and one PHP, together perform the tasks. The `showsites.php` script composes a SQL query "on its own" and uses the results to create the HTML document to be displayed by the browser. The pair `showsitesbycategory1.php` and `showsitesbycategory2.php`, and the pair `removesites.php` and `completeremovesites.php` each start by using PHP to compose a query, with the result used to compose an HTML document containing a form. The second member of the pair acts on the input to the form. Form action is discussed more in the next section.

Since the tasks of PHP often involve creating character strings representing SQL queries or HTML markup, the language has special features for text. The one that is the most unusual for me is that variables can be referenced inside of character strings. That is, if the variable $name holds the string Jeanine, then after the following statement is executed:

```
$greeting = "My name is $name.";
```

the value of the variable $greeting is My name is Jeanine.

The PHP language also accepts single quotes inside of double quotes, and vice versa. Making a small change in the previous example:

```
$greeting = "My name is '$name'.";
```

the value of the variable $greeting is now My name is 'Jeanine'.

Here are two examples from the code. The addsite.php script constructs a SQL query to check if a finder's username and password are in the database. The statement is

```
$query = "SELECT * FROM finders WHERE username='$un' AND epw='$epw'";
```

The single quotation marks around the value of the variable $un and the value of the variable $epw will appear in $query. A short while later in addsite.php, the code constructs another SQL query to perform the insertion of a new record in the database.

```
$query = "INSERT INTO $tname values ('0','$stitle','$sdate','$surl','$sdesc','$scat','$fid')";
```

The string concatenation operator is a period (.), not the + used in JavaScript. Because of the feature of inserting variable references inside strings, the . operator isn't necessary much of the time, but it has its uses.

The PHP language includes the join function, similar to the join method of JavaScript. I will show an example of the join function in the next section.

A PHP task is preparing character strings representing SQL queries. What if someone wanted to input a site with the title (which I have allowed to be made up by the finder) of "Who's on First?". The ' could prove troublesome when it is made part of a string or when the data is handed over to MySQL. The PHP language has two ways to handle this. One is that the installation of PHP can be set to do what is termed *escaping* or *magic-quoting* certain characters, including single and double quotes, when they occur in GET or POST data. That was *not* the case with my installation, so I needed to do something else.

The PHP language includes a function called addslashes. This function would turn Who's on First? into Who\'s on First?, and I used it for handling the title, description, and category input in the addsite.php script.

■ **Tip**   You will need to check out whether you need to use the addslashes function with your server support staff. It may be available using a command called phpinfo(), which displays considerable information on the PHP installation. However, some installations do not allow this command.

A PHP script generally is not all written in the PHP language. Because a PHP task composes an HTML document, a PHP script can contain straight HTML. The PHP is indicated (delimited) by the presence of <?php and ?>. The following is the complete showsites.php script. Notice that it starts and ends with standard HTML5. The code after the `<?php` and before the `?>` will be explained following, in the "Results from SQL Queries" section. Briefly, the `showsites.php` script invokes an SQL query and uses the results to construct an HTML table to be displayed by the browser on the client computer.

```
<!DOCTYPE html>
<html>
<head>
<title>List sites with finder ids</title>
</head>
<body>
<?php
require("opendbo.php");
$query="SELECT * FROM sitesfinders as s JOIN finders as f where s.finderid = f.finderid  ORDER
BY sdate DESC";
$result=mysql_query( $query, $link);
print("<table border='1'>");
print("<tr><th>Title</th><th>URL</th><th>Date </th><th>Description </th><th>Category
</th><th>Finder </th></tr>");
while ($row=mysql_fetch_array($result)) {
print("<tr>");
 print("<td> ".$row['stitle']."</td>");
 print ("<td><a href='".$row['surl'] ."' target='_new'>".$row['surl']."</a></td>");
 print ("<td>".$row['sdate']."</td>");
  print ("<td>".$row['sdescription']."</td>");
   print ("<td>".$row['scategory']."</td>");
   print ("<td>".$row['username']."</td>");
 print ("</tr>");
}
mysql_close($link);
?>
</table>
</body>
</html>
```

The document can go into and out of PHP any number of times. In particular, what may seem especially strange is that you can have a PHP `if` statement and brackets for the clauses, and go out of PHP to write straight HTML, and then back into PHP for more PHP statements, including closing up the brackets. You will see an example of this in the `addsite.php` script.

Form Action

HTML forms represent a way for users to interact with an application. The user input can be referenced by validation code built into the browser in the case of HTML5 form validation. The input can also be referenced and, perhaps, changed by a JavaScript function specified by the `onSubmit` attribute in the `form` tag. Lastly, the input can be passed to a function specified by the `action` attribute in the `form` tag. The passing of data can be done using the `GET` method or the `POST` method. Input passed using the `GET` method is passed using what is called the *query string*, and is visible on the web location toolbar. You probably have noticed a web site address followed by a string like this one:

`…..?first=John&last=Doe`

You also can look ahead to Figure 10-26. Checking out the query string can be helpful during debugging. Information passed using the POST method is not visible, but is passed along as part of the HTTP protocol. The POST method presents a less cluttered appearance to the user, and this is what I use for most of the scripts for this project. The form tag for the register.html script, for example, is

```
<form name="f" action="completereg.php" onSubmit="return encode();" method="post">
```

In completereg.php, or any of the other scripts that retrieve form input, the code references with the $_GET or the $_POST associative arrays. For example, to extract the contents of the form input field named pw, the PHP statement is

```
$epw = $_POST["pw"];
```

Forms can contain groups of input fields. Look back at Figures 10-17 and 10-18; the HTML markup for each of the check boxes has the name group[ ]. The markup is created using information from the database, and will be explained in the next section. With this definition of the input field name, the code to extract the array of input values is the same as a simple variable:

```
$ids = $_POST['group'];
```

I spoke about a join function in the previous section. I use it in the completeremovesites.php function to take the values in the $ids array and create a character string with a separator that has the value indicated in the first operand. So, if the $ids array contains a 10, 20, and 30, then after these two lines

```
$deletelist = join (', ',$ids);
$query = "DELETE FROM sitesfinders WHERE sid IN ($deletelist)";
```

the $deletelist will be the character string "10,20,30" and the DELETE statement will remove from the sitesfinders array the three elements with a primary key sid equal to 10, 20, or 30.

■ **Note** Early versions of PHP allowed developers to refer to POST input, GET input, and cookies one simple way: just using a dollar sign and the name. This was and is considered a bad practice with respect to security, since a knowledgeable hacker could jump into a script using the query string without going through prior programs. It is possible to change the settings of the PHP implementation to continue doing this, but it is not recommended.

I created several pairs of programs:

- register.html and completereg.php

- changepassword.html and completechangepassword.php

- addsite.html and addsite.php

- showsitesbycategory1.php and showsitesbycategory2.php

- removesites.php and completeremovesites.php

The first script in each pair contains a reference to the second in the action attribute of a form tag. The first script is an HTML file if it does not need access to the database and a PHP file if it does. I could have combined each pair into one script by checking if a form input field was defined. This is a standard practice, described as using *self-referential scripts*. The benefits are fewer files and, probably, an easier time making changes, because you do not have to refer to multiple files. However, the negative factors are that the scripts are more complex.

Results from SQL Queries

An SQL query produces two types of results: an indication on the success or failure of the operation *or* a recordset (a table with each row an associative array). The names or keys of the associative array are the field names in the database tables.

Simple Results

Let's cover the first type of result. The task of the `completereg.php` script is to insert a new record into the `finders` table. Please accept that the variables `$finder` and `$epw` contain the username and the encoded password. The fact that I assume that the username is an e-mail address is not significant for this part of the program. The `completereg.php` script contains the following lines:

```
$query = "INSERT INTO $tname values ('0','$finder','$epw')";
$result = mysql_query($query, $link);
if ($result) {
        print("The finder was successfully added.<br>\n");
}
else {
        print ("The finder was NOT successfully added. <br>\n");
}
```

The `$query` variable contains the SQL query. The single quotation marks are required. The `0` is a placeholder for the primary key field that is assigned by MySQL. The `mysql_query` function submits the query and returns a result that my code assigns to the variable `$result`. The `$result` is interpreted as `true` or `false`. The `print` statement makes one of the two strings be part of the HTML document returned to be displayed by the browser. The `true` and `else` clauses each could be larger and contain more `print` statements.

Recordset Results

Now we get to the more interesting results from SQL queries. A `SELECT` query may return a substantial amount of information, all available to be used to construct an HTML document. Let's consider what the `showsitescategory1.php` script needs to do to produce what is shown in Figure 10-14 and Figure 10-15. The code makes use of `mysql_query` as just shown, and also `mysql_fetch_array`, a PHP function for extracting the next row of the recordset. The HTML document to be sent to the browser has markup that is independent of what is returned from the database, including the `<form>` tag and the `<select>` tag. The form tag specifies the `GET` method. The results with the query string displayed are shown in Figure 10-26. Notice that `pickedcategory` is set to be "academic." Also, the `submit` input value is part of the query string. The `%21` stands for an exclamation mark.

Sites in academic category

Title	URL	Date	Description	Finder
Purchase College	http://www.purchase.edu	2011-08-01	Purchase College website	larry@gmail.com
Jeanine at Purchase	http://faculty.purchase.edu/jeanine.meyer	2011-07-28	JM's academic info	moe@yahoo.com

Figure 10-26. *Showing the query string for the GET method*

The material that is dependent on the contents of the database consists of the `value` attributes of the option elements and the contents of the option elements. Here is the entire `showsitesbycategory1.php` script. Notice the `<?php` and `?>` delimiters.

```
<!DOCTYPE html>
<html>
<head>
<title>List sites in a category</title>
</head>
<body>
Pick the category you want:
<br/>
<form action="showsitesbycategory2.php" method="get">
Choices: <select name="pickedcategory">
<?php
require("opendbo.php");
$query="SELECT DISTINCT scategory FROM sitesfinders";
$categories = mysql_query($query, $link);
while ($row=mysql_fetch_array($categories))
{ $cat=$row['scategory'];
   print ("<option value='$cat'>$cat</option><br>\n");
}
mysql_close($link);
?>
</select>
<input type=submit name=submit value="Choose!"> <br>
</form>
</body>
</html>
```

The results of the `mysql_query` call are assigned to the variable `$categories`. The `while` state has as the condition the expression assigning to `$row` the results of `mysql_fetch_array`. This PHP function does what the name applies: it fetches the next row from `$categories`. An internal index keeps track of the next row. When there are no more rows, `$row` is assigned a value that is interpreted as `false`, and the `while` clause is exited.

So, say that `$row` has a valid value. This value is an associative array. There is only one item per row since the `SELECT DISTINCT` query just asked for the `scategory` values. The line

```
$cat = $row['scategory'];
```

extracts the value and assigns it to $cat. The next line prints a line of HTML. At this point, I need to remind you (because I often need to remind myself) that PHP extracts the value of variables when the variable names occur in strings. If the value of $cat is media, then the line

```
print ("<option value='$cat'>$cat</option><br>\n");
```

would cause the following line to be printed as part of the HTML document:

```
<option value='media'>media</option><br>
```

The \n would cause a line break to appear in the HTML document. You will often see <br> and \n together. The <br> means the browser will include a line break in the display, and the \n means that the HTML document will have a line break, making it easier for the programmer to read.

After the while statement has caused these lines to be added to the HTML document, the connection is closed and the PHP coding ends. The rest of the HTML document follows, including the <input type=submit...> and the closing tags for form, body, and html.

The showsitesbycategory2.php script is similar, but somewhat more complicated; however, the bulk of the work is done for us by the SQL. The goal is to produce something like what is shown in Figure 10-16, where the rows are all records of a category that has been specified by the user responding to the user interface presented by showsitesbycategory1.php. The while loop creates the HTML markup for a row of a table. The loop is

```
while ($row=mysql_fetch_array($result)) {
print("<tr>");
 print("<td> ".$row['stitle']."</td>");
 print ("<td><a href='".$row['surl'] ."' target='_new'>".$row['surl']."</a></td>");
 print ("<td>".$row['sdate']."</td>");
  print ("<td>".$row['sdescription']."</td>");
  print ("<td>".$row['username']."</td>");
 print ("</tr>");
}
```

Notice that the first thing printed out is a <tr> tag, and the last thing for each row is a </tr> tag. In between, the code prints out td elements. The material is from different elements from the $row associative array. The . operator is used to concatenate strings. The rows of the table include markup for an a element. The $row['surl'] value occurs twice in the HTML markup: for the href value and for the contents of the element. I could have chosen to make the $row['stitle'] be the contents—that is, what starts off being blue and underlined—but I decided to show the URL that had been entered by the finder. The <a> tag contains a target attribute of '_new', indicating that if someone clicks the link, a new window is to be opened.

■ **Caution** The PHP print statements (you also can use the command echo) are intricate things to produce, but you can do it! Be patient and keep track of the single quotation marks and the HTML opening and closing tags, and make sure you use the right names for the variables.

With this exposition on the features of HTML5, JavaScript, PHP, and SQL, and how they work on the client and server computers, it is time to put it all together.

Building the Application and Making It Your Own

You can make this application your own by using it as is and inserting the web sites that are of interest to you or a group for which you are building the project. You can also make it your own by building a totally different database. The task of defining the tables may take time, as it may not be obvious what the entities and relationships are.

An important consideration for this project is which scripts are intended for end-users and which are for database administrators. The createresearchtables.php and the register.html scripts may be things that only the database administrator runs. You may even want to remove them (and completereg.php) from the web site and only upload for a short time for each use. Similarly, removesites.php and completeremovesites.php may not for general use, even though they require a registered finder. Once you decide what is appropriate, you may want to create an HTML file with links to the scripts you are making available to the world.

The basic web site project demonstrated and discussed in this chapter consists of 15 scripts. One of them is the sha256.js script that you need to download from the www.webtoolkit.info site yourself. Another is the opendbo.php script that I showed with several fields empty in the previous section. I have included the file opendboToBeFixed.php as one of the downloads available from the publisher. You need to determine the four pieces of information, edit the file, and then save it with the name opendbo.php. The remaining 13 scripts also are available as downloads, and are given here with annotations.

In the projects described in the previous chapters, I started this section with a brief outline of the functions, and a table describing the functions invoked and called. The appropriate overview for the database project is different. Table 10-1 gives the rows corresponding to the distinct tasks. When two scripts are listed together in a row, the second script is invoked by the first through the mechanism of the action attribute in a form tag. A file with JavaScript is included in an HTML file through the use of a script element. This is done for the sha256.js file and the drawroundarrowbox.js file. A similar inclusion operation is done for PHP scripts. The opendbo.php file is brought into all the PHP files using the require function, as described previously in the "Relational Databases" section.

Table 10-1. *Tasks by Scripts in the Web Site Database Project*

Script(s)	Task	Uses	Called or Used
opendbo.php	Set up a connection to the database		All scripts accessing the database (i.e., all the PHP scripts)
createresesearchtables.php	Create tables	opendbo.php	Called directly by the person setting up the project; this is invoked once for production, but generally several times during debugging
register.html and completereg.php	Register the finder	register.html uses sha256.js completereg.php includes opendbo.php	register.html is called directly by the person setting up the project to register finders

Script(s)	Task	Uses	Called or Used

`changepassword.html` and `completechangepassword.php`	Change the password	`changepassword.html` uses `sha256.js` and `drawroundarrowbox.js`
		
		`completechangepassword.php` includes `opendbo.php`
			`changepassword.html` is called directly by the finders

`addsite.html` and `addsite.php`	Add a web site to the database	`addsite.html` uses `sha256.js`
		
		`addsite.php` includes `opendbo.php`
			`addsite.html` is called directly by the finders

`showsites.php`	Show all sites	Includes `opendbo.php`	Can be called directly by anyone; there is a link in the HTML constructed by `addsite.php`
`showsitesbycategory1.php` and `showsitesbycategory2.php`	Show sites in a category	Both scripts include `opendbo.php`	`showsitesbycategory1.php` can be called directly by anyone; there is a link in the HTML constructed by `addsite.php`
`removesites.php` and `completeremovesites.php`	Remove sites	Both scripts include `opendbo.php` `removesites.php` uses `sha256.js`	`removesites.php` can be invoked by anyone, but only registered finders will be able to make deletions
`sha256.js`	Encode passwords		Invoked in `register.html`, `changepassword.html`, `addsite.html`, and `removesites.php`
`drawroundarrowbox.js`	Draw the fancy shape		Invoked in `changepassword.html`

I'll now present tables with the annotated code for 13 of the 15 scripts. The code for the scripts takes up many pages, but when you look them over, you will see that there is much repetition of code. An encode function, for example, appears in several of the scripts. It is not identical across the different files, but similar. The scripts that create tables to display information on sites (`showsites.php`, `showsitesbycategory2.php`, and `removesites.php`) also have significant similarities.

Table 10-2 shows the code for `createresearchtables.php`.

Table 10-2. Code for createresearchtables.php

Code Line	Description
`<?php`	Start PHP
`function createtable($tname,$fields) {`	Header for `createtable`; used for two tables
`global $DBname, $link;`	These two variables refer to the ones set in `opendbo.php`; the $DBname is not used
`$query = "DROP TABLE $tname";`	Delete any existing table with the name $tname
`mysql_ query($query,$link);`	For the current database and link, do the query
`$query="CREATE TABLE ".$tname."(".$fields.")";`	Now create a query to create a new table with the name held by $tname and with the fields as defined by the parameter $fields
`if (mysql_query($query,$link)) {`	Do the query, and if successful . . .
`    print ("The table, $tname, was created successfully. \n");`	. . . print out that the table was created successfully
`    }`	Close clause
`else {`	Else
`    print ("The table, $tname, was not created.  \n");`	Print out that the table was not created
`    }`	Close clause
`}`	Close function
`?>`	Close PHP
`<!DOCTYPE html>`	Standard doctype
`<html><head><title>Creating order project tables </title></head>`	Standard HTML

Code Line	Description
`<body>`	Body tag
`<?php`	Start PHP
`require("opendbo.php");`	Bring in `opendbo.php` to make a connection to the database
`$tname = "sitesfinders";`	Set the name for the `sitesfinders` table
`$fields="sid INT UNSIGNED NOT NULL AUTO_INCREMENT PRIMARY KEY, stitle char(50), sdate DATE, surl char(100), sdescription TEXT, scategory char(30), finderid INT ";`	Set the definition of the fields for the `sitesfinders` table
`createtable($tname, $fields);`	Invoke the `createtable` function to do the creation
`$tname = "finders";`	Set the name for the `finders` table
`$fields = "finderid INT UNSIGNED NOT NULL AUTO_INCREMENT PRIMARY KEY, username char(50), epw char(64)";`	Set the definition of fields for the `finders` table
`createtable($tname,$fields);`	Invoke the `createtable` function to do the creation
`mysql_close($link);`	Close the link to the database
`?>`	Close the PHP
`</body>`	Closing body tag
`</html>`	Closing `html` tag

I grouped together the five scripts concerning registration and changing passwords: `register.html`, `completereg.php`, `changepassword.html`, `completechangepw.php`, and `drawroundedarrowbox.js`. The last is only called from `changepassword.html` and is more general than it needs to be. Table 10-3 shows the finder registration scripts.

Table 10-3. *Scripts Concerning Finder Registration*

Code Line	Description
`register.html`	
`<!DOCTYPE html>`	Not strictly necessary, but this is the standard header and may be required in the future; you can use HTML5 elements and features
`<html>`	html tag
`<head>`	Head tag
`<meta http-equiv="Content-Type" content="text/html; charset=utf-8" />`	Meta tag (may be required in the future)
`<title>Register</title>`	Complete title element
`<script type="text/javascript" src="sha256.js"></script>`	Bring in the sha256.js file holding the function for one-way encryption
`<script type="text/javascript">`	Script tag
`function encode() {`	Header for encode function
`    var pw1 = document.f.pw.value;`	Extract the password
`  if ((document.f.un.value.length<1) ||(pw1.length<1)) {`	Check if both the username and password have been entered
`        alert("Need to enter User Name and Password. Please try again.");`	Present an error message
`        return false;`	Return false (don't go on to PHP)
`    }`	Close clause
`    else`	Else

Code Line	Description
`if (pw1 == document.f.cpw.value) {`	Check if the password and confirming password match
`document.f.pw.value = SHA256(pw1);`	If so, encode the password and replace it in the form
`document.f.cpw.value = document.f.pw.value;`	Use the same value for the confirming password
`return true;`	`return true` means that control will go on to the PHP file cited in the `action` attribute
`}`	Close clause
`else {`	Else
`alert("passwords do not match. Please try again.");`	Show the error message for no match
`return false;`	Return `false`, preventing control from going on to the PHP
`}`	Close clause
`}`	Close function
`</script>`	Closing script tag
`</head>`	Closing head tag
`<body>`	Opening body tag
`<form name="f" action="completereg.php" onSubmit="return encode();" method="post">`	Form tag setting up the server-side and client-side processing; set the method to `post`
`<table>`	Table tag for layout

Code Line	Description
`<tr>`	Start row
`<td>User id (email address) </td><td><input type="email" name="un" required /></td></tr>`	Display the label (descriptor) for the un field and the input field; specify as type email and required
`<tr><td>Password </td><td><input type="password" name="pw" required /></td></tr>`	Display the label for the password and the input field; specify as type password (dots instead of characters) and required
`<tr><td>Confirm password </td><td><input type="password" name="cpw" required/></td></tr>`	Display the label for the confirming password and the input field; same specifications as the first password field
`</table>`	End table
`<input type="submit" value="Register"/>`	Submit button
`</form>`	Closing form tag
`</body>`	Closing body tag
`</html>`	Closing html tag
`completereg.php`	
`<!DOCTYPE html>`	Not strictly necessary, but this is the standard header and may be required in the future; you can use HTML5 elements and features
`<html>`	html tag
`<head>`	Head tag

Code Line	Description
`<title>Complete registering finder</title>`	Complete title
`</head>`	Closing head tag
`<body>`	Body tag
`<?php`	Start PHP
`require("opendbo.php");`	Bring in the opendbo.php script that connects to the database
`$tname = "finders";`	Set the table name
`$finder = $_POST["un"];`	Extract the un input field
`$epw = $_POST["pw"];`	Extract the password field; I named the variable $epw to remind myself that this is an encoded password
`$query = "INSERT INTO $tname values ('0','$finder','$epw')";`	Create a query to add a new finder—that is, INSERT a record with the values as indicated; The 0 is a placeholder for the primary key field that MySQL supplies
`$result = mysql_query($query, $link);`	Send the query to MySQL
`if ($result) {`	Check if the result is OK
`    print("The finder was successfully added. \n");`	Print the success message; Include to produce a line break for the display and \n to produce a line break in the HTML source
`}`	Close clause
`else {`	Else

Code Line	Description
print ("The finder was NOT successfully added. \n");	Print the not-success message
}	Close clause
?>	End PHP
</body>	Closing body tag
</html>	Closing html tag
changepassword.html	
<!DOCTYPE html>	Doctype
<html>	html tag
<head>	Head tag
<meta http-equiv="Content-Type" content="text/html; charset=utf-8" />	Meta tag
<title>Change password</title>	Complete title
<script type="text/javascript" src="sha256.js"></script>	Bring in the sha256.js file holding the function for one-way encryption
<script type="text/javascript" src="drawroundedarrowbox.js"></script>	Bring in the drawroundedarrowbox.js function
<script type="text/javascript">	Script tag
function encode() {	Header for the encode function
var ctx= document.getElementById("canvas").getContext("2d");	Set up ctx for writing on the canvas
ctx.clearRect(0,0,600,600);	Clear canvas

Code Line	Description
`var pw1 = document.f.oldpw.value;`	Set password value
`var npw = document.f.newpw.value;`	Set new password value
`if ((document.f.un.value.length<1) ||(pw1.length<1)) {`	Check if the password and username have each submitted
`alert("Need to enter User Name and Password. Please try again.");`	Display message
`return false;`	Return `false` to prevent going to PHP
`}`	Close clause
`else`	Else
`if (npw == document.f.cpw.value) {`	Is the new password the same as the confirming password?
`document.f.oldpw.value = SHA256(pw1);`	Encode the original password
`document.f.newpw.value = SHA256(npw);`	Encode the new password
`document.f.cpw.value = document.f.newpaw.value;`	Assign that to the `cpw` field; this will not be used, but we want the value to prevent any default action if the field is empty
`return true;`	Return `true` so control passes to PHP
`}`	Close clause (passwords match)
`else {`	Else
`drawroundedarrowbox(ctx,10,30,40,300,80,` `"Passwords do not match.",30,"black","pink");`	Invoke the function to draw the fancy box to indicate the problem

Code Line	Description
`return false;`	Return `false` to prevent action going to PHP
`}`	Close clause
`}`	Close encode function
`</script>`	Closing script tag
`</head>`	Closing head tag
`<body>`	Body tag
`<form name="f" action="completechangepw.php" onSubmit="return encode();" method="post">`	Form tag indicating server-side action and what happens before that, client side, on the submit button
`<table>`	Table tag; used for layout
`<tr>`	Row tag
`<td>User name </td><td><input type="email" name="un" required /></td></tr>`	User name label and input field (note `required` and type `email`)
`<tr><td>Current password </td><td><input type="password" name="oldpw" required /> </td></tr>`	Current password label and input field (note `required` and type `password`)
`<tr><td>Password </td><td><input type="password" name="newpw" required /></td></tr>`	Place for the new password; label and input field (note `required` and type `password`)
`<tr><td>Confirm password </td><td><input type="password" name="cpw" required/></td></tr> </table>`	Place for entering the password again for confirmation; label and input field (note `required` and type `password`)
`<input type="submit" value="Change pw"/>`	Submit button

Code Line	Description
`</form>`	Closing form tag
`<canvas id="canvas" width="600" height="600">`	Canvas element
`Your browser does not recognize canvas`	Message for old browsers
`</canvas>`	Closing canvas tag
`</body>`	Closing body tag
`</html>`	Closing html tag
`completechangepw.php`	
`<html>`	html tag
`<head>`	Head tag
`<title>Complete change finder password</title>`	Complete title
`</head>`	Closing head tag
`<body>`	Body tag
`<?php`	Start PHP
`require("opendbo.php");`	Bring in file to make a connection with the database
`$tname = "finders";`	Set the name of the file
`$finder = $_POST["un"];`	Extract the username
`$epw1 = $_POST["oldpw"];`	Extract the original password, encoded
`$epw2 = $_POST["newpw"];`	Extract the new password, encoded

Code Line	Description
`$query = "UPDATE $tname SET epw = '$epw2' WHERE username = '$finder' AND epw = '$epw1'";`	Form the query to UPDATE (i.e., change) the epw field of any record with the indicated username equal to $finder and epw equal to $epw1; the query will make a change if the username and original password are present in the database
`$result = mysql_query($query, $link);`	Send query to MySQL
`if ($result) {`	Check result; If OK . . .
`print("The password was changed. \n");` `}`	. . . print OK message
`else {` `  print ("The password was NOT successfully changed.  \n"); }`	Else print the message indicating no success; line break for display and line break in the HTML document
`?>`	End PHP
`</body>`	Closing body tag
`</html>`	Closing html tag
`drawroundedarrowbox.js`	

`function`
`drawroundedarrowbox(ctx,x,y,rad,width,height,text,arrow,colorstroke,`
`colorfill) {`
	Header for the drawroundedarrowbox function; parameters indicate the context, the (x,y) position, the radius of the curved corners, the width and height, the text, the size of the arrow, and the color of the outline (stroke) and the fill

Code Line	Description
`ctx.lineWidth = 4;`	Set the line width
`ctx.strokeStyle = colorstroke;`	Set the stroke color
`ctx.fillStyle = colorfill;`	Set the fill color
`ctx.font = "bold 16px sans-serif";`	Set the font
`ctx.beginPath();`	Start the path
`ctx.moveTo(x+rad,y);`	Move to just beyond the upper-left corner
`ctx.lineTo(x+.5*width-arrow,y);`	Draw line to arrow closer than the middle
`ctx.lineTo(x+.5*width,y-arrow);`	Draw a diagonal line above the box
`ctx.lineTo(x+.5*width+arrow,y);`	Draw a diagonal line back down
`ctx.lineTo(x+width-rad,y);`	Draw to just short of upper-right corner
`ctx.arc(x+width-rad,y+rad,rad,-.5*Math.PI,0,false);`	Draw an arc, a quarter of a circle
`ctx.lineTo(x+width,y+height-rad);`	Draw a line down to just short of the lower-right corner
`ctx.arc(x+width-rad,y+height-rad,rad,0,.5*Math.PI,false);`	Draw an arc, a quarter of a circle
`ctx.lineTo(x+rad,y+height);`	Draw all the way left to just short of lower-left corner
`ctx.arc(x+rad,y+height-rad,rad,.5*Math.PI,Math.PI,false);`	Draw an arc, a quarter of a circle
`ctx.lineTo(x,y+rad);`	Draw up to just short of the upper-left circle

Code Line	Description
`ctx.arc(x+rad,y+rad,rad,Math.PI,-.5*Math.PI,false);`	Draw an arc, a quarter of a circle
`ctx.closePath();`	Close path
`ctx.fill();`	Fill in
`ctx.stroke();`	Draw outline
`ctx.fillStyle = colorstroke;`	Change the fill style to the outline (stroke) color
`ctx.fillText(text,x+rad,y+rad);`	Draw the text
`}`	Close function

The group of scripts in Table 10-4 handles the adding and removing of sites by registered finders.

Table 10-4. *Adding and Removing Site Records*

Code Line	Description
`addsite.html`	
`<!DOCTYPE html>`	Doctype
`<html>`	html tag
`<head>`	Head tag
`<title>Add website info, login</title>`	Complete title
`<script type="text/javascript" src="sha256.js"></script>`	Bring in the sha256.js file holding the function for one-way encryption
`<script type="text/javascript">`	Script tag
`function encode() {`	Header for the encode function
`var pw1 = document.f.pw.value;`	Set pw1 with the input value

Code Line	Description
`if (document.f.saveok.value!="No") {`	Check if the user changed the saveok field
`try {`	Try to do localStorage
`localStorage.setItem("researchun",document.f.un.value);`	Save the item under the name researchun with the value the un value
`localStorage.setItem("researchpw",pw1);`	Save the item under the name researchpw with the value of the password
`}`	Close the try clause
`catch(e) {`	If there was an error . . .
`alert("error on local storage "+e);`	. . . display the error
`}`	Close the catch clause
`}`	Close if saveok has changed
`else {`	No saving, so remove anything saved previously
`try {`	Try
`localStorage.removeItem("researchun");`	Remove item
`localStorage.removeItem("researchpw");`	Remove item
`}`	End try
`catch(e) {`	Catch
`//alert("error on local storage "+e);`	For now, no message
`}`	Close catch
`}`	Close the else for no saving

Code Line	Description
`if ((document.f.un.value.length<1) ||(pw1.length<1)) {`	Check if the user did not enter something for both un and pw1
`alert("Need to enter User Name and Password. Please try again.");`	Display the message
`return false;`	Return false to prevent going to the PHP script
`}`	Close clause
`else {`	Else
`document.f.pw.value = SHA256(pw1);`	Encode the password
`return true;`	Return true so action does go to the PHP script
`}`	Close the else clause
`}`	Close the function
`function retrieveinfo() {`	Header for function that attempts to retrieve info from localStorage
`var savedun;`	Used for the un
`var savedpw;`	Used for the pw
`try {`	Try
`savedun = localStorage.getItem("researchun");`	Attempt to get localStorage data named "researchun"
`savedpw = localStorage.getItem("researchpw");`	Attempt to get localStorage data named "researchpw"
`if (savedun) {`	If savedun is not null . . .

Code Line	Description
`document.f.un.value = savedun;`	. . . then set it as the un value in the input field
`document.f.pw.value = savedpw;`	Also assume **savedpw** is good, and use it to set the pw value in the input field
`document.getElementById("greeting").innerHTML="Welcome Back.";`	Fill in "Welcome Back" at the top of the document
`document.f.saveok.value = "Yes";`	Set the **saveok** to Yes; the user can change it
`}`	Close the `if (savedun)` clause
`}`	Close the **try** clause
`catch(e) {}`	**catch** clause; if there are problems in trying to use localStorage, do nothing
`}`	Close function
`</script>`	Closing script tag
`</head>`	Closing head tag
`<body onLoad="retrieveinfo();">`	Body tag; invoke **retrieveinfo** after loading
`<div id="greeting"></div>`	Div that is a place to put the "Welcome Back" greeting
`<form name="f" action="addsite.php"  onSubmit="return encode();" method="post">`	Form tag; sets the server-side action to be **addsite.php**; sets the client-side response to the submit button to be **return encode()**; the method is **post**

Code Line	Description
`Site: <input name="stitle" placeholder="Your name for site" required/> `	Label and input field for site name
`Date: <input name="sdate" type="date" placeholder="YYYY-MM-DD" required/>    `	Label and input field for date
`Site description:  `	Label for site description; line break
`<textarea name="sdesc" cols="30" rows="2">`	textarea element
`</textarea>  `	Closing textarea; line break
`URL:   <input name="surl" type="url" placeholder="http://   " required/> `	Label and input field for URL
`Category: <input name="scat" type="text" required/><hr/>`	Label and input field for category
`Username: <input name="un" type="email" required / >  `	Label and input field for username
`Password: <input name="pw" type="password" required />  `	Label and input field for password
`Save on this computer next time you invoke addsite? <input name="saveok" value="No" />`	Question and input field for user opt-in to saving on local computer
`<input type="submit" value="Submit Site"/>`	Submit button
`</form>`	Closing form tag
`</body>`	Closing body tag
`</html>`	Closing html tag
`addsite.php`	
`<html>`	html tag

Code Line	Description
`<head>`	Head tag
`<title>Complete adding site to research table</title>`	Complete title
`</head>`	Closing head tag
`<body>`	Body tag
`<?php`	Start PHP
`require("opendbo.php");`	Bring in the file to connect to the database
`$tname = "sitesfinders";`	Set the variable with the table name
`$stitle=addslashes($_POST["stitle"]);`	Extract the title and escape pesky characters such as '
`$sdate= $_POST["sdate"];`	Extract the date
`$sdesc= addslashes($_POST["sdesc"]);`	Extract the description and escape pesky characters such as '
`$surl= $_POST["surl"];`	Extract the URL
`$scat = addslashes($_POST["scat"]);`	Extract the category and escape pesky characters such as '
`$un = $_POST['un'];`	Extract the username
`$epw = $_POST['pw'];`	Extract the password
`$query = "SELECT * FROM finders WHERE username='$un' AND epw='$epw'";`	Form the query to see if this is a registered finder; That is, SELECT from the finders table all records where username equals $un and epw equals $epw
`$result = mysql_query($query, $link);`	Send the query to MySQL

Code Line	Description
`if ($row=mysql_fetch_array($result)) {`	If there were any results, take the first one
`$fid = $row['finderid'];`	Extract the `fid` field
`$query = "INSERT INTO $tname values ('0','$stitle','$sdate','$surl','$sdesc','$scat','$fid')";`	Form the query to insert a new record into the `sitesfinders` table using all the data, including the `fid` just determined from the SELECT statement
`$result = mysql_query($query, $link);`	Send the query to MySQL
`if ($result) {`	Check if the result is OK
`print("The site was successfully added. \n");`	Print the success message
`?>`	Leave PHP (still in the success clause)
`Add [another] web site?  `	Display the invitation to add another site
`<form name="f" action="addsite.php"    method="post">`	Form, with action to go to `addsite.php`
`Site: <input name="stitle" placeholder="Your name for site"/> `	Place for title
`Date: <input name="sdate" type="date" placeholder="YYYY-MM-DD" /> `	Place for data
`Site description:  `	Label for description
`<textarea name="sdesc" cols="30" rows="2">`	Text area for long(er) description
`</textarea>  `	Close `textarea`; line break
`URL:    <input name="surl" type="url" placeholder="http:// "/> `	Place for URL
`Category: <input name="scat" type="text"/><hr/>`	Place for category

Code Line	Description
`<?php`	Restart PHP section
`print ("Username: <input name='un' type='email'  value='");`	Using data sent
`print ($un."' />");`	Display username
`print ("Password: <input name='pw' type='password'  value='$epw' />");`	Display dots for each character of encoded password (this is 32 characters)
`?>`	End PHP
`<input type="submit" value="Submit Site"/>`	Submit button
`</form>`	Close form
`<a href="showsites.php">Show all websites </a>  or <a href="showsitesbycategory1.php">Show sites for a category </a>`	Hyperlinks to go to showsites or showsitesbycategory1.php
`<?php`	Restart PHP
`    }`	Closing } for the if-OK test
`  else {`	Else
`        print ("The site was NOT successfully added.  \n");`	Print error message
`    }`	Close clause
`  }`	Close clause on no-problem-with-finder info
`  else {`	Else
`        print ("Problem with username and/or password and/or data.");`	Print the message for problem-with-finder info
`  }`	Close clause
`?>`	End PHP

Code Line	Description
`</body>`	Closing body tag
`</html>`	Closing html tag
`removesites.php`	
`<!DOCTYPE html>`	Doctype
`<html>`	html tag
`<head>`	Head tag
`<title>Delele some sites</title>`	Complete title
`</head>`	Closing head tag
`<script type="text/javascript" src="sha256.js"></script>`	Bring in the sha256.js file holding the function for one-way encryption
`<script type="text/javascript">`	Script tag
`function encode() {`	Header for the encode function
`    var pw1 = document.f.pw.value;`	Set pw1 with the password
`  if ((document.f.un.value.length<1) ||(pw1.length<1)) {`	Check if un and pw1 have not been entered
`        alert("Need to enter User Name and Password. Please try again.");`	Display the error message
`        return false;`	Return false to stop action going to the PHP script
`    }`	Close clause
`    else {`	Else

Code Line	Description
`document.f.pw.value = SHA256(pw1);`	Encode password
`return true;`	Return `true` to send control to the PHP script
`}`	Close clause
`}`	Close the `encode` function
`</script>`	Closing script tag
`<body>`	Body tag
`<?php`	Start PHP
`require("opendbo.php");`	Connect to the database
`$query="SELECT * FROM sitesfinders as s JOIN finders as f where s.finderid = f.finderid  ORDER BY sdate DESC";`	Form the query to get `SELECT` all the records from tables joined where the `finderid` values are equal; order by the `sdate` field in descending order, meaning most recent first
`$result=mysql_query($query, $link);`	Send the query to MySQL
`print("<table border='1'>");`	Output to the HTML document table tag
`print("<tr><th>Remove?</th><th>Name</th><th>URL</th><th>Date</th><th>Description </th><th>Category </th><th>Finder </th></tr>");`	Output to the HTML table column header row
`?>`	Close PHP
`<form name="f" action="completeremovesites.php" method="post" onSubmit="return encode();">`	Form tag
`<?php`	Restart PHP
`while ($row=mysql_fetch_array($result)) {`	`while` based on rows extracted from the result of the query

Code Line	Description
`print("<tr>");`	Print HTML markup to start row
`print ("<td><input type='checkbox' name='group[]'` `value='".$row['sid'] . "'/></td>");`	Print HTML check box; the value is the ID for the site record
`print("<td> ".$row['stitle']."</td>");`	Print HTML with the site title
`print ("<td><a href='".$row['surl'] ."'` `target='_new'>".$row['surl']."</a></td>");`	Print HTML with the hyperlink; the surl date from the table is used twice
`print ("<td>".$row['sdate']."</td>");`	Print HTML showing the data
`print ("<td>".$row['sdescription']."</td>");`	Print HTML showing the description
`print ("<td>".$row['scategory']."</td>");`	Print HTML showing the category
`print ("<td>".$row['username']."</td>");`	Print HTML showing the finder name
`print ("</tr>");`	Print HTML closing tr tag
`}`	Close the while loop
`mysql_close($link);`	Close the link to the database
`?>`	End PHP
`</table>`	Closing table tag
`Username: <input name="un" type="email" required />  `	HTML for finder signing in
`Password: <input name="pw" type="password" required />  `	HTML for finder password
`<input type="submit" value="Delete selected sites" />`	Submit button

Code Line	Description
`</form>`	Closing form tag
`</body>`	Closing body tag
`</html>`	Closing `html` tag
`completeremovesites.php`	
`<!DOCTYPE html>`	Doctype
`<html>`	`html` tag
`<head>`	Head tag
`<title>Delele some sites</title>`	Complete title
`</head>`	Closing head tag
`<body>`	Body tag
`<?php`	Start PHP
`require("opendbo.php");`	Bring in `opendbo.php` to connect to the database
`$un = $_POST['un'];`	Extract the un input
`$epw = $_POST['pw'];`	Extract the pw input (it is the encoded password)
`$query = "SELECT * FROM finders WHERE username='$un' AND epw='$epw'";`	Form a query to check if the finder is registered; SELECT all records in which the username equals $un and the epw equals $epw
`$result = mysql_db_query($DBname,$query, $link);`	Send to MySQL
`if ($row=mysql_fetch_array($result)) {`	If anything was returned, take the first (probably only) row

Code Line	Description
`$ids = $_POST['group'];`	Extract the group input (this is an array)
`$deletelist = join (', ',$ids);`	Join the array elements together to form a string with commas in-between and assign to $deletelist
`$query = "DELETE FROM sitesfinders WHERE sid IN ($deletelist)";`	Form a query to delete all records where the sid is contained in the $deletelist; the $deletelist is a comma-separated character string
`$result=mysql_query($query, $link);`	Send to MySQL
`if ($result) {`	If true result . . .
`        print ("The " . count($ids)." selected sites were deleted.");`	. . . print out the message, giving the number of sites deleted
`}`	Close clause
`else {`	Else
`        print ("Problem with deletion.");`	Print out the problem message
`}`	Close clause
`}`	Close clause for check-on-finders info
`else {`	Else
`        print ("Problem with username and/or password.");`	Print out the message indicating the problem-with-finder info
`}`	Close clause
`mysql_close($link);`	Close connection

Code Line	Description
?>	End PHP
</body>	Closing body tag
</html>	Closing html tag

The last group of scripts, shown in Table 10-5, includes the three for displaying the contents of the database. Now, I need to be clear as to what is meant by the term *table*. The PHP code creates HTML tables. The PHP uses information returned for SELECT statements concerning the MySQL sitesfinders table and the MySQL finders table. Look back at Figure 10-13 and Figure 10-16 for clarification.

Table 10-5. Displaying Information on Sites in the Database

Code Line	Description
showsites.php	
<!DOCTYPE html>	Doctype
<html>	html tag
<head>	Head tag
<title>List sites with finder ids</title>	Complete title
</head>	Closing head tag
<body>	Body tag
<?php	Start PHP
require("opendbo.php");	Bring in the file to make the connection to the database
$query="SELECT * FROM sitesfinders as s JOIN finders as f where s.finderid = f.finderid ORDER BY sdate DESC";	Form query to SELECT all the fields from all the sites from the sitesfinders table, joining with it all the fields from the finders table; the code will only use the username from the finders table fields
$result=mysql_query($query, $link);	Send to MySQL

Code Line	Description
`print("<table border='1'>");`	Print the table tag to the HTML document
`print("<tr><th>Title</th><th>URL</th><th>Date </th><th>Description </th><th>Category </th><th>Finder </th></tr>");`	Print the row with column headings to the HTML document
`while ($row=mysql_fetch_array($result)) {`	while loop to iterate over the values returned by the query
`print("<tr>");`	Print the tr tag to HTML
`print("<td> ".$row['stitle']."</td>");`	Print as a td element the stitle field from the sitesfinders table
`print ("<td><a href='".$row['surl'] ."' target='_new'>".$row['surl']."</a></td>");`	. . . a hyperlink, with the surl value present as the href value and as the visible contents
`print ("<td>".$row['sdate']."</td>");`	. . . sdate field
`print ("<td>".$row['sdescription']."</td>");`	. . . sdescription field
`print ("<td>".$row['scategory']."</td>");`	. . . scategory field
`print ("<td>".$row['username']."</td>");`	. . . username field (from the finders table)
`print ("</tr>");`	. . . ending tr tag
`}`	Close the while loop
`mysql_close($link);`	Close the connection to the database
`?>`	End PHP
`</table>`	Closing table tag
`</body>`	Closing body tag
`</html>`	Closing html tag

Code Line	Description
showsitesbycategory1.php	
`<!DOCTYPE html>`	Doctype
`<html>`	html tag
`<head>`	Head tag
`<title>List sites in a category</title>`	Complete title
`</head>`	Closing head tag
`<body>`	Body tag
Pick the category you want:	Text instructions
` `	Line break
`<form action="showsitesbycategory2.php" method="get">`	Form tag, indicating the action and the method
Choices: `<select name="pickedcategory">`	Choices text and select tag
`<?php`	Start the PHP
`require("opendbo.php");`	Bring in the file to connect to the database
`$query="SELECT DISTINCT scategory FROM sitesfinders";`	Form query; this SELECT statement picks up all the scategory fields, but reduces the list to the distinct ones—that is, there are no repeats, even if a category appears for more than one record in the table
`$categories = mysql_query($query, $link);`	Send the query to MySQL; the results are assigned to $categories
`while ($row=mysql_fetch_array($categories))`	while loop iterating over categories
`{ $cat=$row['scategory'];`	Set $cat

Code Line	Description
`print ("<option value='$cat'>$cat</option> \n");`	Print out to HTML an option element, with the $cat as the value and the visible contents
`}`	Close the `while` loop
`mysql_close($link);`	Close the connection to the database
`?>`	End PHP
`</select>`	Closing `select` tag
`<input type=submit name=submit value="Choose!">`	Submit button
`</form>`	Closing form tag
`</body>`	Closing body tag
`</html>`	Closing `html` tag
showsitesbycategory2.php	
`<!DOCTYPE html>`	Doctype
`<html>`	`html` tag
`<head>`	Head tag
`<title>Show sites in selected category</title>`	Complete title
`</head>`	Closing head tag
`<body>`	Body tag
`<?php`	Start PHP
`$scat = $_GET['pickedcategory'];`	Extract the `pickedcategory` input and assign it to the `$scat` variable

Code Line	Description
`print "Sites in $scat category  ";`	Print out to HTML text for the display; line break
`require("opendbo.php");`	Bring in the file to link to the database
`$query="SELECT * FROM sitesfinders as s JOIN finders as f WHERE s.finderid = f.finderid AND scategory = '$scat' ORDER BY sdate DESC";`	Form query; this is picking up all the fields from the sitesfinders table, joined with the finders table, when the finderid fields are equal, where the scategory field is equal to $scat; order by sdate, descending (most recent first)
`$result=mysql_query($query, $link);`	Send the query to MySQL; assign the results to the $result variable
`$NoR=mysql_num_rows($result);`	Set $NoR to be number of rows
`if ($NoR==0) {`	Check if this is zero
`        print ("No sites in that category");   }`	Print the message (this should not happen because the list of present categories was just generated)
`else {`	Else
`print("<table border='1'>");`	Print to HTML the table tag
`print("<tr><th>Title</th><th>URL</th><th>Date </th><th>Description </th><th>Finder </th></tr>");`	Print to HTML the column headers
`while ($row=mysql_fetch_array($result)) {`	while loop to iterate over the value returned
`print("<tr>");`	Print the tr tag
`print("<td> ".$row['stitle']."</td>");`	Print as a td element, the stitle value
`print ("<td><a href='".$row['surl'] ."' target='_new'>".$row['surl']."</a></td>");`	Print as td element, a hyperlink with the surl value appearing as the value of the href and as the visible contents

Code Line	Description
`print ("<td>".$row['sdate']."</td>");`	. . . sdate
`print ("<td>".$row['sdescription']."</td>");`	. . . sdescription
`print ("<td>".$row['username']."</td>");`	. . . username
`print ("</tr>");`	Print closing tr tag
`}`	Close while
`print ("</table>");`	Print closing table tag
`}`	Close the else clause
`mysql_close($link);`	Close the connection to the database
`?>`	End PHP
`</body>`	Closing body tag
`</html>`	Closing html tag

Testing and Uploading the Application

The project for this chapter requires you to have a server account that supports your use of PHP and provides access to a MySQL database. Testing a database program is a challenge! First of all, you do need to upload everything to a server, or perform the intricate process of setting up a server on your own computer. Second, you need to be aware of the state of the system as a whole. Data persists, which is the whole point. For example, you may need to remove items added to tables in the database to test a particular script. If your application involves the use of localStorage, this is part of the system as well, and you may need to remove saved items. When the project includes a login/password subsystem, you need to remember the passwords.

Do keep in mind that you need to create your version of the opendbo.php file. Use opendboToBeFixed.php as a base. You need to consult with your server organization to do this. You also need to download the sha256.js file from www.webtoolkit.info/javascript-sha256.html or obtain an equivalent program. If you use a different program, you will need to search for the function named sha256 and change it to what you included.

Summary

In this chapter, you learned techniques in HTML5, JavaScript, MySQL, and PHP, including the following:

- SQL commands for creating tables for a database
- SQL commands for inserting, updating, selecting, and deleting records
- PHP commands and techniques for composing SQL queries from form inputs and taking the results of SQL queries to compose HTML pages
- Using localStorage to save and retrieve information

This is the last chapter. I hope you have enjoyed the examples, and you will go on to build exciting and beautiful projects on your own.

Index

E

F

G

Mary R Drabik

MRN: 02249989

Today's Visit

White Bear Lake Internal Medicine with Caroline M Tahara, MD on 7/17/2013.

Reason(s) for Today's Visit

Fatigue   - Primary

Muscle pain

Vital Signs Today

BP	Weight	BMI
111/70	122 lb 3.2 oz (55.43 kg)	20.97 kg/m2

To-Do List

Visit Instructions/Information

We'll check the blood counts, lyme test and CK or muscle enzyme test. If everything is okay, then I think we'll have you hold the pravastatin for a month to see if your symptoms improve. If your symptoms improve, I'd think about switching your statins

Recommended Lab Test(s)

Future Labs/Procedures	Complete On/After
CK, TOTAL	7/17/2013
HEMOGRAM/PLTS	7/17/2013
	7/17/2013

WESTERN BLOT(IF NEEDED)

Medications

Instructions

Please let us know if any of the medications or instructions below are incorrect or missing. If you are unsure, please contact the provider who prescribed them. For refills, please contact your pharmacy.

Current Medications as of Today

Medication

aspirin 325 MG tablet (Taking)   Take 1 Tab by mouth once as needed for Pain for 1 dose.

pravastatin (AKA PRAVACHOL) 40 MG tablet (Taking)   THS

Healthcare Contacts

Have questions? Call 651-653-2100
Need care after hours or on weekends? Call 612-339-3663
Need to make an appointment? Call 952-967-6614
Prefer to do all of this online? Visit www.healthpartners.com
For other helpful phone numbers visit www.healthpartners.com/clinics

Thank you for visiting us today!

CPSIA information can be obtained at www.ICGtesting.com
Printed in the USA
LVOW020229210313

325312LV00025B/167/P